VARIETIES OF CORPORATISM

A Conceptual Discussion

This book provides a comprehensive discussion of the concept of corporatism. It seeks to develop models of the different types of corporatism against the background of a general model of corporatism. It represents the first systematic attempt to clarify, rather than simply discuss, the concept of corporatism in its various usages.

It examines the three varieties of corporatism: the body of nineteenth- and twentieth-century prescriptive economic and social thought; the practice of certain authoritarian regimes with private ownership of the means of production and wage labour; and a theoretical tool of analysis employed to study relations between organised groups and the state in ostensibly liberal democracies. It draws on a wide range of historical and contemporary writing on the subject, and includes a detailed study of the ideas behind and nature of corporatism in Fascist Italy and in Portugal under Salazar and Caetano. The discussion of the varieties of corporatism is clearly related to current debates in the social sciences on the nature of corporatism.

This book will be of interest throughout the social sciences to those studying corporatism.

VARIETIES OF CORPORATISM

A Conceptual Discussion

PETER J. WILLIAMSON

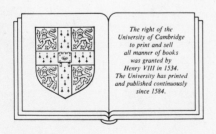

The right of the
University of Cambridge
to print and sell
all manner of books
was granted by
Henry VIII in 1534.
The University has printed
and published continuously
since 1584.

CAMBRIDGE UNIVERSITY PRESS

Cambridge
London   New York   New Rochelle
Melbourne   Sydney

Published by the Press Syndicate of the University of Cambridge
The Pitt Building, Trumpington Street, Cambridge CB2 1RP
32 East 57th Street, New York, NY 10022, USA
10 Stamford Road, Oakleigh, Melbourne 3166, Australia

First published 1985

Printed in Great Britain at the University Press, Cambridge

Library of Congress catalogue card number: 85 11365

British Library Cataloguing in Publication Data

Williamson, Peter J.
Varieties of corporatism: theory and practice.
1. Corporate state
I. Title
321.0   HD3611

Library of Congress Cataloguing in Publication Data

Williamson, Peter J.
Varieties of corporatism.
Based on the author's thesis (Ph. D. – Aberdeen
University).
1. Corporate state.   I. Title.
JC478.W553 1986   321.9   85–11365
ISBN 0 521 26805 2

CE

For Mo

'Give a small boy a hammer and everything looks like a nail'

Grant Jordan summarising the promiscuous application of the concept of corporatism, *Scandinavian Political Studies* Vol. 7 (1984), p. 141.

Contents

Preface

This book is based partly upon work that I conducted for my doctoral thesis at Aberdeen University, and in part upon work carried out subsequent to that which sought to resolve some of the inevitable outstanding issues from my Ph.D. My concern in writing this work has been very much with the conceptual angle, though I have consciously sought to avoid excessive abstraction and always attempted to discuss the concept of corporatism in relation to its potential analytic utility. That stated, however, the actual analytic utility in any particular empirical context remains something that is not fully addressed. Instead, what I have attempted to achieve is a reasonably clear and substantial conceptual basis from which empirical consideration of corporatism can benefit. Whether or not this has been realised is not for me to judge, but I do firmly believe in the present need for some greater clarity to be gained in conceptualising corporatism. Undoubtedly some people may be of the opinion that lengthy scholastic deliberations upon concepts without their ever actually being applied will not lead to theoretical advances. And I would certainly not demur from this view that an integral part of theoretical development involves placing testable propositions against empirical evidence and drawing operating hypotheses from the 'real world'. Theory, however, cannot solely be abstracted from empirical data; it needs to encompass certain premises if it is to be manageable and one or more attendent theories if it itself is a sophisticated theory. Moreover, a theoretical model requires a conceptual boundary within which to operate, otherwise the language of analysis becomes so malleable as to be redundant. There is, therefore, a case for conceptual-theoretical deliberation because the above issues are fundamental to the eventual understanding gained from analysis. Discussions of corporatism could certainly benefit from further consideration of these issues.

In carrying out the work and formulating many of the ideas that have gone into this present volume I have received valuable assistance from a number of quarters. Frank Bealey, who supervised my Ph.D. at Aberdeen University, merits special mention for the range of knowledge he provided to me on many topics, thus enabling me to use the materials I accumulated in a far more effective manner. Likewise Dr Mick Moran, who externally examined the thesis, pinpointed a number of areas where my arguments were not as convincing as they might have been, and I am greateful for the undoubted improvements that have resulted from following his advice. Grant Jordan provided quite gratuitously a forum for discussing ideas, a source of many references and a humorous slant on many other writers' products.

A number of people were generous enough to readily provide me with copies of their own work on the Portuguese *Estado Novo*, namely: Prof Howard Wiarda, University of Massachusetts, Amherst; Prof Harry Makler, University of Toronto; Dr Peter McDonough, Institute of Social Research, University of Michigan; and Dr Joyce Riegelhaupt, Sara Lawrence College, New York University.

Colin Crouch, Wyn Grant and Alan Cawson have been kind enough both to read an earlier draft of my work on neo-corporatism and to provide me with copies of their own work. Prof Philippe Schmitter similarly has kept up a stream of his essays through the post, despite the fact that he disagrees fundamentally with my presentation of his ideas. I would also like to thank Joan Stringer for her help in many ways, and to her and Clive Gray for being able to incorporate some ideas from work we have jointly done.

Morag Williamson not only had to endure many of the costs of the project for few of the benefits, but also assisted greatly with the translation of many of the texts cited below. Her enduring support is very genuinely appreciated. This book is dedicated to her.

Finally, I would like to thank Francis Brooke of Cambridge University Press for his valuable support. And, in the absence of anyone else being kind enough to step forward, I take full responsibility for all the errors, of which I remain happily oblivious.

Aberdeen   PETER WILLIAMSON
December, 1984.

Part I

Varieties of corporatism

1

Varieties of corporatism: an introduction

During the past decade or so there has developed in Britain and several other countries an extensive interest in the concept of corporatism. The concept has been most widely employed in political science, but has infiltrated a number of the other social sciences. Since the mid-1970s corporatism has come very much into vogue, gaining at least an honourable mention in a wide range of contexts. Many such contexts are seemingly dubious, but corporatism has a quality akin to celebrities who have walk-on parts on other people's shows: they don't contribute to the shows but they increase the audience and status.

In Britain, corporatism has been the subject of intense interest, providing for many analysts a new and more utilitarian framework for examining the contemporary British politico-economic system both *in toto* and in its many parts. Probably the most significant indicator that reflects the poignance of such interest has been the establishment by the (then) Social Science Research Council of a Research Panel on Corporatism and Accountability in 1980 backed by not insubstantial funding and overseeing a plethora of research projects. Outside Britain attention has likewise been keen as corporatism has emerged as the 'analytic tool of crises'. As Gabriel Almond has noted: 'What distinguishes the contemporary concern for corporatism is its centrality in a growing debate over the causes of and remedies for the economic and political crises in advanced industrial societies.'[1] Yet despite its prevalence in the literature, corporatism remains an ambiguous concept in the political vocabulary encompassing a wide range of all too often imprecise definitions. For example, corporatism has been employed to describe significant phenomenon in such seemingly diverse political systems as the United States[2] and the Soviet Union.[3] Far too regularly for its own good, corporatism is applied as a very generalised concept, providing a handy label that will stick to almost any surface,[4] but severely curtailed in its analytic utility and significance.

The more one notices the term 'corporatism' leaping from the pages of published essays and books, the more one is inclined to regard corporatism as beyond redemption. However, excessive diversity and generality, and the resultant confusion and superabundant application, eclipse a reasonably substantial core to modern corporatism. In a sense corporatism's new-found star quality has led to it being dissipated by its utilisation as an 'all-rounder' concept to be applied anywhere, at any time. Yet despite the remaining ambiguities which surround modern corporatism, there exists within the major works of contemporary corporatism a range of ideas presented and issues raised that are both interesting and significant in respect of the relationship between the state, organised interests and civil society in advanced industrialised polities. Nevertheless, while modern (or more preferably neo-) corporatism provides, potentially at least, a valuable and sophisticated framework for the analysis of advanced industrial political systems, corporatism has been distinctively employed in a number of other contexts, all of which pre-date what can be regarded as the genesis of modern corporatist theorising with the publication of Philippe Schmitter's famous essay 'Still the Century of Corporatism?' in 1974.[5] Firstly, corporatism has been a designation applied to a body of prescriptive economic and social theory that gained prominence in a number of European countries from the period approximately 1860 to 1940. Corporatist ideology, which drew heavily on the moral philosophy of Roman Catholicism, was regarded as one of the great 'isms' of industrial society, standing alongside liberal capitalism and socialism. In many ways corporatism was the Catholic riposte to the protestantism of liberal capitalism and the atheism of socialism. Overall though, corporatist ideology never achieved the same status as its two illustrious counterparts. For one thing it did not flourish in countries where there was not a conspicuous, continuing Catholic tradition. After the Second World War it died out in many western and central European countries through its 'guilt by association' with the defeated authoritarian axis powers. Indeed, the propaganda machine of Mussolini's Italy had gone a long way to implanting in European minds the view that corporatism and fascism were virtually synonymous.

One, however, suspects that under the post-war welfare states of western Europe, corporatism, certainly as it stood, would have lost much of its basis of appeal. Nonetheless, during the period from the middle of the nineteenth to the middle of the twentieth century, in those countries where corporatist ideology was formulated and developed, it did gain a reasonably substantial foothold in the world of economic and social ideas. Furthermore, in Iberian and certain Latin American countries corporatist ideology remained prominent long after the last war.

The second form of usage of corporatism relates to the politico-economic system practised in a number of authoritarian regimes in the twentieth century. Included amongst such regimes are most notably Fascist Italy, Austria 1934–8, Portugal 1933–74, Vichy France, and post-1945 Brazil, Peru and Mexico. In addition, corporatist experiments have at least been initiated, if not sustained, in a host of other countries during this century.[6] These regimes which adopted various corporatist practices not surprisingly all laid claim to following the prescriptions of the economic and social theorists. True, there had to be modifications and elaborations in the process of translating ideology into political activity, but corporatist theory was alleged to have provided the central framework. In reality, even in the most mature of corporatist systems, with which we shall be principally concerned, ideology provided only a partial blueprint. To the time-served political analyst, the failure of ideology to live up to its promise in practice hardly comes as the most startling piece of news of recent years. Our present purpose, however, is not to reveal the unusual and amazing, but to clarify, and hopefully develop, the concept of corporatism. In the advanced corporatist regimes, as will be discussed in Part III, one does not just find the rubble of pious ideological hopes, but a distinctive form of corporatism. This distinctive form drew in part upon the ideas of corporatist economic and social theory, but additionally developed from the ideas or doctrines of the political leadership in control at the time. The doctrines of the leaders were themselves moulded by the contemporary balance of political forces. Nevertheless, without going off presently to elaborate the sources or content of such political practice, the important point is that we are faced with another variety of corporatism that necessitates recognition and further consideration.

A final usage of corporatism is of more recent origin, but one which predated the 'take-off' of neo-corporatism in the mid-1970s, though it has subsequently continued to enjoy a certain degree of attention. This usage has treated the concept of corporatism as a form of political culture or as a societal phenomenon of political significance. Unlike the other usages referred to here, the focus is primarily on the 'psychology' rather than on the structure of political systems. Such cultural or macro-societal conceptualisations of corporatism, while interesting and no doubt purveyors of greater insight into Latin American and Iberian politics than certain other models, appear rather lacking in analytic precision.[7] Most importantly, the concept is underdefined in such usages so that its empirical application looks to be based upon impressionistic and circular arguments. If corporatism in this form was to fly past the window one would be hard pushed to recognise it as such.[8] Moreover, the 'corporatist tradition' is presented as closely allied with other traditions (e.g. authoritarian, elitist, patrimionialist, organicist) such that even its significance is difficult to discern.

Finally, the generality of this usage of corporatism is sharply reflected in the fact that the empirical linkages between corporatist 'traditions' or 'modes of action'[9] and corporatist structures is vaguely specified. So in this respect as well, 'culturalist' conceptualisations of corporatism assume a form lacking in analytic value or conceptual solidity.

The above represents the four general categories of usage of corporatism. It is the purpose of this book to examine, elaborate and clarify three of these four usages, or varieties, of corporatism. Specifically, this discussion of the varieties of corporatism will seek to determine the central components of each variety and also to establish the elements common to each of them, that is the basic constituents of corporatism. The reasons for not pursuing the fourth variety, that relating to characteristics of political culture or politically significant societal features, have already been partially put forward, namely a rather insubstantial central core, both definitionally and analytically. Therefore, any discussion of this employment of corporatism would merely involve outlining the reasoning behind the conclusions set out above. The critique would be largely negative, providing no residual basis upon which to rebuild.[10] (Those readers who have any doubts on this point are recommended to read the literature and judge for themselves.)

There are, however, three further reasons for taking diversionary action here. Firstly, I am not convinced that the employment of the term corporatism to the concepts used in this manner is valid. In cases where it relates to a single phenomenon it appears that the language of politics already has an adequate term, and so it is no more than 'new labels on old bottles'. Where it is employed as a generic term, on the other hand, it is hard to see what is the generic quality that leads to applying the term 'corporatism'; in other words, it is not evident, particularly given other usages of the term, what is specifically corporatist about the various characteristics listed. Indeed, drawing out a particular generic quality from such listings would preclude any discussion of corporatism as being applicable to advanced industrialised western polities, instead tying the term to specific and limited geographic locations. Secondly, because this usage is concerned with culture it is difficult to tie it meaningfully in with the other, structural usages. Finally, the cultural-societal employment of corporatism, in fact, covers a range of quite different conceptualisations. It is not, therefore, a variety of corporatism but a set of (minor) varieties. So, there would be no real opportunity for consolidating, for distilling central components, and hence ultimately achieving greater clarity, that I will be arguing is possible in the other three cases. It is to begin the process of determining the components of the three varieties of corporatism that we now turn.

Three varieties of corporatism

The discussion this far has suggested that three widespread usages of the term corporatism can be regarded not only as forms of usage, but can be refined and developed into three varieties or types of the same general concept. That is, it is possible to construct models of the three varieties which are subsets of a more general model. Obviously the moment one begins to construct a model one has to justify the inclusion and form of the chosen components, and in some cases support the reason for excluding other suggested or possible components. The thought processes entailed in such an exercise of constructing a model are inevitably disordered and sporadic, and certainly not very readily explainable. Instead, all one can attempt to do is to present an argument in support of conclusions that emerged not so much from reasoned reflection, but were the result of intuitive groping. Some of the propositions arrived at in this manner could be sustained by argument, others live their lives in earlier drafts of this work. Given the somewhat anarchic process by which the propositions to be presented here were initially arrived at, and that while a jig-saw is being put together the overall form of the picture becomes of secondary concern, I will give a brief resumé of the development of this work.

My study of the concept of corporatism began, after an interest had been aroused by the works of the earliest proponents of neo-corporatism, with an examination of nineteenth- and twentieth-century corporatist economic and social theory. The purpose of this examination was not to provide a history of a body of thought, but to extract the central tenets of corporatist prescriptive theory. This was duly done with the product being a model of corporatism consisting of a reasonably wide range of components. The second stage in the exercise was to apply empirically the model developed to three politico-economic systems, namely two noted corporatist regimes, Fascist Italy and Portugal 1933–74, and contemporary Britain 1960–80.[11] In all three cases the model was by no means a perfect match, and failed to significant degrees, particularly in the case of Britain, adequately to describe and explain political phenomena in these systems. The analysis did, however, leave two important questions only partially answered.

In the first place, Italy and Portugal, and for that matter other corporatist regimes, despite clear divergencies between themselves and the model, also displayed certain significant similarities. Moreover, these regimes had professed to being guided by corporatist ideology and had called themselves 'corporatist'. The issue was one of whether such regimes should be regarded as failed corporatist regimes or a variant of corporatism not explicitly revealed by the original model. Second, a question arose as to why there was continuing interest in corporatism as applicable to Britain (as well as other western polities) when the model extracted from prescriptive corporatist theory drew a virtual blank. Again the central matter was the one of whether there were any substantial linkages between the model applied and the phenomena encompassed under neo-corporatism, such that they could be regarded as a genus of the same species, or whether they were different conceptual entities sharing the same name. Clearly, given what has already been said about the amorphous nature of neo-corporatism, such links could not be expected to lie with every brand of corporatism currently on the market, but there remain certain more substantial approaches within the literature which could (and should) be the focus for extrapolating any such linkages.

Interestingly, dimensions common to the three usages of corporatism were discernible that were specific enough to mark corporatism off from other political models. The common ground between corporatist ideology and authoritarian practice was not perhaps so terribly surprising, but the connections between them and certain leading neo-marxist and radical writers on neo-corporatism was something that had only been vaguely suggested, not substantiated by any means. What was discernible in each usage of corporatism were four major dimensions. The first of these is particularly valuable because it goes a long way to help clarify which segments of the neo-corporatist writings can be considered legitimately corporatist (in historical terms at least) and which cannot.

The first of the common dimensions relates to the role of the state. In the three usages of corporatism the state's function is to establish and maintain a particular economic and social order. Such economic and social orders, moreover, are not compatible with a free market or managed market economy. So, the state is concerned to directly regulate and influence the behaviour of individual actors in the economy such that their behaviour is compatible with the goals of the economic and social order. Finally, and crucially, in seeking to sustain a particular economic and social order, the state's performance of this function is not to be subject to effective challenge from popular or particularistic demands. In this respect, therefore, the corporatist state is a dominant state.

The second dimension of corporatism follows on from the final point above. Given that a corporatist state is dominant in the econonic and social domain, there is a severe limitation placed upon liberal democratic institutions in authoritative decision-making. Indeed, it may be the case that such institutions do not exist at all, but this is not imperative to a corporatist system; it is possible for democratic institutions to play a significant role outside the economic and social sphere. Of course, by some definitions the economic and social sphere can be so wide as to leave outside only a very small and insignificant arena of political decision-making. In actual fact, there are reasonably tight limits to those economic and social matters with which corporatist structures are directly concerned. Briefly, one can say that corporatist structures are principally concerned with the regulation of productive processes, not distributive processes, though there will be concern for the manner in which productive processes impinge upon distribution. This relationship with productive processes is not the result of the obscure ideological predilections of some nineteenth-century writers, but reflects the constraints placed upon the state's mode of operation when seeking to regulate the productive process because of its lack of direct control of certain essential resources in that process.

Following on from that last point leads us directly to the third dimension of corporatism. Obviously where the state has direct control over the resources of the productive process then the mode of operation adopted – for these reasons at least – are not so constrained, and hence the desirability of corporatist structures is reduced. In such circumstances where such direct control does not pertain, yet the state is responsible for some overall economic and social order, then there is a need to bring about the requisite degree of control. All three varieties of corporatism are, in differing ways, concerned with the need to create such control in circumstances where there is a predominance of private ownership of the means of production and wage labour. This is not to deny that where private ownership does not pertain, and there is for whatever reason an inadequate level of state control, corporatist (or more accurately corporatist-type) structures may be relevant. However, corporatism as a system of ideas or as a description of political systems is directly concerned with the *problématique* of how a state can sustain an economic and social order within a predominantly privately owned productive order: corporatist ideology adhered to moral and productive principles in support of private property; corporatist states encompassed interests that gave widespread support to private property; and neo-corporatist analysis is concerned with the role of the state in advanced capitalist economies. This link between corporatism and the predominance of private capital employing wage labour is all but universal and, therefore, will be regarded as an essential dimension of corporatism.

The fourth and final dimension common to all varieties of corporatism is the ascribing, prescriptively or descriptively, of an intermediary function to 'representative' organisations. Under corporatism producers' organisations cease to be exclusively voluntary representative bodies, but also acquire a substantial role as a regulatory agency on behalf of the state. The organisations no longer solely act as a link between the state and economic

Table 1.1 *General model of corporatism*

1   The state has a principal function of establishing and maintaining an economic and social order. Such an order is not compatible with an essentially market-based economy. The performance of this function must override any conflicting popular or particular demands; the state is dominant in the economic and social sphere.
2   The economy is predominantly constituted of private ownership of the means of production and wage labour.
3   There is at least a circumscription upon the role of liberal democratic institutions in authoritative decision-making. Indeed, liberal democratic institutions may not exist at all.
4   Organisations of producers undertake an intermediary role between the state and societal actors, performing not only a representative function but also operating as a regulatory agency on behalf of the state.

and social actors in terms of performing a function of articulating the interests of their members to the state authorities. Under corporatism they additionally act as a link between the state and societal actors through being delegated regulatory powers by the state over their members. Importantly, these regulatory powers concern not just the internal relations of the organisation, but are more directly concerned with ensuring compliance to allocations made by the state authorities. In short, these organisations are transformed such that they lose their exclusively private character, becoming agencies enforcing political decisions and thereby, in some form, they control the members' behaviour on behalf of the state authorities. Given that these organisations have a functional duality – sending demands up, passing directions down – they will be termed *intermediaries* throughout to distinguish them from conventional interest organisations, on the one hand, and conventional public agencies on the other.

The above represent the four core dimensions of corporatism and hence provide us with a basic model of corporatism. (See Table 1.1)

The three varieties of corporatism which we will be discussing in this work are, therefore, elaborated types of the general model. Of course, any general model provides the potential to develop a wide range of types, but the present intention is to clarify those types that already have in different contexts been widely used. The major differences between the three types rest predominantly on the fourth part of the general model, namely the basis upon which the intermediaries control their members and the intermediaries' general relationship to the state. There are, nonetheless, other differences between the types relating to the extent to which liberal democratic institutions are circumscribed and the nature of the economic and social order the state seeks to sustain. However, as the major differ-

Table 1.2 *Varieties of Corporatism*

Usage		Central characteristics	Type
1 Prescriptive economic and social theory	(a)	State licences intermediaries, and intermediaries in turn licence economic and social actors. This is the basis upon which the state controls and hence sustains a particular economic and social order.	Consensual-licenced
	(b)	There is an assumption that a corporatist system will both generate and attain a high degree of consensus about its underlying values and goals. Such a consensus will result in limited need for state to exercise control and a notable degree of autonomy for intermediaries and societal actors.	
	(c)	Corporatist structures are so established as to enhance degree of consensus.	
2 Politico-economic system as adopted practice in a number of authoritarian corporate states	(a)	State licences intermediaries, and intermediaries in turn licence or otherwise restrict freedom of economic and social actors. This is the basis upon which the state controls societal actors and hence sustains a particular economic and social order.	Authoritarian-licenced
	(b)	It is assumed that there is limited support for the underlying values and goals of the corporatist system and that the economic and social order will have to be imposed.	
	(c)	Corporatist structures are so established as to secure the greatest level of state control practicable.	
3 Models of analysis applied to western industrialised polities (neo-corporatism)	(a)	State achieves domination by securing favourable 'contracts' or exchanges with producer groups through bargaining. Producer group leaders in turn secure compliance of their members to terms of contract by various means (sometimes aided by state); weaker means employed may display tendency to breakdown.	Contract
	(b)	There is a general consensus in support of existing order, but particularistic demands and conflict threaten stability of the order.	
	(c)	Corporatist structures are so established as to generate a high degree of voluntary consent to authoritative decisions. In consequence corporatist structures are institutionally less formal than under the other two types	

ences relate to the position of the intermediaries, I will distinguish them in terms of nomenclature upon this basis. Thus while each variety of corporatism will be discussed in the context of its usage, the fact that these different usages amount to different types will be given terminological recognition.

In one sense, it is somewhat premature to slap labels on the types of corporatism when they remain to be examined. Nevertheless, there is a benefit in introducing them here because the terms do provide a general indication of the direction of the discussions and do set down from the outset a basis for distinguishing between them. The titles of the three types are as set out in Table 1.2.

Before going on to outline the general methodology to be employed in the examination of the three varieties of corporatism it is necessary to return briefly to the general model, and its application. Not only does the model provide the basic skeleton to types of corporatism, it does also supply a set of criteria by which to assess whether the utilisation of the term is legitimate. This ability to apply a set of elements upon which, or define a general context within which, discussions of corporatism should be conducted is desirable given the already-mentioned diverse forms of corporatism doing the rounds. Once corporatism is discussed outside the context suggested here it rapidly falls into a state of excessive malleability as a concept. The consequence of this pliability is that corporatism travels too far, too easily, treading on the toes of many other analytic concepts *en route*. In particular, the boundaries set by the general model should allow for clarification of the presently uncertain dividing-line between neo-corporatism and pluralism. Further, the general model should place a limit on the nomadic existence of corporatism, *whereby one aspect of an existing corporatist model* is found in some unrelated context and hence *corporatism* is found in some previously unrelated context. After all, political models are not made up of mutually exclusive components, but this does not mean the components need be mutually interchangeable.

The inevitable outcome of laying down the 'house rules' of corporatism is the expulsion of a large number of the present membership. Some of these cases of expulsion will be discussed further in Part IV. At the moment, the general *raison d'être* upon which this more selective attitude is based is that of historical precedent, that is these forms of corporatism do not accord at all precisely with the concept as it has been historically employed. So, the onus is on these writers to come up with some substantial reasons why their particular description of certain phenomena as 'corporatist' is valid.

The methods of investigation

The three varieties of corporatism to be discussed in this book are not just different types but are related to divergent usages. Therefore, the method by which these three types are elaborated and the main components identified must itself be different in each case. For each usage examined, however, the overall purpose will be the same: the intention will be to examine the literature, whether theoretical or empirical, to establish what are the components common to each usage, so that these components can be regarded as the model of that type.

In respect of extracting the components of nineteenth- and twentieth-century corporatist economic and social theory the procedure has entailed three stages. The first stage, aided by authoritative texts on the history of ideas, was to establish a range of materials, both by corporatist theorists and about corporatist ideas, that could be regarded as legitimately wide enough to represent what corporatist ideology *in toto* was consistently prescribing as a set of ideas. Obviously, the limits imposed upon the range of writers *ipso facto* fixed what is, and what is not, corporatist thought. However, the limits set were neither arbitrary nor expedient. Instead, the objectives were to delimit corporatist thought in terms of a set of reasonably coherent and inter-related prescriptions while also remaining largely in accord with the view taken by authorities on the subject of corporatist thought. Therefore, the boundaries were in the first instance demonstrated by reference to authoritative texts on corporatist thought. Thereafter, the limits were clarified when examination of the theorists' ideas revealed common traditions, metaphysical bases and prescriptions that in a sense established an 'identikit' corporatist theorist. The result is that corporatist ideology is discussed in more restricted terms than is sometimes the case.[12] But it is defined in terms of a system of ideas and not as a category of ideas whereby the only degree of commonality is the categorisation itself.

The second stage in the extraction process was to identify within the body of literature common areas of concern such as the role of the state, the establishment of intermediaries between the state and societal actors and the role of capital and labour. These areas of common concern provide the categories within which the analysis of corporatist thought is placed. The final stage involved putting the ideas of the writers into these categories and distilling the lowest common denominator. So it was established what were the concrete prescriptions generic to corporatism. The discussion that follows in Part II of the book entails drawing upon evidence from the theorists' works and other secondary sources to support the conclusion reached about the prescriptions. Clearly to keep the exercise down to manageable proportions the evidence employed is selective but I have continually tried to cite a range of authors in terms of era, nationality and overall philosophy thereby avoiding suggestions of evading distinctive, and hence different, ideological viewpoints.

Turning now to the second type of corporatism, that is its utilisation as a description of the politico-economic system of certain authoritarian regimes, necessitated a reasonably well organised and precise method of extracting a model from empirical material. For the study of authoritarian-licenced corporatism two regimes have been chosen, Fascist Italy and Portugal 1933–74. These two regimes were chosen because to all intents and purposes they represented the most developed corporatist regimes to have existed. It must be added that these are also two regimes whose corporatist aspects have been widely studied, and while different interpretations exist and will continue to exist, there is an extensive range of hard empirical material to be drawn upon. Not surprisingly, these 'corporatist states' were not developed overnight but graudally evolved over a number of years. Therefore, they will be judged in the main on their latter, more mature period. Nonetheless, given their process of evolution provides a good deal of insight into their overall character, and that many of the crucial decisions were taken early on, the regimes' development will be given due attention.

The means by which the central components of the authoritarian-licensed type will be established involves utilising the model of the consensual-licensed type, to study the actual practice of the regimes. Given that it has already been acknowledged that we will be dealing with a different type of corporatism, this method has been adopted for reasons other than there being a good match between model and empirical data. Instead, the model has been applied first and foremost as an interpretative framework, a means of organising the analysis. Further, because we are studying authoritarian-licensed corporatism through the application of a model of consensual-licensed corporatism the differences (the consensual/ authoritarian aspects) and similarities (the licensed aspects) between the two types are clarified, which in itself is important. Finally, the employment of the consensual model has set down some reasonably precise bounds to where the discussion of corporatism in these regimes ends and examination of non-corporatist aspects begins. So, for those reasons listed, the model gives some clearer focus to studying corporatism as practised in Italy and Portugal than would be the case with a less structured approach.

In the case of the third variety of corporatism, that is neo-corporatism, there is less need to spell out the method by which the model of this type will be established. This reflects the point that the exercise here will not solely involve distilling certain components from a body of literature, as is the case with the other two types, but also entails extrapolating from certain contemporary theoretical discussions a more substantial and developed theory that fits the criteria of analytic utility, operational potential and accords with the general model of corporatism. Therefore, methodology is not so much a basis for, but a substantial part of, the discussion. However, it is pertinent to note at this juncture that the concern will not be to develop what at face value are necessarily the most amenable models on offer, but instead attention will be paid to those most amenable to development within the framework laid down by the general model of corporatism. The intention here is not just to develop a theory of corporatism with a pedigree, but to construct one that is an explicit alternative to pluralism. Overall the construction of a model within such a framework poses two questions: One, what is wrong with developing 'mongrel' models if they increase analytic insight and, two, is there any need to have an explicit alternative to pluralism? These are valid, not to say crucial, questions. So the discussion on neo-corporatism will not just be concerned to follow a particular path of development, but will begin by justifying the choice of path over other routes available. In other words, the construction of this particular model of neo-corporatism will not be justified on the sole grounds that it is possible to do so within the confines of the general model of corporatism; it will also be vindicated, one hopes, on grounds of analytic validity.

Outline of the work

It may have appeared somewhat pedantic to have engaged in a discussion of methodology in the manner above, but, as one might say, there was method in it. The reason was to present the basis upon which the ensuing discussion and clarification are to be conducted, thereby indicating why a particular line of argument has been followed. Much of this book involves presenting evidence in support of what amount to pre-determined conclusions. What is precluded, therefore, from the discussion is any other evidence that might support different conclusions about conceptualising corporatism. The discussion of methodology, particularly that on corporatist ideology, sought to indicate that the evidence selected (and hence that rejected) was done so for reasons other than that it supported the desired conclusions. Instead, the evidence drawn upon conforms to a set of criteria that have applied to corporatism in different historical usages which can be argued, therefore, to be the defining characteristics of corporatism. This argument is supported further in the absence of any alternative characteristics having been proposed.

Lastly, before going on to the much heralded discussion of the varieties of corporatism, a brief outline on the work is desirable. Part II, on corporatist thought, will be structured into four chapters. Chapter 2, after a brief overview of corporatist thought, will be concerned to elaborate the prescribed role for the state, that is its economic and social responsibilities. The third chapter will be focussed upon the status, structures, membership and functions of the licenced intermediaries, while the following one discusses the nature of the corporatist political system, essentially dealing with representative and responsible government. Part II will be concluded with a brief chapter which draws the previous three together, and makes some overall conclusions on and sets out a model of *consensual-licenced* corporatism. Each of the three substantive chapters will be divided into sub-sections that conform to the subject matter of the model's components.

The next part deals with the analysis of corporatist practice in Italy and Portugal, both countries being dealt with in a single chapter. While the model of consensual-licenced corporatism is to be employed as an interpretative framework to assist with the establishment of the *authoritarian-licenced* type, there will be a change in the ordering of the subjects discussed from that which they came off the production line in Part II. This reflects the logical necessities of setting out the model of authoritarian-licenced corporatism. Therefore, to present in a more satisfactory format what corporatist practice entailed, each chapter will begin with a brief discussion of the development of corporatism, then go on to look at corporatist structures in more detail, concluding with the socio-economic impact of such structures. To maintain a basis for comparison between the consensual and licenced types the chapters will be broken into the same general subject headings. This part of the book will finish with a short chapter that draws together general conclusions about and constructs a model of authoritarian-licenced corporatism. To further support the conclusions, reference will be made to other such corporatist regimes.

The fourth part deals with neo-corporatism. The first chapter on neo-corporatism is to be essentially directed towards discussing the story to date, by outlining the growth of neo-corporatism, the response of adherents to pluralist approaches and the present limitations of certain substantive theories of neo-corporatism. The following chapter will pick up where the previous one left off and seek to develop a general model of *contract* corporatism by drawing on major theories of neo-corporatism that are centred upon bargaining between the state and organised interests, and will aim to develop them through theoretical discussion of power and the state. In addition, the chapter will consider present discussions of organised interests as intermediaries and attempt to clarify the picture.

Part V will attempt to put the discussion of the varieties of corporatism into some overall perspective. In particular, there will be an assessment of what contribution corporatism can make to contemporary political analysis, especially in respect of ostensible liberal democracies, and will discuss how corporatism may be theoretically developed and possibly broadened.

Part II

Corporatist thought: consensual – licenced corporatism

2

Corporatist thought: the state's economic and social responsibilities

This chapter is primarily concerned to examine the corporatist theorists' view of the economic role of the state, which in turn necessitates consideration of the role of the market. In addition, there is a more specific study of what responsibilities the state sought to ensure capital and labour exercised. However, before proceeding to these issues it is necessary to provide an overview of corporatist economic and social thought, thus giving a general background to the process of extrapolating the components. It is particularly important to do this because the components so extracted will concentrate on the concrete structural and functional prescriptions, not on the metaphysical dimensions of the body of thought. It is, nonetheless, desirable to have some flavour of these dimensions so the components can be better understood within their wider context.

Corporatist thought: an overview

Corporatist thought emerged as a response to the disappearance of the *ancien régime* in several continental European countries. The response came most immediately from those who had lost out in the development of industrial capitalism and incipient liberal political institutions. It is hardly surprising, therefore, that the earliest theorists were either exclusively Catholics or aristocrats, or both. Although much emphasis was initially placed upon the alleged benefits of medieval society, with landlord and peasant locked into an 'organic community' which was harmonious and ordered, the theory even in the early days cannot be characterised as exclusively reactionary. Instead, the organic nature of society, with its attendant harmony and order, was to be recognised in the political and economic arrangements of industrial society, thereby ending the class conflict and injustice that industrial capitalism had wrought. Thus, the social bonds between landlord and peasant it was suggested pertained in medieval times would be transposed to the relationship between capitalist and worker.

It is this notion of a harmonious medieval society being reborn in the era of industrial capitalism that underpins much of the writers' prescriptions. Simply put, they took the view that, if the social bonds could be restored by certain changes to the politico-economic arrangements of industrial society, harmony would prevail and conflict would abate; society would be significantly consensual in character. The moral basis of this consensus concerning economic and social life would be either Catholicism – serving the greater glory of 'God' – or nationalism – serving the greater glory of the nation.

While corporatism was an intellectual response to the advent of industrial capitalism in what was held to be liberal politico-economic systems, and the writers were often scathing of the impact it had upon the proletariat, the theory strongly defended the maintenance of private property as the most desirable form of ownership of the means of production. Corporatism was, in effect, anti-liberal rather than anti-capitalist. Liberalism had broken down social bonds and turned society into a mass of atomistic, self-seeking individuals devoid of any higher moral purpose. As two French corporatists of the inter-war period colourfully put it, liberalism aimed 'to direct man towards the material world, to drain him of all notion of eternity, or social life, to make him a brute wanting sentiments of charity, pity, altruism'.[1] In terms of this line of argument, it was not private property that was at fault, but the 'amoral' nature of liberalism that left property without any moral, that is social, responsibilities. This emphasis on social responsibilities meant, however, that while corporatism strongly defended the existence of private property, it would be wrong to see the theorists as strongly allied with bourgeois interests.

In addition to breaking down the social bonds of medieval society, liberalism was indicted for granting political and economic equality to individuals who in corporatist eyes were manifestly unequal. For corporatists, society had to be hierarchically structured, a person's rights and duties reflecting their status within society. Corporatism was to be a system of status set against the contract system of liberalism, inverting Sir Henry Maine's dictum 'from Status to Contract'. The corporatist theorists were thus in fundamental disagreement with Maine's assessment that social progress occurred where relations of persons are no longer summed up in the relations of the 'Family', but in relations arising from the free agreement of individuals.[2] It is important to note that this emphasis upon status relations not only set corporatism apart from liberalism, it similarly painted a thick dividing line between itself and socialism.

So, in place of the liberal individualistic socio-economic order was to be a collectivist and status-based hierarchical one. Central to the establishment and maintenance of this order was to be the state. To corporatists the state was not to be restricted to a Spencerian 'hindrance of hindrances' or a slumbering nightwatchman. Instead, the corporatist state can best be characterised as one of guardianship. This reflected the theorists' proposition that the state had a definite moral base drawn either from 'God' or from the nation's past; indeed the moral and political bases of the state were seen as closely fused. The state was, therefore, endowed with a moral authority to serve the greater glory of 'God' or the nation's interest, and had the right to intervene in economic and social affairs whenever they conflicted with 'God's' will or the national interest. There were, nonetheless, limits to the authority of the state and its right to intervene. The application of 'God's' will or principles of national interest in economic and social affairs was not boundless: 'God' was concerned with seeing justice prevail, not product design and innovation, while national glory was reflected in national output not in the means adopted to produce it where producers should enjoy a relatively free hand. Yet, as we shall see in due course, the actual boundaries to the state's intervention into the economy remained an uncertain and ambiguous dimension of the body of thought. This itself was a reflection not only of the amorphous character of translating moral principles into practice, but also of the capriciousness amongst the theorists about how far the establishment of a corporatist state would generate a corporatist society; that is, how far it would generate a consensus allowing for extensive delegation of economic decision-making. There was near universal belief on the part of the writers that a significant degree of consensus would emerge, such that delegation and self-regulation would be a notable attribute of corporatist regulation, but a handful of theorists (as opposed to apologists for corporate states) did cross the fence into the authoritarian-licensed camp.

Into the later part of the nineteenth century and on into the twentieth, there was within corporatist thought – while no fundamental altering of the basic tenets – a general change in the weight of emphasis. There was less harking back to some bygone idyll and more prominence was given to corporatism as a system valid in its own right as a prospectus for industrial society. The arguments for corporatism became, to a greater degree, pragmatic rather than metaphysical. This practical approach, although it was never an exclusive part by any means, reached its zenith after the Great War. Much of the driving force behind this came from an increasing awareness of the shortcomings of capitalism and the rise of the challenge of socialism. Corporatism was fighting a doctrinal battle on two fronts, hence Auguste Murat's description of corporatism as the 'third solution'.[3] In one distinctive way, however, socialism posed the longer term ideological and political threat because corporatists largely believed that 'liberal capitalism' contained the seeds of its own destruction and that socialist revolution would ensue if capitalism remained unchecked.

Socialism, of course, was no less anathema to corporatists than liberalism. It threatened private property, preached class conflict, proffered equality, was internationalist, which nationalist corporatists found unacceptable, and was agnostic, which similarly displeased Catholics. The corporatist attack on what are regarded as conventional socialist values and principles was a sustained and widespread feature of the writers' work. This is an important feature of the body of thought, because it is often suggested that corporatism is closely associated with forms of socialism,[4] where in fact they were part of different traditions of thought[5] separated by divergent underlying values. A note of caution, however, should be added because certain corporatist writers, like Catholic socialists or monarchical socialists were not averse to using 'socialism' as a flag of convenience.

In respect of the above point, it is worth reiterating that corporatism was based on one of two underlying philosophies, Catholicism and nationalism, neither of which is noted as contributing to socialist thought. These two distinctive tendencies within the theory pose a question concerning the unity of the body of thought. To some extent nationalist corporatist clearly adopted, then adapted, Catholic ideas for generating a harmonious and hence unified society. Often atheist nationalist writers read very much like their Catholic counterparts, providing, like the positivists (whose sociology clearly inculcated corporatism), a form of 'secularised catholicsm'.[6] Quite simply, corporatist theory is essentially not found outside countries where there is a strong or dominant Catholic intellectual tradition. This is not to deny there were differences between the two groupings. Catholic and national corporatist states served different overall moral purposes and their corporatist societies were bonded together upon divergent principles. The Catholics saw their edifice bound together by Christian love, the application of justice and the following of 'God's' will. Nationalist corporatists, on the other hand, saw society held together by individual sacrifice to the national good, usually as it was to be interpreted by some self-appointed leader. Below this level of abstraction there was an extensive coming together, not only in terms of institutional arrangements, but also in relation to generating harmony and applying principles of justice within society.

One difference in tone between the two groupings that is detectable, if far from universal, was that nationalists seemed to be less tolerant of potential nonconformity, though Catholics themselves did not regard the opportunity for dissent as welcome and were ambivalent, if not hostile, towards democracy. This is not to say that corporatists believed in an absolutist state. It is most noticeable in French writings, but almost all theorists wished to see constraints placed upon the authority of the central state through the regulation of society and the economy by means of semi-independent, self-regulating professions. The central state was to lay down broad principles that would set a general framework within which the professions would regulate their ambit of responsibility. Thus the heavy hand of bureaucratic centralization associated with corporatist practice, was in fact something the theorists consciously sought to avoid.

By the time regimes were being established in a number of European countries that overtly claimed to be corporatist, beginning with Fascist Italy, corporatist economic and social theory had come a long way from medieval resurrection. Indeed, most later writers had called into question the motion of a medieval harmony. But the writers remained true to the Greco-Roman, Christian-Thomistic and medieval traditions[7] of their predecessors and convinced that a consensual, harmonious society could be engendered under corporatism. In this period between the world wars, with the economic and political crises in many liberal capitalist polities on the one hand, and the repercussions of the Russian revolution on the other, the 'third way' gained a sharper political edge. However, the popular appeal of the 'third way' probably remained greatest amongst third forces, those squeezed by industrialisation such as artisans and small businessmen.

The summer of corporatist theory ended ironically with the emergence of corporate states in Europe where corporatist writers became apologists for what was, no longer prescribers of what ought to be. Many corporatist theorists, particularly those in France who had time to trace developments elsewhere, however, dissented from the corporatist practice of the authoritarian states. With the defeat of the European axis powers who to varying degrees adopted corporatist experiments, corporatism as a body of thought all but died out in these countries. In large measure, the cause was guilt by association. That is not, however, the full explanation and the issue will be given further consideration in the final chapter, once corporatist thought and practice have been studied. For the moment, the notable point is that the near fatality of corporatist thought meant that no revisionist versions or schools emerged in the light of experience, and so corporatist thought retained its intellectual coherence. With that point in mind we now turn to examine what were the common prescriptions of the theorists.

The state, the economy and the market

The corporatist view of the role of the state in economic and social affairs was grounded in an often extensive critique of the doctrine of *laissez-faire* liberalism, although in actuality they regarded anything approaching a free market in the allocation of resources to determine communal welfare as intolerable. In practice, the attack on economic liberalism was based on the twin grounds of doctrinal incompatibility between the free market and a corporatist order and the harmful consequences observed as resulting from the operation of the market. Therefore, there was a dual-pronged attack – on the doctrine of liberalism and on the practice of capitalism.

Sometimes which prong was being employed was not made clear by the writers. But the message was always explicit – the competitive market was undesirable and should be replaced by other forms of regulation. For example, the Frenchman Georges Valois, writing just after the First World War, attacked the fundamentals of economic liberalism claiming to be in error 'the belief that liberty is the necessary condition of work, of production, of progress'.[8] While, in more pragmatic terms, Pierre Lucius declared during the inter-war depression that the 'disordered initiative tolerable in the last century has become a dangerous anachronism'.[9] But even prior to the Great War, corporatists were not very charitable towards the French economy's condition. For La Tour du Pin, one of France's foremost Catholic corporatists, unrestricted competition was injurious because it resulted in economic waste.[10] In Germany as well, corporatists persistently attacked the unchecked market. Wichard von Moellendorff, in the context of reconstruction after the First World War, argued it was necessary to turn away from *Manchestertum* and that the aims of the country could not be achieved through competition.[11] Earlier in the 1870s, Adolf Wagner held that the immediate task of the German Empire was the struggle of German national economics against the doctrine of the Free Trade School.[12] The Spanish corporatist, Azpiazu, similarly pointed out in the 1930s that a corporate economy would be a directed or controlled economy, although he was careful to add that such direction would not be coercive, but would be what he euphemistically termed a 'gentle bending' towards the common good.[13] Finally, in Austria too, the corporatist theorists ranged themselves against economic liberalism. For example, Othmar Spann, a Viennese professor of political economy, set out in some detail his proposals for an anti-individualistic economy highly organised and extensively regulated,[14] and likewise the Romanticist and authoritarian Vogelsang School condemned capitalism for, among other things, introducing unrestricted competition.[15] As Professor Denis summarised the position in 1941, under corporatism, the vocational groups that were to act as agents of the state would tend 'to conserve or suppress the market' and consequently act as an instrument of a planned economy.[16]

Therefore, in whichever country or era, dating back to 'Romantics' of the early nineteenth century like Adam Müller,[17] corporatist theory is examined, economic liberalism was evidently anathema to and severely criticised by the writers. This point will be emphasised many times over as the discussion of corporatist theory unfolds. In essence, the case against the market was that competition resolved economic matters according to the power of the participants, without reference to any other higher, moral principles.[18] Instead, corporatists argued that economic actors could not have complete liberty[19] in taking decisions but had to be bound by the social duties, as well as rights, it was proffered they held. The theorists were, therefore, not concerned that interference, particularly on an extensive scale, into the market would (on liberal premisses) reduce the social benefit, because it undermines the efficiency of the allocation system away from 'Pareto optimality', and interferes with economic liberty.[20] Even if the corporatists had accepted these liberal premisses, and not many did in any case,[21] it would not have led to any redefining of their attitudes to the market because they were not primarily concerned with efficiency or economic liberty.

The theorists, in consequence, fully supported economic regulation and turned to the state, and as we shall see shortly to its agents, to take on wide economic and social responsibilities. De Michelis, an Italian theorist writing at the height of the Italian corporate state under Mussolini, for example, argued that under a corporative economy, conflict between private interests would not be resolved automatically according to the strength of those involved but by the consciously exercised authority of the state.[22] Azpiazu suggested wide responsibilities for the state with it as the custodian of what is just and controller of the 'commonweal', performing such activities as protecting labour from exploitation, protecting consumers, protecting enterprises against foreign competition and aiding them to break into foreign markets, combatting speculation and also giving some general direction to the economy. Azpiazu's ideas reflect those of other corporatists in that the state was not solely to be concerned with intervening to see justice (or for others the national interest) prevail, but also to perform a general function of economic management.[23] To the social Catholics, indeed, the state's role was central, if not omnipresent, acting as the source of leadership to the economy.[24] According to Paul Chanson, discussing the corporative institutions, 'the state coordinates their activities, arbitrates their respective interests and makes them accord with the general needs of the national economy'.[25] Francois Perroux, the noted French economist, indeed talked in terms of 'corporate planning' under which 'it is the State in collaboration with individuals, and no longer the operation of prices which closes establishments, transfers workers and distributes capital',[26] while Georges Valois saw the state as a source of veto over any economic regulations contrary to the national interest.[27]

Even to earlier writers, the state was of foremost importance, with corporatists like Adam Müller seeing the state as the necessary pinnacle of the hierarchy of the productive forces.[28] Likewise, Adolf Wagner's writings reflect the desire to place the state at the centre of the economy's life using its authority wherever, and however, necessary to strengthen the nation; and, according to the well-known 'Wagner's law', the state's role in the economy would continue to increase as a natural and necessary corollary of increasing national might.[29]

Wagner's view of the state's role stands in contrast to most corporatist writers, although his views were not unique amongst those theorists examined in our study. All the theorists saw the state as ultimately having extensive responsibilities in economic and social affairs. However, to the majority this was not to result in unlimited state invervention as the bulk of the regulation of the economy would fall to the specially constituted corporatist institutions. For these corporatists, their prescriptions offered a way to economic regulation which would not entail an *étatiste* system, with the state as the keystone of the hierarchy of production but not the main institution of regulation. According to Frauendorfer the corporatist institutions would be subject to the general oversight of the state but would possess a considerable degree of autonomy.[30] To the monarchist La Tour, the king was not to be absolute and was to respect the semi-autonomous character of the corporations.[31] In the same tradition Valois, while proposing the state would exercise a veto over regulations contrary to national welfare, argued that the state was not to 'penetrate into the domain of work itself where it is incompetent',[32] and Hubert Ley also 'expressed the general corporatist viewpoint that social insurance and economic regulation could more efficiently be administered by corporations than by the state'.[33] Von Moellendorff even went so far as to say that the 'professional communities' in formulating and carrying out industrial policies designed to advance the national interest should enjoy a virtual immunity from state interference.[34]

What these theorists were arguing for was a 'guardian state' ensuring through limited intervention that other economic institutions benefited the general welfare and applied certain values, such as justice, to their economic and social behaviour. Thus Walther Rathenau maintained that his 'New State' would not be complete until the 'political state' had been relieved of economic, administrative and other extraneous tasks so that it could fulfill its own essential mission of 'giving direction and making final decisions'.[35] Indeed, Rathenau held that the modern state had drawn every human activity into its orbit in a centralized unitary estate, but now its responsibilities had to be redistributed and rationalised.[36]

The question remains concerning those theorists who did not see the intermediary bodies, the corporations, as acting as a check upon the state, but instead saw them as a means of control for a powerful state over economic and social affairs. Adolf Wagner has already been referred to, but he was not alone in his viewpoint. For Gaeton Pirou, Professor of Law at the University of Paris, the idea of semi-autonomous corporations performing regulation essentially without state control was impractical. Other French interbellum corporatists, such as Odette de Puiffe de Magondeaux,[37] agreed with him, although they were clearly only a handful. Probably the most noted of all corporatist theorists, Mihail Manoilesco, for example, saw as a virtue of corporatist doctrine the plurality of public authority and the autonomy of the corporatist organisations it proposed,[38] despite the important role ascribed to the state by him. Wagner apart, amongst German corporatists the idea of organisational autonomy from the state was almost universally adhered to until the Nazi regime came into being, when writers like Frauendorfer attacked the autonomy advocated for corporative organisations for not adequately recognising the supreme authority of the state.[39] In Italy too, the denunciation of group autonomy by theorists came after the advent of the Fascist movement.[40]

There is, therefore, a divide amongst the theorists centred around the degree of autonomy to be enjoyed by corporatist organisations. The issue was not over whether the state was to be powerful or not, for those, such as Lucius, who wanted control of the economic system to remain chiefly in the hands of producers also demanded a strong state.[41] The difference centred, as a result, on how limited the exercise of authority granted to the state was to be in practice, or, put another way, how extensive the powers delegated to the intermediaries were to be. These views were themselves founded upon judgements as to the extent a corporatist consensus would emerge, and hence how far responsibilities could be delegated by the state. Such divergences of opinion are hardly surprising, but the vast majority of theorists held that the degree of consensus engendered would make a significant level of delegation feasible. A few theorists, however, had no faith in a consensus being generated, or perhaps they were dubious about the compatibility between their view of what the social order ought to be and the extent to which society would share such values. Whatever the grounds of their case, they held that the order would need to be imposed and thus advocated something more akin to authoritarian-licenced corporatism. This issue of the authority of the central state is pertinent to a full understanding of corporatist theory, and indeed it greatly occupied the theorists themselves, and so it will be returned to after the status and structure of the intermediaries have been discussed. Before turning to elaborate upon what the theorists prescribed in relation to the state's role in regulating capital and labour, over and above the more general view of the economic function of the state, it is necessary to clarify further the corporatist assessment of the market. Corporatism was not to result in the total abolition of the market and its replacement by comprehensive state planning. Instead, the market was to be constrained by collective interests. Spann, who was no admirer of economic liberalism, for example, recognised that some form of competitive market would have to continue, though it would not be all-pervasive, instead being bound by corporatist values. Franz Hitze spoke in similar terms. He argued that in bringing production and distribution under social control 'competition is not to be abolished, but it is to be brought within bounds'.[42] Likewise, Azpiazu pointed out that when the corporatist system was established it would not result in the disappearance of competition, it being necessary only to regulate the market according to the principles of 'right reason' and 'common sense'.[43] Indeed, among the theorists there was, having attacked free competition in strong terms, almost a back-tracking, because although they wished to see established 'just prices', they also recognised certain benefits of competition. Georges Valois, who was concerned to see greater and greater production at lower and lower prices, for one was in no doubt that competition was a spur to technical progress.[44] Spann had also noted the benefits of competition for developing individual talents.[45]

Such a paradoxical situation was reflected apparently in the works of Mathon and Lucius, who advocated both the continuance of competition and, simultaneously, the regulation of prices and production.[46] In effect, however, the paradox is non-existent, because the corporatists were distinguishing between competition based on the pursuit of self-interest as occurred under liberalism, which was anathema to them, and corporatist competition based on ethical principles that would require regulation only on occasion. As Johannes Messner asserted, it was not possible to develop economic ethics on the basis of general moral norms but one must take into account actual economic conditions and economic theory with the respective scope of each having to be recognised.[47] Therefore, the corporatists were not prescribing a certain level of economic regulation. As Dobrestberger argued it would vary according to the conditions prevailing adding that regulation would be necessary where ethical, or socially responsible, competition failed to achieve the desired objectives.[48]

Like the variation in views among the corporatists concerning the limits to the state's exercise of authority, there were divergences over where the dividing line between regulation and the market would be. Some theorists appeared to be of the opinion that the market would remain largely intact, but the behaviour of economic actors would be bounded by some *esprit de communauté*, instead of spurred exclusively by self-interest. Others emphasised the need for regulation and planning. Indeed, one can detect the same sort of differences in relation to the regulation of international trade. Obviously, all theorists recognised the fundamental point that unrestricted international commerce was a potential threat to domestic regulation and 'ethical markets'. However, such a point of concern evoked a range of responses. For example, Johann Fichte, one of the first writers in Germany after the French Revolution to outline corporatist proposals, proclaimed the virtues of a 'closed commercial state' where foreign trade would be conducted through a state monopoly aiming at the highest degree of autarky.[49] Writers like Müller,[50] Baader,[51] and Wagner,[52] under the influence of German nationalism, leaned in the same direction. Other writers were less extreme in their outlook, but nevertheless not averse to protectionism to achieve specific objectives: La Tour wanted protection to assist French agriculture,[53] while Georges Valois argued for it to ensure a steady increase in national output to achieve the twin objectives of expressing the glory of France and to combat a regenerated Germany.[54] Yet a further group of corporatists went beyond rather personal preferences for protectionism and actually incorporated the case for protectionism directly into their corporatist scheme. Into this category fell Spann[55] and Walther Rathenau,[56] and most notably Manoilesco, whose whole corporatist edifice rested on an economic theory of competition between nations.[57] It is perhaps not surprising that these three writers' corporatist ideas were based much more on a political-economic, rather than philosophical, approach.[58]

The writers, therefore, adopted quite variable standpoints *vis-à-vis* the role of the market, both in terms of domestic and international economic activity. These differences reflected the divergent goals they espoused – and the different emphasis they gave to these goals – and their somewhat diverse assessments about how far regulation would be necessary to attain these goals. The commonality in all their positions was the primacy of the goals to be pursued by the state authorities over and above any allocations decided through the market. Contrary to liberalism, the market was not hallowed, because the corporatists did not highly value efficiency or liberty. Instead, they sought to apply communal principles of justice and the national interest. It is to the elaboration of how these principles were to affect capital and labour respectively that attention is now directed.

The role of capital

Central to the concerns of the corporatist writers was outlining how and upon what basis a private capital economy could be rendered compatible with overall state responsibility for economic and social well-being.

Evidently the exercise of such responsibility not only impinges upon the operation of the free market, but also places constraints upon the rights of private property. However, despite often attacking the irresponsibility of capitalists and wishing to see restraints put on their behaviour, the theorists staunchly defended the right to hold capital. Indeed to Catholic theorists, private property was an inviolable right of natural law. For Bishop von Ketteler, the maintenance of private property was fundamental. He stated that 'if there is to be peace and order in the world in the use and dispensing of the goods of the earth [...] the private property rights must be acknowledged to possess the same dignity as a law of nature as for instance the right to breathe'. Any challenge to the right would inevitably lead to conflict, which would completely destroy the 'development of mankind itself'.[59] Azpiazu,[60] de Mun and La Tour[61] added their voices in support of private property. Indeed, Azpiazu cited not only natural law in support of his case, but also the more practical argument that it offered the best opportunity for society to prosper. Common among Catholic corporatists in addition to support for private property, however, were arguments in favour of extending ownership to include the workers. Certainly, La Tour and de Mun[62] put forward proposals for collective, corporatist property to be held by the workers: the former in such an ambiguous manner[63] that he opened himself to the charge of being a socialist.[64] Further, the two 'corporatist pontiffs', Leo XIII and Pius XI, in their encyclicals on the social question, *Rerum Novarum*[65] and *Quadragesimo Anno*[66] respectively, backed the twin nostrums of defending and extending private ownership. Not surprisingly, often coupled with the argument for diversification of ownership was criticism of the increasing concentration of capital.[67]

Non-catholic corporatists did not have natural law upon which to draw but, different premises apart, there was little difference in their outlook. Walther Rathenau, for example, saw nationalisation as being out of the question because it would deprive the economy of any driving force,[68] for, however uncongenial it appeared, it was of great importance from the economic point of view that private property continued to exist, as it alone could shoulder the risks of the economy. The state could not act as entrepreneur,[69] so his *neue Wirtschaft* was to be a 'private economy'.[70] Rathenau's one-time colleague, Wichard von Moellendorff, took a similar view but further proposed a property taxation should be inaugurated which would allow the Reich to become a shareholder in a number of corporations, though this was not to form the basis of the state's regulatory powers.[71] Other German nationalist corporatists, like Marlo,[72] Schäffle[73] and Wagner,[74] sought to defend private property, largely on the grounds that it was essential for generating the economic leadership and competence to ensure increased prosperity. Their French counterparts were less inclined to staunchly defend private ownership, probably reflecting the French writers' lesser obsession with the threat of socialism, which the Social Democratic Party placed in German minds. Indeed, the French attitude was in part critical following on from La Tour's attack on financial and large-scale capital.[75] However, the proposals for dealing with the *sociétés anonymes* was to strengthen the position of the owners, the shareholders, over management.[76]

While the corporatists supported the private ownership of capital, and usually praised its economic, as well as moral, value, there was never any absolute advocacy of its ascendancy; in certain circumstances other forms of ownership would be desirable. Manoilesco for one argued that the form of ownership was a 'pragmatic' matter, depending on its social function. If it was proved that for a particular category of production the best results were achieved by socialised property, state property or corporative property, then such an evolution would not be opposed under corporatism. Although there is a degree of ambivalence in Manoilesco's position, there is nothing in his work to suggest that private property would be abolished wholesale; instead transfer away from private ownership would only occur when it wholly failed in its social mission.[77] Likewise De Michelis took a pragmatic view, but he did add that in his epoch private property was the best form to subserve the general interest,[78] and his compatriots Vito and Feraldi concurred.[79] Even staunch supporters of private property recognised that there would have to be exceptions to the rule, including those drawing upon the natural law traditions like the Thomist Heinrich Pesch[80] and Pius XI.[81] Indeed, several writers – Marlo, Konstantin Frantz and Schäffle among them[82] – took the view that there were certain 'natural' public industries and that they had to be clearly demarcated from the private sectors. More specifically Wagner proposed the railways for nationalisation.[83] Overall, the picture was one of public ownership being restricted to special cases, those where functional requirements such as natural monopolies or defence industries prevailed, though there was never any consistency as to what exactly these functional requirements were to be.

There was, however, another sense in which the corporatist defence of private property was not absolute. Private property can be defined as the right of an individual (or a corporate entity) to exclude others from some use or benefit of something.[84] Under capitalism, private property is subject to certain limits on the uses to which it can be put with regard to creating a nuisance, endangering life and health, and so on. It, nevertheless, remains an absolute right because it entails a right to dispose of, as well as to use, and it is a right which is not conditional on the owner's performance of any social function.[85] The corporatists wished to end property as an absolute right by making it conditional upon the performance of certain social functions. Franz Baader set out the general view of Catholic corporatists when he stated: 'Christianity has also fundamentally reformed all doctrines and notions of acquisition, possession and consumption of property by doing away with the pagan concept of absolute property without, however, barring individual acquisition and possession [...] No Christian may declare, this property, this right, this office are mine, to handle as I please; for in reality these are God's gifts and tasks, and a Christian may therefore handle them only as it pleases God, which in a truly Christian community makes of every possession only an *ex officio* possession [...]'.[86] Other Catholics took up this point and emphasised that property could not be used or consumed without due regard to common welfare, particularly giving assistance to the poor.[87] As Heinrich Pesch stated, private property was only legitimate so long as it met the 'demands of the common welfare' on both the productive and distributive sides.[88] Not unexpectedly, the Catholic writers placed most of their emphasis upon owners fulfilling their obligations to their employees, not simply in terms of wages but also in respect of working conditions, though certain specific issues, like the ten-hour day and child labour, are now only historical curiosities in Western societies. Nevertheless, with the possible exception of Ketteler, the obligation to the wider welfare of society was prominent too in Catholic works. For example, La Tour argued that private capital would have to meet the social needs of production, including producing better quality products and charging a 'just price'.[89]

On the other hand, the non-catholic corporatists put greater weight upon production than allocation. Rathenau is a good case in point; the organisation of production was always his central theme. He proposed that the large joint-stock corporations, with their depersonalised ownership, should come to be motivated by considerations other than high profit. Instead, they should be motiviated by a sense of community subject, of course, to the general supervision of the state.[90] For his part, Manoilesco was less munificent, more straightforward than to assume any change in capital's motivating force. Property, it was asserted, had a social function and had, therefore, to be subject to the social ends established by the state.[91] Wagner was also in accord with this viewpoint, as ever stressing the authority of the state.[92] But De Michelis did point out that productive processes could not be shackled by the state; rather capital would be subject to 'limitations' and 'adaptions' to subserve the general interest.[93]

Generally, the tendor of corporatist writers was to talk of putting bounds upon the internal decision-making of firms. For example, quotas might be set to prevent what is regarded as 'over-production', or prices fixed within limits, or capacity determined. Within the constraints set by the number and range of these limits, firms would compete through the market.[94] It is important to stress that because property had a social obligation, the public authorities were not expected to cushion the effects of or encourage through incentives the meeting of such obligations. Nowhere in theory was it ever suggested that the state had a reciprocal obligation to private capital. Of course, the theorists were of the view that capital under the new order would be socially responsible in its outlook, and the state would not need to impose such obligations on a significant scale. Where capital did, however, ignore its social obligations, then it would be in breach of public law and subject to the appropriate penalties. In cases of persistent transgression – a difficulty the theorists for obvious reasons never considered in any depth – then the most obvious course would not be public appropriation, but to transfer to more responsible owners. In other words, the theorists largely adhered to the Thomistic concept of the stewardship of property.[95] It was the Romantics, like Othmar Spann, who most explicitly set out proposals for stewardship of property. In his 'true state' the majority of property would be held in the form of *Lehen* (enfeoffed property) with individuals having the use of the property, in return for rendering services to the community, but never having full title to it.[96] The other theorists took a less manifest position, resting their case on the grounds that the right of property was not an inalienable right and hence could ultimately be forfeited.

Before going on to discuss the corporatist view on the role of labour, one final aspect of the position of capital needs to be considered, that is profits. Evidently the *raison d'être* of the behaviour of private firms was not to be solely that of profit maximisation. Further, capital was to be subject to regulation of price, investment and production and, therefore, given that the source of capital was to be mainly private, some consideration had to be given to the subject of return on investment. In point of fact there was not much in the way of precision on the matter. Presumably profit rates would have to attain a rate that brought forward the desired level of investment, but whether the return would be above such a 'normal rate' was scarcely touched upon.[97]

In general, the theorists' position was that the social obligations would have to be borne by capital and as a consequence profit rates would overall be lower than that prevailing at the time of writing.[98] Instead, capital would be less materialistic[99] and guided by higher principles,[100] though in any case under a regulated economy profits would probably fall because of reduced risks. Despite the view held by theorists that profit rates would on average be significantly lower than under 'capitalism' there was never any suggestion that profits were not a legitimate means of motivation and form of reward in themselves.[101] However, not all profits could be regarded as legitimate. It was made explicit, as we shall see in the next section, that profits based on the exploitation of labour were not legitimate; nor, likewise, were those which were earned through consumer exploitation. In actuality, the writers devoted what appeared to be a disproportionate amount of attention to the abuses of monopoly power and inequities of speculation and usury; nor was this largely a concern of earlier writers, but was consistently prominent throughout the history of corporatist thought.[102] This partly is explained by the fact that as the corporation could be traced back to medieval guilds, all writers sought to reassure that the malpractices of the *ancien régime* would not be reinstituted. Overall, though this was the only aspect concerning profits about which the theorists deemed it necessary to elaborate upon. Otherwise one has to look elsewhere for implicit indications, particularly to the theorists' view of the social obligations of capital to labour.

The role of labour

There is no room for doubt that one of the principal concerns of corporatist theorists was the position of the working class under capitalism. Such a concern was double-sided: on the one side the conditions of poverty and alienation from society endured by the proletariat made it impossible to talk of a harmonious society; on the other, there was a fear that such conditions combined with democracy or revolutionary agitation would lead inevitably to socialism. The 'social question', as it was euphemistically called, therefore, evoked a double-sided response. There were series of proposals to remedy the worst excesses of the proletarian condition, as we will presently examine, but there were also lengthy critiques-cum-tirades against the nature of socialism[103] combined with continuous emphasis upon the workers' duties towards a particular social order. Not to put too fine a point on it, under corporatism the worker would enjoy a degree of material protection, but in return he had to accept his position in the social hierarchy. In terms of improving the workers' security, the corporatists proffered that they had rights in relation to wages, welfare when not employed and employment protection.

The theorists started from the premiss that the worker performed a social, as well as an individual, function and as such he should enjoy certain social rights, in contrast to his duties.[104] The foremost right of labour was to receive a wage that did not simply reflect market forces, but which also took into account the social position of the worker. This was usually presented in terms of the medieval and scholastic concept of a 'just wage',[105] although some outlined their proposals without direct reference to that term. Wages had to provide the worker with the basic necessities of food, clothing and shelter for himself and his family. Furthermore, it was often suggested that wage-levels should also allow the worker to save to enable him to support the family when he was not in employment. The operation of the market was not able to ensure such a state of affairs universally prevailed. Indeed, Bishop Ketteler was of the opinion that it never could, as he accepted the iron law of wages popularised by Lasalle, which held that wages could never rise for long above a minimum because population increases would increase the labour supply and consequently lower wages.[106] The corporatists, however, did not turn to state assistance or enhanced trade union activity, but to corporatist institutions (see following chapter) to secure a 'just solution' between employer and employee.[107] A number of the Catholic writers extended their definition of the just wage beyond distributive justice to include social and communative justice principles in accord with scholastic teaching.[108] In line with the application of these principles Azpiazu, for example, argued that there should be equal pay for equal work; that is pay should correspond to the value of the employee's working capacity measured not by individual transactions but by the value of each grade of labour in each labour market as a whole.[109]

The non-Catholic corporatists did not cite principles of natural justice to support their propositions, though a number were clearly influenced by Catholic teaching.[110] Others preferred, nonetheless, to talk without reference to justice, instead advocating some minimum to meet the basic necessities of life such that, as Rathenau stated, the 'most disastrous' forms of poverty and want are eliminated.[111] It is true that nationalist writers, while acknowledging the needs of the workers, laid more emphasis on the additional needs of the national economy in the determination of wage levels than the Catholics, but it was never suggested that the minimum for the worker would be wholly sacrificed to such requirements.[112] In any case, Catholic theorists themselves did not ignore the point that the determination of wage levels would have to reflect general economic imperatives. Messner for one argued that a 'just wage' could not alone be developed on the basis of general norms, but had to take into account the prevailing economic conditions. He opined that wage levels had to be calculated by other aspects of the common good, and he mentioned investment needs for future growth, social investment and monetary stability as being pertinent to the common good.[113] In similar vein, Azpiazu recongised the wider context within which wages would be settled,[114] while Pius XI, not noted for his grasp of economics, wrote that wage rates had to be regulated so as to be concommitant with full employment.[115]

Concern with principles relating to the national economy were not, however, the only factors over and above the workers' needs to be considered. La Tour indicated that a worker's salary would have to be limited to the real value of his product and that he would have to endure the consequences of industrial crisis.[116] On a similar tack Ketteler noted that the level of wages should be tied to the ability of the capitalist to pay.[117] The general corporatist line was one that workers could not expect to be cushioned in times of crisis to such an extent that this imperilled the capitalists's position though there were some suggestions that workers should not suffer simply because of mismanagement.[118] However, what the theorists were equally clear about was that the financial interests of the capitalist could not overrule, as happened under capitalism, the material rights of the worker, which were based upon the social utility of his labour, whatever the economic conditions prevailing.[119]

In addition to proposing that wage levels should meet the needs of workers and their families, including provision for periods when the earning of wages was not practicable, the writers further supported the case for a welfare, or income maintenance, service. Such prescriptions in a contemporary context can hardly lay claim to novelty, but in their time the theorists were consistently in advance of developments within their societies with their proposals. Nor did the corporatists stand alone among their contemporaries in arguing for advances in welfare provision. They did, nonetheless, have one claim to being reasonably distinctive. The theorists did not look to the state *per se* to expand welfare services, but instead suggested that its actual operation should be the responsibility of corporatist institutions – the corporations – with capital and labour working together to administer such assistance. One suggested benefit of this scheme would be the greater identification of the workers with their vocational grouping, that is it would induce, as 'just wages', greater solidarity. This was certainly the view of Emile Durkheim, the French solidarist whose corporatist ideas widely influenced twentieth-century French theorists. He advocated that the corporations would administer a wide range of funds for insurance, assistance and retirement.[120] La Tour reflected the widespread concern on this issue amongst French writers by putting the administration of a patrimony at the head of the corporations' functions.[121] His one time associate, Count Albert de Mun, similarly gave great prominence to proposing welfare benefits that could be provided through corporative funds.[122] Indeed, both de Mun and La Tour had collaborated together in the establishment of a number of *Œuvre des Cercles Catholiques d'Ouvriers* designed to distribute alms and bring employers and employees together in a spirit of understanding. Their 'corporatist experiment', however, soon lost its early momentum despite de Mun's enduring commitment.[123]

Later French corporatists were more concerned with the improvement, than the establishment, of welfare schemes, but the same range of benefits – for sickness, unemployment, injury, retirement, and widows and orphans – were referred to throughout the history of French corporatism.[124] In other countries the theorists were not markedly different in their basic intentions, though in Germany in particular, there was less of a tendency to combine them with criticisms of existing provision.[125] One writer worthy of mention was Bishop Ketteler who devoted so much of his writing to the development of an effective welfare system, providing a good deal in the way of practical proposals.[126]

It is important to emphasise that there was not just common ground among the theorists about the need for welfare provisions and the contingencies that were generally to be covered. There was also accord that such provision, and further wage levels, were not to be so generous as to bring about a fundamental redistribution of income and wealth. The outlook was essentially minimalist, the emphasis was still placed on the iniquities of equality. Walther Rathenau went a good part of the way in summarising the corporatist outlook when he stated that the 'goal' was not equality but the abolition of the proletarian condition.[127] For him 'human inequality could never be abolished'.[128] Manoilesco too regarded equality as not feasible, being *antifonctionnel*,[129] while Azpiazu reflected Catholic principles that equality was 'social injustice'.[130] In fact, several writers went further and re-emphasised the hierarchical nature of corporatism. Equality of economic rights was itself unjust and detrimental.[131] Indeed, many theorists tended to take much off their 'radical sheen' in respect of welfare provisions by appearing to ally themselves with the *status quo* of social structure, often specifically so with threatened social groups whose corporatist rights would impede their decline as was happening under capitalism.[132]

One final right the theorists sought to grant workers was that of employment protection. Overall in the writings there is a lack of concreteness as to what exact form these rights would take, but the general tenor was to argue that a worker was to enjoy rights beyond those afforded by the normal contract of employment. Obviously the model of medieval guilds was prominent in corporatist minds, combined with the emphasis upon status over contract. Thus one of the major concerns of Othmar Spann, for example, was that under capitalism the worker had been rendered *standlos*. The answer to this particular problem for him lay in applying the principles of medieval times, thereby turning membership of corporatist institutions into a form of property,[133] what French writers termed *propriété du métier*. For La Tour capital was not the only form of property, because: 'The possession of a career or trade can also partake the character of property when it is guaranteed by law [...]', and hence can only legally be removed. He found the essential features of possession of a career in the system of *brevet* of professional capacity and this he wished to establish for all classes of employment except labourers.[134] Albert de Mun also referred to the 'corporate property' owned by both classes.[135] La Tour, de Mun and indeed later French writers,[136] were rather imprecise as to the advantages afforded. It was nonetheless evident that possession of a *brevet*, or certificate, meant that a worker whose work was redundant would be redeployed or retrained instead of losing his employment. The other benefit would be that the *brevet* would afford the right to participate in the activities of corporatist institutions. Some writers went so far to suggest that those higher up the profession would enjoy a greater say, through having more votes and so on.[137]

Outside France the writers also emphasised that employment was more than just a contract, but was a capacity that needed to be afforded protection in its own right. In this vein, one finds theorists such as Messner talking of the 'right to work',[138] and Wichard von Moellendorff boldly calling for the exclusion of unemployment.[139] In fact, without much elaboration the theorists gave the impression that such employment rights would go a long way to solving unemployment, though in effect they were advocating work-sharing as the solution.[140]

Of course, as with the other rights of workers already discussed there were to be limits upon them. For one thing, there were voices of concern that such a system of privileges would lead to the abuses of medieval times[141] where, for example, jobs became the property of families. However, there was never any suggestion that such rights would be allowed to conflict with justice[142] or the functional requisites of the economy.[143] This is not to deny that the corporatists did not attach a good deal of importance to such rights as they regarded them as a positive step towards reintegrating the proletariat into (certainly a hierarchical) society, thereby achieving greater social stability and harmony.

That concludes our examination of the corporatist view of the state and the economy, and the related matters of the role of capital and labour. Having already referred to them *en passant*, the next chapter proceeds to discuss the corporatist institutions through which the state was to carry out its economic and social functions.

3

Corporatist thought: state licenced intermediaries

In the previous chapter the corporatists' prescriptions about the state's economic and social role were examined. However, a more notable trait of the body of thought was the institutional arrangements which were proposed for carrying out in large measure these regulatory activities. The state was to delegate most regulatory authority to specially constituted 'self-regulating' agencies which would sit as intermediaries between itself and societal actors. In essence, the state authorities would not regulate the economy directly, they would instead regulate the regulatory agencies. This part of the theory was not just the writers' views upon public administration. The intermediaries or corporations, like the state had a moral base and were regarded through the perspective of an organic state and society. Therefore, the corporations were not discussed in terms of effectiveness and efficiency *per se*, but in terms of their 'natural' relationship to the rest of society, and as 'natural' entities, their contribution to social harmony. Moreover, as 'natural' entities with a life of their own, the corporations' relationship with the state was not to be so straightforward for them to be purely subordinate administrative agencies of the state. There will, in consequence, be a reasonably lengthy discussion of the corporations' status and overall character, before proceeding to look at their membership and functions.

State licenced intermediaries

The corporation was envisaged as being a means of resurrecting the positive attributes of the medieval guild in industrial society. Instituting such a structure would practically re-establish the corporate principle of medieval thought of 'the supremacy of unity over plurality'.[1] The corporation was a body to engender unity and solidarity. Therefore, in line with the imperatives of industrial society, the essence of the corporation was in it being an organisation that brought those representing capital and labour together in one association, reflecting the object of replacing class loyalties, and hence eliminating industrial and class conflict, with new loyalties based on function instead of class. To La Tour, Christian social justice was not possible 'with the absence of ties of solidarity between men united by the same social function',[2] and the corporation would be 'the society which unites the diverse elements of the same profession, i.e., its employers, its white collar and manual workers, in a society perfect from the professional point of view'.[3] Albert de Mun, one time associate of La Tour, described the corporation as 'a community formed among employers and workers of the same profession held together, first of all by acceptance of the principle of social justice, which imposes on the former, as well as on the latter, reciprocal duties'.[4] Another Catholic, Ketteler, also emphasised the need for such integrated associations.[5] Pierre Lucius could have been speaking for all corporatists when he defined the corporation as 'an organism which groups all those – employers, employees, directors, foremen, technicians – who participate in the production of the same category of products and are bound, consequently, by a common interest superior to the interests which divide them'.[6] Even '*völkisch*' theorists in Germany emphasised the need for worker–employer organised collaboration.[7]

The corporation was to the theorists, therefore, an organization based on a particular function (trade, profession or industry), but in accord with medieval guilds, vertically integrating all those who compose a common activity such as the manufacture of leather goods.[8] The corporatists did not accept as desirable, certainly as compared to the corporation, associations which divided within, or even across, the function. Such associations as trade unions and employers' organisations were regarded as leaving unnaturally incomplete economic and social organisation. The basis behind and the aims of such designs for integrated functional organisations will be examined presently, but firstly it is necessary to examine the relationship between the corporations and the state envisaged by the theorists.

Despite claims that such bodies as the corporations were 'natural', the theorists had little faith that under the prevailing 'liberalism' these organisations would emerge:[9] 'liberalism' indeed, by breaking up social bonds would work against such developments. La Tour, one of the earlier writers being considered, was, nevertheless, cautious about legal compulsion. He realised that few of these mixed associations were in existence, yet he was not anxious to see the state step in and enforce such groupings. Instead, he placed emphasis on a process of 'learning by doing' where all associations in a particular *corps d'état* would be given representation in a chamber and from this, he ambiguously maintained, as these free corporations were to be legally recognised, they would 'by the force of things' tend to become obligatory[10]. La Tour's outlook was basically shared by the other writers. The difference that existed amongst them was over the state's role in establishing the corporations. There was no doubt that corporations should and would be legalised and nurtured by state fiat. These theorists as a result regarded as desirable a gradual approach over a transitional period. Others contended that the state should organise the corporative system from the outset.[11] So, for example, Rathenau saw using the authority of the state to bring about compulsory grouping of all German industry as the only means of accomplishing corporatist organizations[12]. Corporatist theory has thus presented two distinct means of establishing corporations; one by state encouragement, the other by state command. In the final analysis the means by which the corporations came into being is not of primary importance, however. The important point is, whether created by state encouragement or state command, the corporation was granted by the state legal recognition, not simply to exist as a corporatist body, but to exercise certain public powers and to encompass a particular constituency. Such a structure of organisations requires, unlike private organisations such as trade unions or trade associations, that to what extent and in what areas these organisations can perform public functions be de-limited; and the grant of public authority can be made only by the state. The state, for example, would have to determine where one corporations's responsibilities ended and another's began and decide what division of groups or individuals was eligible for membership of a particular corporation. No matter to what extent such groupings emerged voluntarily, the state would have to lay down a basis for their external relations with both each other and the state itself. The corporations would not just be nurtured and facilitated by the state, they would be *licenced* by it and the overall structure would be its creation. It needs no further elaboration that the corporatists were making prescriptions not for particular industries but for all economic activity and the system of corporations would, therefore, be more or less comprehensive.

The theorists' support for the state's licencing and overall structuring of the corporations reflected more than a need to 'tidy up the loose ends' of voluntary developments of such integrated associations or the need for the state, in the absence of any other forces, to create such organisations. Such ideas reflected that the corporation was more than an organisation for bringing capital and labour together. The corporation was also prescribed to function as an intermediary between the state and economic and social decision-makers. The corporations were the means through which the state's overall economic and social responsibilities were to be realised. Widely influential to German corporatists like Rathenau were the writings of Otto von Gierke, particularly his four volume *Das deutsche Genossen-schaftsrecht* ('The German Law of Associations') of which the third volume (1881) dealt with the theory of State and Corporation in classical and medieval times.[13]

Gierke made an earnest assault upon the fiction theory and concession theory of group personality, denying that all groups receive their personality as a concession from a state. His sociological presuppositions were sympathetic to the idea of a real personality of a group, arguing that a group has a real existence which is more than the sum of parts, with it possessing many of the characteristics of individual men. On this basis he set out in opposition to the mechanical viewpoint, that of the Germanic Middle Ages when: 'The thought of a concentration at a single point of the whole life of the Community not only stood in sharp contradiction to actual facts and popular opinions, but also was opposed in theory to what might seem an insurmountable bulwark, namely to the medieval thought of a harmoniously articulated Universal Community whose structure from top to bottom was of the federalistic kind.'[14] He then went on to attack modern theories of the state that 'had nothing to say of groups that mediated between the State and the Individual' with the consequence that 'all intermediate groups were first degraded [...] and in the end obliterated'[15]. Von Gierke saw in the resurrection of these intermediate groups a solution to many of the political and social problems of his day through counteracting the centralised state and overcoming the antagonisms fostered by individualism.

Gierke did not resurrect such concepts for corporatists, as many had been drawing upon the medieval basis of such premises before his work was published, but he was extremely influential in reinforcing the notion of the intermediate groups. He, therefore, laid down in a seminal form what corporatists writing before and after him had laid great emphasis on, namely that groups, such as corporations, had a personality of their own and, as natural and permanent forces, they should carry out public economic and social functions.[16] In his book *The New Economy*, Rathenau, under the influence of Gierke,[17] despite a manifest desire not to restore the medieval guilds, set out proposals for organisations of producers which would carry out the management of day-to-day affairs of industry so that the new economy would not be a 'state economy'.[18]

Likewise, Hegel's discussion of the individual, society and the state in *Philosophy of Right* (1833) gave support to the concept of the corporation as an intermediary and acted as a source of inspiration to many of the corporatists who later tried to outline a synthesis between the extremes of individualism and collectivism. As with Gierke, he opposed the abolition of the medieval 'corporations', and argued that: 'Under modern political conditions, the citizens have only a restricted share in the public business of the state, yet it is essential to provide men – ethical entities – with work of a public character, over and above their private business. This work of a public character, which the modern state does not always provide is found in the corporation.'[19] Hegel's concern was centred upon the atomisation and alienation of the individual, and to him the corporation would redress the balance by creating intermediate groups between the state and the individual.[20] Many of the elements in Hegel's 'civil society', an idealised description of the essentially rural and handicraft society in which he lived, to a large degree reflect many of the prescriptions set out by corporatists subsequently, although despite his inspiration there remained fundamental differences between the ultimate objectives he embraced and the more rigid system the corporatists outlined. Nevertheless, he was a source of support for many corporatists.

Many other corporatists put great weight on the idea of the corporation regulating economic and social affairs between the state and the individual. In Germany, Karl Marlo proposed that the state would maintain a general supervision, but would refrain from detailed interference, leaving to federated guilds, enjoying a large measure of independence, responsibility for the 'self-government of industry', thereby avoiding bureaucratic centralisation in the economy.[21] Similarly Ernst Gerlach saw a hierarchy of corporations which would act as a check on monarchical authority by being self-governing organisations.[22] Even Adolf Wagner, whose concept of the state's limitations was out of line with most corporatists, saw corporate organisations as a means through which the state could rule and coordinate economic life.[23']

French corporatists were no less supportive of the corporation as an intermediary than their German counterparts. La Tour while advocating the need for economic regulation was attracted to the idea of states within the state, with the corporation limiting the sovereignity of the central authority and thereby preventing centralisation.[24] Apart from La Tour, also influential upon later French corporatists with regard to this point was Léon Duguit,[25] who suggested pluralism be brought about by giving certain of the state's economic and social functions to syndical organisations. Duguit supported fully the development of autonomous groups as the norm of social organisation which would be both the cause and consequence of the disappearance of the authoritarian Jacobin State, so long as these syndicates were instruments of cooperation among classes.[26] Many of the inter-war corporatists repeated, in modified form, Duguit's arguments. Valois, as already seen, in his schema gave the state a right of veto over the corporations when they transgressed certain principles, but added that it was not to become involved in production 'where it is incompetent'.[27] Casimir de la Rocque, despite his fascist sympathies, held that the corporations were not simple extensions of the state's administration but were semi-autonomous from the state,[28] while Pierre Lucius, from similar sympathies, declared that the state's sphere of action 'would be limited by the statutes of the constituted bodies – families, association, *corporations*, communes, provinces',[29] reflecting the seriousness with which corporatists felt *étatisme* should be avoided. Louis Baudin, however, emphasised the corporatists' difference with Duguit by stating that, as intermediaries between the state and the individual, syndicates and cartels had not fulfilled the hopes expected of them, and only the corporation with bonds with the nation could fulfil this function of avoiding excessive individualism and total *étatisme*[30].

Corporatists outside France and Germany also shared the contention that corporatism would be able to combine economic regulation without *étatisme* through the intermediary corporations. The Spanish corporatist Azpiazu maintained that it would be necessary for the corporations to preserve their autonomy and develop their strength to serve as intermediaries between the individual and the state. In Austria one romantic Social Catholic, with not a little ambiguity, opined that the state 'alone has the power to overcome the instinctive and tendentious leadership', but qualified it by adding that 'at the same time the state leadership must resist the temptation to influence social reforms in a one-sided political manner and to regard the occupational corporations as mere tools of power politics and subjects of the state'.[31] In an attempt to demonstrate that fascism should not monopolise the appeal of corporatism, Hendrik de Man, the Belgian corporatist theorist, whose goals were socialistic in character, argued that the idea of autonomous groupings based on a trade or profession offered the necessary organisation if 'socialism' was to avoid bureaucratisation and centralisation.[32]

It has been desirable to detail at some length the concept in the theory of the corporation, which is specifically licenced by the state and which is based on the 'natural' community of a function thereby bringing together (representatives of) capital and labour, as an intermediary between the state and the individual, so allowing economic regulation at the productive level without recourse to an all-embracing state. Further this is of importance, because it is the other side of the issue, which was touched upon in the previous chapter, regarding how circumscribed the state should be. The vast majority of theorists suggested that the state's role would be limited to one of overall 'coordination', by which was meant giving a general direction, arbitrating conflicts that could not be resolved by the corporations and ensuring that decisions taken were not contrary to the interests of the nation or social justice.[33] The theorists frequently recognised that to ensure that the state was able to fulfil this role it would have to be strong with effective ultimate authority. They were as such not just expressing their support for countervailing sources of power to the state but for a hierarchy of responsibilities with the state placed firmly at the top.[34] Thus, the state would set out basic principles and rules which the corporations would elaborate and add detail to, and so be able to apply them to the individual economic actors. Just as the individual economic actors would have to conform to the constraints of the corporation's regulations, so the corporation would have to conform to the (more basic) regulations of the state and, if it did not, the state would intervene. The corporation's 'autonomy', as the corporatists called it, was not absolutely determined but was relative to the extent that they conformed to general state principles. Thus, while the corporation as an intermediary was held by the theorists to be a system which would avoid *étatisme*, this was only true to the extent that the corporations were 'conformist'. It is evident enough from the anti-*étatisme* of the writings of those theorists that they held that the conformity would more or less be the rule, taking refuge in the point that the corporation as a natural community would develop an ethos supportive of the general interest.[35]

These corporatists were, therefore, advocating that the corporation's natural legitimacy would act as a check on arbitrary and illegitimate interference by the state and, because the corporations shared the same values as the state, they would not need to be subject to much interference from it. This latter premiss was not drawn from any empirical basis but emanated from acceptance of medieval natural law theories and the works of those in related schools, like Durkheim's solidarism, as well as other theorists. To those theorists, corporatism would generate, or more accurately bring to the surface, a widespread consensus of economic and social values, previously latent, of which the state would be the final guarantor, because it too would share such values. A few theorists, such as Rocco, Wagner, Frauendorfer and Pirou, did not believe that such a consensus would emerge and, therefore, they questioned whether the limited state would prove practicable. For example, Pirou who gave the issue serious consideration predicted that under corporatism as widely proposed there would be disharmony, not harmony prevailing. Thus the state would either be bound continually to interfere in the work of the corporation or be submerged in the conflict between corporatist inter-ests.[36] He concluded, as a result, that the only possible form corporatism could politically take was that of a dictatorship with the corporations clearly subordinated to the state, and he cited the Italian experience under Mussolini as a 'prototype'.[37] Pirou and a few theorists who adopted such a perspective were, in consequence, closer to being authoritarian – licenced corporatists. However, they were not in a position identical to that variety of corporatism because they adhered to certain values which were never applied in corporatist regimes. These writers, none of whom were Catholic corporatists, can be regarded as being in some hybrid category between the consensual and authoritarian variants. They are too few in number to suggest that we need to formulate a further variety of corporatism, or at least they can be recognised in terms of a hybrid which does not undermine our present classification of varieties of corporatism.

Interestingly, Michael Manoilesco in his work *Le Siècle du Corporatisme* did make a distinction between the mainstream majority and the critical minority. While Manoilesco's typology of corporatism does not detract from the efforts to classify forms of corporatism being presently undertaken here, they are worthy of mention because it clarifies the nature of the division through reference to one of the most noted theorists and because his typology has re-surfaced in discussions of neo-corporatism.[38] The Romanian writer, in fact, identified three types of corporatism. The first type was what he termed *corporatisme subordonné*. As the term suggests, under this type of corporatism the corporation would be completely subordinated to the state as argued for by Pirou. This could occur either under a constitutional parliamentary system, contrary to Pirou, or under a one-party dictatorship. Manoilesco, however, for different reasons saw both as incompatible with the corporatist organic conception of the nation.[39] The second type, termed *corporatisme pur*, he regarded as 'the true solution and the only possibility'. Under this type the state is itself regarded as a corporation which has proper functions to carry out. The first functions are those independent of other corporations, namely defence, foreign affairs and public order, which places the state on the same level (*plan*) as the other corporations. The second category of functions takes the form of coordinating and disciplining the other corporations, which places the state on a superior level to the other corporations.[40] This type of corporatism evidently corresponds to what the bulk of the corporatists envisaged in their scheme. The third and final type identified by Manoilesco was that of *corporatisme mixte*, where the corporation is on the same level as the political state because they are represented in a corporative senate alongside a chamber based on universal suffrage, which he regarded would be in conflict with each other.[41] This type was really a hybrid, if an unsatisfactory one to Manoilesco, of *corporatisme pur* and *corporatisme subordonné*. For our present considerations, this hybridised type is rather ambiguous for the reason that Manoilesco did not determine, presumably because it would depend on the effect of the conflict between the two chambers, whether the corporation was to be autonomous, within the limits of state co-ordination, or not. Most theorists, including Manoilesco himself clearly fall into the *pur* camp, while Pirou and company are in agreement with the *subordonné* type.

In addition to having a good deal to say on the decision-making relationship between the corporation and the state, the theorists also outlined the legal status of the corporation. Obviously the corporation sponsored by the state and carrying out public regulation of the economy was not a purely private association. For Azpiazu the corporations would have a 'full juridical personality' and thus were separate legal entities from the state, being entities of public law,[42] thereby distinguishing them from the state bureaucracy and private associations and presenting them as a kind of economic and social police force. Other social Catholics, like Albert de Mun also demanded that institutions of public law be established[43]. For his part Manoilesco argued strongly that 'true' corporations would only exist if they had their own distinct legal personality and had the character of a public organization with the legal right to impose certain rules on the members and even those outside the corporation[44]. Baudin indicated that in the corporatist future beside the legislative, judicial and administrative sources of law would be the corporative source, and common law would be progressively reduced in favour of corporative law[45].

It is generally true that the theorists did not bother to elaborate enough upon what type of public body the corporation would be, particularly for those not acquainted with continental legal traditions, although they were clearly drawing from the precedent of medieval guilds. To turn to La Tour again, he defined the corporation as a 'social institution which holds a determined place in the organisation of the commune, and more or less directly that of the state'.[46] La Tour reflects a general ambiguity that is found in all the theorists referring to this aspect of thought. However, this ambiguity is indicative of what was seen as the unique character of the corporations. The writers continually emphasised, at least the majority who adhered to *corporatisme pur*, that the corporations were not just instruments of the state and were not representatives of particular interests. It was, therefore, neither simply a private body nor simply a normal public body. Instead, it was a quasi-public body reflecting, as Azpiazu points out, that the personality of such organisations is not derived entirely from the state.[47] Such ideas were derived from natural law theory, but for our purposes 'quasi-public' will be employed in a more limited sense to reflect that such organizations should have autonomy with regard to their internal organisation and rule making so long as it did not breach the general principles laid down by the state. The idea of self-governing corporations was a strong one amongst the theorists, and to simply present the intermediary organisations as public bodies would not so accurately pinpoint their character as 'quasi-public', despite their evident public functions[48].

The intermediaries' membership

In addition to the corporation's status in relation to the state, as examined in the previous part, there is the important issue of whether membership of such organisations was to be voluntary or not; after all, there is little point in establishing a structure for regulating the economy if there are no, or only a few economic actors, whose behaviour can actually be regulated because most do not fall within the orbit of the regulatory agency. Logically, therefore, because corporatism was concerned to regulate economic and social behaviour according to certain universal principles, universal regulation necessitated universal jurisdiction. In addition, as the corporations were supposed to encompass producer self-regulation there were strong imperatives to have universal membership. In the event, the theorists realised that their system could only operate on the basis of universal membership of the corporations and this would, in turn, necessitate an element of compulsion regarding membership. Bishop von Ketteler thought that membership of the vocational corporations should be compulsory for all workers, stressing divine sanction for the authority that would restrict individual occupational freedom,[49] while his compatriot and fellow Social Catholic, Franz Hitze, emphasised that each workman would have to pass an examination in professional capacity organised by the corporation before being legally empowered to perform his trade[50]. The limitation of compulsion to workers by Ketteler and Hitze reflects their primary concern with the conditions of labour. Most other theorists' schemes were concerned with wider economic and social regulation. Karl von Vogelsang urged the creation of compulsory corporations composed of all different groups in the profession. Furthermore, he outlined a means whereby the compulsion would be fully effective through the state granting a legal monopoly to the corporation for the sale of its products.[51] Albert de Mun,[52] Walther Rathenau,[53] Paul Chanson,[54] and not surprisingly Gaetan Pirou[55], were similarly assertive that compulsory membership was essential. Few corporatists gave much countenance to any ideas that corporations based on voluntary membership were compatible with the broader aspects of their schema.

Nevertheless, some corporatists did elaborate further upon the issue of compulsion by coming down in favour of some (undetermined) period of transition. La Tour, for example, held that in the first place the state should grant privileges to freely formed corporations so they could continue to exist, but added that the corporations' increasing prerogatives would eventually make them obligatory.[56] What La Tour was attempting to reconcile was the conflict between the idea of the corporation as a 'natural community' and that membership of this body should be obligatory, although of course, he only side-stepped the issue. He did, however, clearly envisage that the corporation should not just be introduced in an artificial and obligatory form, but that gradually as corporations enjoyed more and more privileges, the cost to an economic actor of not joining would become prohibitive: such corporations would, La Tour surmised, originally be formed upon a voluntary basis generated by the leadership offered by people like himself. Azpiazu similarly felt the power of Catholic teachings was more desirable, even if its impact was to be gradual, than outright force.[57] Manoilesco went even further than these two. He stated that his definition of the corporation would not prejudge the question of whether the corporation must comprise, obligatorily or not, all those exercising the same function or only a part of them.[58]

The division of opinion about the obligatory nature of the corporation amongst the theorists was essentially one of whether this would be brought about by the gradual means or immediately. Apart from the chronological factor, the theorists were agreed that the means to compulsion lay in the granting of privileges to members of corporations. Ultimately these privileges would amount to a 'licence' to carry out a particular economic function, in much the same manner as medieval guilds exercised, and certain modern professions exercise, a monopoly over a particular function. Thus, the most important element in the state's licencing of the corporations would be the granting and guaranteeing of this monopoly.[59] Whether membership of the corporation was to be pre-entry or post-entry was, however, a point which divided the corporatists enough to make it impossible to draw a precise viewpoint: some were of the opinion that certain qualifications were a necessary pre-requisite to membership, while others did not mention the issue at all. Fermin Bacconnier, the principle economic and corporatist theoretician of the *Action Française*, claimed that admission to the corporation would only be possible on 'proof of capacity, of solvency, of morality, and of willingness to accept the discipline and regulation of trade'.[60] Some other writers were less concerned with moral aspects of admission and simply with that of capacity to do a particular job,[61] which was no more than a statement of the obvious, laced with corporatist emphasis on craft and skill as an important element in production. Thus further division amongst those who discussed 'entry qualifications' exacerbates the difficulties of drawing a component for the model on this issue.

The question also arises as to what happens to the various associations representing the different groups within the profession or function, such as trade unions and employers organisations, once all members of the profession had been integrated into the one organisation. Despite the fact that the activities of such groups of pursuing exclusively particularistic interests and of taking part in 'class conflict' were anathema to corporatists, they were not intent on seeing such organisations withering away. To La Tour, the ultimate goal was the integrated organisation, the corporation, but the various group associations, or syndicates, were to form component parts or categories within the all-inclusive organisation[62]. To Emile Durkheim, whose solidarist principles and other corporatistic ideas were picked up by twentieth-century French corporatist writers, the 'agents' of a profession which were all integrated into the corporations would be divided into a syndicate of employers and another of employees for the purpose of electing representatives to the corporative assembly, the governing body of the corporation.[63] Durkheim was, therefore, suggesting that possibly certain syndicates would themselves have to be sponsored from outside to allow for representation within the corporation.

Interbellum corporatists in France echoed the idea of subdivisions within the corporation. George Valois, who covered many pages describing the structure of the corporations, outlined how the corporation was to include syndicates of foremen, technicians, clerks and departmental heads.[64] Turning to agriculture, Bacconnier divided these corporations into unions of farmers, farm workers and sharecroppers.[65] From a somewhat different perspective, De La Rocque saw such syndicates, being the sole collective organisations actually in existence, as the only means to build the corporations. However, despite the desire he held not to see the disappearance of such associations whose cooperation was 'absolutely indispensable', De La Rocque held that they would have to be purely apolitical, occupational organisations.[66] In arguing for the continuance of syndical associations, but under certain conditions, De La Rocque was in line with almost all French inter-war theorists[67].

Elsewhere the emphasis was similarly on maintaining the divisions of the existing associations, if integrated and absorbed into the new functional organisations. Even those theorists having connections with fascist regimes like Rocco[68] and Frauendorfer,[69] in theory at least saw a continued existence for the syndicates, while Wagner advocated that the state should encourage workers' and employers' associations because it was a step towards corporate representation.[70] Likewise, so that it could be clearly determined which groups were entitled to take what decisions in the corporation, Manoilesco discussed at length how the corporations should be divided into syndicates because different types of decisions pertained to different groups or combinations thereof.[71] The continued existence of syndical associations reflects the different groups within the corporation would be of different status and would in consequence require separate representation. In addition, it was recognised that within the function certain specific interests would continue to exist. The syndicates were therefore, to be both administrative and representative units within the corporation. Beyond that the corporatists were none too unified in their proposals, and it is not possible to reach firm conclusions on whether syndical membership was compulsory or not. (On balance, more theorists were in favour of compulsory membership, or at least discrimination against those who were not members.) Certainly, it is clear that the syndical associations, because of the decisions taken by the corporations, would *de facto* enjoy a monopoly of representation and would be licenced by the state or, more likely, the corporation itself under authority granted by the state. The syndicates would be fully under the jurisdiction of the corporation and as a result their character would be different to that of a system where their activities were not subordinated to the aims of a higher authority, but to members' specific interests.

To conclude, therefore, on the position of the intermediaries and their membership: corporatists advocated that membership of the intermediary organisations would be compulsory for all who wished to engage in a particular economic activity over which these organisations would exercise a public monopoly and that the membership would be organised in a number of producers' associations. These associations were to be integrated into the intermediary organisation, and be granted a monopoly of representation by, licenced by and subordinated to that organisation.

The intermediaries' functions

Having discussed the organisational nature of the corporations it is now necessary to turn to the broad functions the theorists generally proposed their intermediary bodies should carry out. The functions so prescribed can be divided into two broad categories, economic and social functions and industrial relations functions.

a) Economic and social functions

Before discussing the basic economic and social functions the corporatist theorists argued should be the responsibility of the corporations, it is worth noting that it was in the details of such proposals that many of the differences between the theorists became most marked. Therefore, because the present exercise is concerned to draw out the areas of agreement amongst the theorists, the examination will largely involve a listing of the functions. However, without getting bogged down in the detail of proposals, an attempt will be made to highlight some of the differences, and also some of the shared concerns. For the record it should be noted that in addition to the five basic functions to be presently outlined, corporatist writings are littered with individual theorists' pet functions they felt should fall within the corporations' remit.

The first function to be ascribed to the corporations was that of price regulation. Of particular concern to many writers in respect of this function was the need to give reassurances that the corporations would not abuse their monopoly position. The successful precedent of the guilds of the *ancien régime*, was enough for La Tour that these monopolies could under public surveillance, fix a 'just price'.[72] Rathenau, in stark contrast, sought to give reassurances that the anti-social privileges would not be reinstituted.[73] More reassuring than either, Louis Baudin afforded a lengthy analysis to the determination of *le prix normal* under conditions of monopoly and of monopoly and monopsony which would prevail in an economy where unitary corporations regulated prices.[74] However, Baudin's approach was largely the exception and few writers, including those like Manoilesco[75] entered into detailed accounts of how prices would be computed. Many theorists simply called for a system of just prices, borrowing extensively from the theory of St Thomas Aquinas and the Middle Ages, whereby the price of the commodity was based upon what it was intrinsically worth, which 'the community was supposed to determine regardless likewise of temporary fluctuations in the market'.[76] On this basis, the price of a commodity was computed upon the cost of production and both buyer and seller were to reap reciprocal advantage from a transaction, neither exploiting the other's position. To this end, the corporatists argued that the corporations would present each other with a countervailing force which would prevent one group exploiting another, while consumers were to be protected either by, somewhat unrealistically, organisations of consumers, or more probably by the state in some guise or another[77]. Despite the emphasis often being placed on abstract conceptionalisations of price rather than on clear principles for price determination, it is clear that there was quite a wide divergence amongst writers on their overall view of price regulation. For example, for Georges Valois the notion of corporatist price regulation was one of a collectivised market where fluctuations would be smoothed out by the transfer of information from one collectivity to another,[78] while to Walter Rathenau price regulation was to be part of a much more extensively planned system of which the state was to be the directing force.[79] Clearly some writers envisaged the corporation would be involved in detailed price regulation while others suggested that the corporation would impose certain general constraints upon the operation of the market.[80]

The second function specifically ascribed to the corporation was that of the regulation of production. Once more there arises the problem that beyond a general area of agreement the corporatists' prescriptions began to divaricate into individual theses about what would be required. As in the case of prices, the difference concerned the extent of the regulation envisaged, or what it was felt necessary to outline. The two principal theorists of the 'German Economy', Rathenau and von Moellendorff, both delineated extensive lists of the areas where the intermediaries would be involved in regulation, including sales promotion, raw material procurement, dissemination of scientific expertise, improving efficiency through enforced rationalisation and increased capacity, setting down standardisation, setting quotas for output and, finally, selling the products at home and abroad.[81] It is important to note, if not to actually fathom, that Rathenau believed that within this scheme of regulation free competition and the spirit of private enterprise were to be preserved, indeed to some extent further encouraged, and this to him would have a stimulating effect.[82] Moellendorff, who had worked with Rathenau during the wartime planning, put forward the same kind of regulatory functions with regard to production – such as the acquisition of raw materials, standardisation, regulation of distribution channels, to promote better production methods and to carry out technical research, as well as setting output targets – that Rathenau had propounded. Moellendorff, despite drawing from Rathenau's ideas, however, did not envisage the continuation of the competitive element Rathenau had argued for, and this, aided by personal resentment between the two, formed the basis for a mutual denunciation of each other's proposals.[83]

Other theorists were, for a variety of reasons, less particular with their references to the corporations and regulation of production than the two principal architects of the German Collective Economy. Nonetheless, the theorists often outlined the kinds of functions to be exercised by the corporations in this sphere under consideration. Manoilesco simply presented a list of such tasks the corporations would exercise. Those he set included regulating raw material purchases, concentrating production in the most efficient enterprises, dividing production nationally between the various branches, controlling capital investment, organising credit necessary for the enterprises, organising the sale of products and generally regulating agreements between enterprises.[84] Manoilesco, Rathenau and Moellendorff illustrate the general areas of jurisdiction the corporation was to be granted, although a number of writers did not attach so much importance to some of the functions that have just been set out above. In fact, most theorists did not usually specify much more than that the corporation would regulate production, however, and whenever necessary. Thus La Tour merely stated that the governing body of the corporative organisation would 'fix the conventions relative to work, [...] in such a manner as to favour the establishment of good customs of the profession [*métier*] and their successive modification in accordance with the industrial situation and the economic circumstances'.[85] He did, in addition, throughout his work conceive of the corporation as regulating, but not managing, industrial enterprises. The theorists in effect preferred to profess the general principle, and in certain cases also provide an indicative list. Attachments to general principles, rather than elaboration of the mechanics, is not surprising given that they were economic and social theorists, but it does leave a feeling of incompleteness because the application of such principles posed certain problems of which several writers were aware but few were willing to confront. The detail as ever was focussed upon the issue of the extent of regulation and control over economic actors.[86]

The third function in the economic and social sphere the corporation was delegated concerned the determination of wages. In the cases of price and production there had been a divergence of opinion among the writers as to whether these would remain the prerogative of management or whether they would be under the auspices of joint capital/labour decision making;[87] but in the case of wages, which was generally put into the category of social affairs, it was to be one of *mixte* determination. As the issue of the nature of industrial relations will be examined presently and the objectives of wage regulation have already been discussed in the previous chapter there is, at this juncture, no need to elaborate beyond noting that this was one of the ascribed functions of the corporation and that it extended to conditions of work as well as to remuneration.[88] In fact, the corporation was not just to be responsible for the remuneration and conditions of labour but also for the placement of labour in particular enterprises, although this was given more emphasis by those corporatists, such as Manoilesco[89] and Rathenau,[90] who were concerned to increase national production rapidly. There was inevitably a degree of vagueness as to the extent of compulsion involved in such placement.

A fourth economic and social function, if one of obvious significance, was that of regulating the profession upon which the corporation was based. In this regard, the corporation, rather than the state and/or the firm, was to determine who had the requisite qualifications to perform a particular occupation in the industry concerned. Moreover, this was not to be of limited application to certain occupations usually associated with an apprenticeship system. De La Rocque called for a 'fight against the false conception that apprenticeship should be limited to some few chosen occupations' as for him, 'every branch of labour demands an apprenticeship'.[91] Such an all-embracing system of qualifications for almost all occupations very much reflects the corporatist adherence to the idea of a hierarchy of status within each occupation. Thus, Firmin Bacconnier of the *Action Française*, stated that 'The certificate of professional capacity can be delivered to all the agents of production, to the engineer as well as to the worker; without this certificate no one can be an active member of the corporation or raise himself above the lowest rank of the professional hierarchy'.[92] It is also true to say that such an apprenticeship system was viewed as part of an increasing proliferation in craft- and skill-based labour in the productive process. However, such a scheme was not simply based upon a desire to see the most competent placed in the occupations demanding the most ability, but was also part of a method of internal discipline. It has already been noted above that Bacconnier was interested not just in a worker's capacity but also in his good conduct;[93] indeed, he went further and also added a nationality requirement.[94] Bacconier's proposals to a marked degree, with some elaboration, correspond to those put forward by La Tour some fifty years earlier. He too emphasised that the worker would be able by skill and good conduct to rise in the profession, although compared to Bacconnier he placed greater weight on the possession of a professional *brevet* as a legal guarantee of particular rights.[95] Needless to say, the corporation was to provide the necessary training for such qualifications.[96]

It is hardly surprising that the corporations, drawn from the precedent of the medieval guilds, should have been granted such a task as the regulation of the profession, although the institutions of which the theorists had more intimate knowledge, like the Church, the Army and the University, also furnished them with examples of 'self-regulation'. More importantly, though, such a procedure for designation and discipline was essential to the operation of the corporation because of its divisions into different groupings with differing rights and duties, its systems of remuneration and its need to have some sort of control over its members' behaviour. Thus, Manoilesco, while not concerned in any way to engage in some form of medieval restoration, did nevertheless outline an almost identical system.[97] The regulation of the profession is, therefore, an important function for the corporation, it being fully enmeshed in the operation of its other economic and social functions.[98]

The final economic and social function emphatically granted to the corporation was one of administering a social welfare system. As has been already discussed, much of the theorists' writings were directed to outlining a system that would ameliorate the poor conditions of the workers and

their families. For the moment, the important aspect is how the corporatists envisaged such assistance would be administered. Again Casimar de
La Rocque reflected, if somewhat crudely, the position of all corporatists
when he asserted that the French social security system in the 1930s was
inadequate and that 'In place of this capitalisation, the logical thing would
be to substitute a process of redistribution within the industry itself, thus
permitting an immediate allocation of the necessary funds'.[99] The Catholic Azpiazu thought that, apart from protecting the family, the corporation
would bring about the defence of what he termed the 'less competent',
such as the poor and the labourer, against the difficulties of life.[100] Later
on in *The Corporative State* he added that given the nature and the role of
the corporation, it should be entrusted with the institutions for 'improving
wage-reparation funds' which would tend towards the better development
of the corporation itself.[101] By this he clearly meant that such social
assistance provided by the corporation would help to engender a greater
feeling of solidarity amongst that institution's membership, particularly
with regard to those whom it was held would feel most alienated otherwise
because of their conditions. As a Social-Catholic-cum-Royalist, La Tour
had advocated similarly that assistance be given through the corporation.
He suggested the idea of a patrimony constituted and managed by the
corporation itself. The fund was to be raised as a tax on production at a
rate to be shared equally by capital and labour according to a number of
possible procedures.[102]

The ideas of La Tour, which owed much of their origins to other Social
Catholics such as Emile Keller,[103] were reiterated by the French theorists
after the war. There were some variations, however, Eugene Duthoit,
whose proposals had continually shown a pro-employer bias, intended
that the fund be managed solely by employers and accountants without
any participation by the workers.[104] With a bias the other way, towards
the employees, Paul Chanson set out a scheme where the patrimony would
be raised from a tax on profits as well as on the output of employers and
employees[105].

Such proposals for a social-security fund administered through the
corporation were most evident, not surprisingly, among Social-Catholic
corporatists. For example Bishop von Ketteler's major work on corporatism, *The Labour Question and Christianity*, deals at some length with the
issue of how social assistance should be administered, although there is
throughout the work doubt concerning the immediate efficacy of introducing a system of corporatist support.[106] Nevertheless, it is evident
enough that Ketteler ultimately wished to see some form of guilds administering such funds.[107] Count Albert de Mun, along with La Tour, to
reiterate a point, attempted to get things moving in a practical manner

through their establishment of *Cercles* which were involved in assistance of workers.[108] Nevertheless, despite the obvious lead taken in the area of corporatist social security, it was not the exclusive property of the confessional corporatists. Many nationalist corporatists, no doubt under some influence from Catholic ideas, also supported such schema. Gaetan Pirou, for one, sketched out such attributes for the corporation.[109] Manoilesco also made reference to such functions, although in a perfunctory manner.[110] Alfred Stoecker, an advocate of German Monarchical Socialism, saw assistance as a means to inculcate the working class with loyalty to the German nation.[111] One notable exception to those advocating such proposals was Othmar Spann. To him the problem of the prevailing order of capitalism was not economic deprivation. Instead, he asserted that: 'Mankind can take poverty in its stride, because poverty will always be with us. But insecurity, rootlessness, and insignificance are conditions nobody is prepared to suffer quietly'.[112] The evil of capitalism was not, therefore, poverty which would be a permanent feature come what may, but that it had rendered the worker *standlos*. Spann's presentation of the social problem in such a confined perspective remains unique, even among the Romantic tradition, of which he was a part, within corporatist theory amongst those who turned their attention to the problems of the working class.

(b) Industrial-relations functions

In addition to the five economic and social functions – regulation of prices, production, wages, professions and social assistance – for which the corporations were to be responsible (albeit under the general supervision of the state), the theorists also envisaged a crucial function for the intermediaries in the domain of industrial relations. This was hardly surprising given their remit to regulate wages and conditions, but it has further to be viewed within the context of the corporatists, wider concerns. If one factor emanating from capitalism, or 'liberalism' as the theorists often labelled it, had to be designated as the most pernicious, the vast majority of corporatists would have plumped for the spread of industrial conflict. The very idea that there should exist conflict between those exercising the same function or profession was totally heretical to them. Indeed, the existence of any form of class conflict was heralded as contrary to the organic nature of society with each individual and group being bonded to each other through social ties of natural rights and duties. The socialists and communists who advocated engendering further class conflict as a means to social change were for this reason alone beneath contempt in the corporatists' eyes. The aim of the corporatists in indus-

trial relations was, therefore, the elimination of conflict and the introduction of a system that generated industrial peace and harmony. Such a
condition was to be brought about by two traits of the corporation. Firstly,
the corporation, by bringing together capital and labour in the same
organisation based on the profession, would restore the social bonds
between different classes that 'liberalism' had destroyed. However, it was
not simply the expedient of bringing the two sides together that would
reintroduce the bonds of solidarity. The bonds would re-emerge because
the ends of the corporation were social justice, or, in the case of nationalist
corporatists, the national interest.

For La Tour the existence of 'social justice' and 'social peace' were
clearly connected; the latter was not possible without the former.[113] La
Tour, like many other writers, throughout his works outlined how social
justice was to be achieved. However, with regard to the achievement of
'social peace', he did specifically mention three facets of the corporation,
namely, amiable fixing of labour conditions, social assistance in times of
need and regulation of industrial forces.[114] The first of these mentioned
suggests that La Tour was of the opinion that even the expedient of
bringing the two sides together, presumably in a spirit of reason, would of
itself contribute significantly to 'social peace'. Azpiazu made his proposals
along similar lines. Apart from stressing justice as a product of the
corporation, he emphasised that the primary business of the corporation
would be the maintenance of social peace by means of an 'equal defense of
unequal rights',[115] by which he meant that equal representation, even
although there existed unequal status, would defend the rights of all
equally. Thus a worker's right to a 'just wage' would be defended or
represented, no more or less than the right of the employer to have a loyal
day's service from his employee. Like La Tour, Azpiazu is maintaining that
the structure and nature of the corporation would create the conditions in
which reason will prevail. For our purposes the ideas remain too abstract
to be of value, but nevertheless, it does indicate that the corporation was
by its very structure and nature held to be supportive of 'social peace'.

Such ideas were not, however, limited to Catholics. Other schools of
theorists and quasi-corporatists took up the point. The Fascist Col. de La
Rocque also laid great faith in bringing together the parties of conflict.
Having argued that the class struggle had been 'artificially fomented by
the Marxists', he proclaimed that 'The spiritual fusion of classes is our
objective. Their intellectual, their occupational interpenetration is the
means.'[116] The basis of this new spirit was to be 'social sense'.[117] More
detailed elaboration than that provided by de La Rocque on the concept
came from the Solidarist school. Most important among this school was
Emile Durkeim, whose rather limited corporatist proposals still greatly

influenced corporatist French theorists between the two World Wars. Durkheim claimed that industrial peace could only be established and maintained by a corporative regime which would furnish 'the system of rules which is at present lacking',[118] by which he means moral rules. To Durkheim only a group based on those devoted to the same work would constitute fully a force for solidarity, because only they adequately integrated the individual while the state, religion and the family were for various reasons imperfect in this respect[119]. In essence, the Solidarism of Durkheim which sought to subordinate the physical law of the strongest to a higher moral law[120] is the same as the Catholicism of La Tour and Azpiazu in that both presented the corporation as a means to achieving a new morality in industrial relations; although of course, they were discussing different forms of morality. Indeed, the ideas of Solidarism were highly influential upon Catholic corporatists. For example, the Austrian Catholic Heinrich Pesch, developed his corporatist ideas on the basis of a conceived solidarity of those engaged in the same trade or profession.[121]

However, whether Catholic, Solidarist, Catholic-Solidarist or whatever, the basic proposals were very much the same. In actual fact, there is little need to draw any distinction between the various schools on this point because their ideas became so entangled with each other, all being variations on a theme. The theme itself, as already discussed, was simple, if not tangible: the corporation would allow a latent morality, which had been suppressed under capitalism, to re-establish itself. The new morality was, however, more than a *deus ex machina*. Certain features would reinforce the solidarity and hence harmony, particularly on the side of the workers because they were seen to be the major protagonists of conflict, although it was felt not without justification. It has already been noted that La Tour and Azpiazu argued that since the corporation would ensure that social justice prevailed, no one concerned would have a genuine grievance and so the causes of conflict would evaporate. Bishop von Ketteler reasoned along much the same lines, but he also insisted that experience under wholesome, Christian leadership would teach the workers that their true interests lay not in 'war between the worker and his employer but at peace on equitable terms between the two',[122] contrary to what the socialist leaders insisted.[123] Count Albert de Mun, apart from a solidaristic argument that a union between worker and master was 'the indispensable condition of social peace and national prosperity', also emphasised that the worker would enjoy greater security.[124] Manoilesco, on the other hand, as a national corporatist, did not emphasise the benefits workers would be guaranteed through the corporation, although he did refer to them as a means to social peace. However, he did state: 'The essential social function of the corporation is to create a new moral environment, favourable to the idea of collaboration between employers and workers. Placing the two classes in a position of symmetry, which signifies an equal submission to the orders of the social and national ethic [*morale*], corporatism reduces the arrogance of employers and raises again the dignity of workers'.[125] Othmar Spann, solidly based in the Romantic tradition, also placed less significance in the melioration the corporation would bring the workers, but laid great weight on the internal regulation of the corporation by a contract embracing all relevant matters which would strengthen the guild characteristic of the organisation and, thereby, encourage cooperation between employers and employees.[126] Elsewhere in *Der Wahre Staat*, Spann mentioned that within the *Stand* the individual would be assured of security[127] although a new spirituality was to him the most distinguishing characteristic of his proposed corporatist order.

In the end, despite references to the security, justice, protection and other more tangible benefits that the corporation would afford its members, the crucial ingredient for social peace was the new spirit of cooperation, however defined, induced by the creation of the corporation and, indeed, the whole corporatist system itself. The assumption among the theorists that consensus would be widespread has already been discussed with regard to the relations between the corporations and the state. In both cases such a consensus was to be generated by adherence to either the principles of nationalism or Christian reason by those concerned. Furthermore, in respect of the corporation-state relationship, it was seen that where such conformity failed to manifest itself, the higher authority – the state – would have the right to enforce its decision upon the subordinate authority – the corporation. The matter of industrial peace was of a different order because it concerned relations internal to the corporation and did not, directly anyway, involve the state. Nevertheless, the theorists did set out a basis whereby industrial peace, or at least an appearance of it, would be enforced by the state if the corporation, or even just certain parts within it, failed to settle differences peaceably.

The result was – based on the premiss that a 'just' solution or one conforming to the national interest was guaranteed, which no one morally had the right to contest – that strikes and lockouts and other forms of industrial action were to be rendered illegal or severely circumscribed. Nobody would be allowed to use their industrial power to breach the principles laid down by the state. Between the theorists there was some dissention as to whether the ban would be absolute. The abbé Hitze felt that under the liberal-individualistic order strikes had a certain measure of justification, but under a corporative order, there would be ample grounds for prohibiting strikes and lockouts, or at least tolerating them only when the two parties to a dispute had failed to agree after a special court of industrial arbitration had rendered its decision. Hitze himself had stressed the need to restore the medieval principles of 'vocation' and 'mutuality' creating a system based on 'true solidarity',[128] but still in the end argued for some prohibition on industrial action. Another Social Catholic, Albert de Mun, congruously noted that when labour is corporatively organised 'strikes will be replaced by arbitration'[129]. In 1891, Pope Leo XIII in his corporatistic encyclical *Rerum Novarum*, gave support to such ideas. He did not assert that all strikes were *ipso facto* illegal, but he did vaguely suggest that 'evil' or 'mischievous' strikes could legitimately be prevented by the state authority,[130] if further arguing that the legitimate causes of conflict should be removed.[131] Gaetan Pirou pointed out that the majority of French inter-war corporatists saw industrial conflict as incompatible with corporatism and called for legal prohibition upon strikes and lock-outs. Indeed, the only notable exception among French writers of this period not to consider such outlawing necessary was Jean Brethe de la Gressaye.[132] In the case of Professor Perroux, he was against the use of force in industrial disputes – 'a testimony of the impotency of the modern state' – but he saw possible dangers in such a prohibitive solution, and much of his work attempts to deal with the problem.[133]

The theorists were basically arguing that where conflict arose it should be subject to compulsory arbitration which would replace either temporarily or, more usually, permanently, the usual sanctions of industrial disputes. The Italian nationalist, Alfredo Rocco, laid down that disputes in the final instance would be delegated to special state tribunals, 'acting with the force of law', which implied precluding absolutely all forms of defensive action, including obstructionism'.[134] His compatriot, de Michelis, in much the same vein pointed out that collaboration was not something groups could refuse to be a part of.[135] Manoilesco did not actually call for legal prohibition, but nevertheless, it was clear that *l'arbitrage automatique* which he proposed was not compatible with belligerent syndical associations.[136] Whether Rathenau would have permitted strikes in his new economy remains an open question, but he did mention establishing special courts to have jurisdiction over wage disputes,[137] which one must assume would have displaced to some extent the normal means for settling disputes.

The position of the theorists was, therefore, in the end that state arbitration would replace strikes, lockouts and other forms of conflict in industrial relations. The role of the state would, however, be limited it was assumed because the corporation, with its granting of equality to capital and labour and its particular nature fostering a new spirit of cooperation, would generally ensure an amicable settlement. The state would act as a court of last appeal on a compulsory basis when the processes broke down.[138] Such arbitration was an obvious conclusion. The corporatists had set out objectives for wages and other labour conditions, on the basis of justice or the national interest, and would have hardly accepted that in the last resort such issues could still be settled by force in the market when the state had to ultimately guarantee that corporatist principles on labour conditions would prevail. In this respect, those few theorists like Brethe de la Gressaye or Messner,[139] who envisaged some residual right to strike, appear to be somewhat inconsistent with the paramouncy of corporatist values.

This concludes the discussion of the corporations' functions. It is not, however, the end of our consideration of the corporations. They will figure in the examination of the corporatists views upon the overall nature of the political system.

4

Corporatist thought: the nature of the political system

In terms of political allegiances and backgrounds the corporatist theorists were widely divergent; the writers ranged from monarchists to republicans, from technocrats to Romantics, from fascists to Social-Catholics. There was in consequence to be no one political type of corporatist regime. Nonetheless, there was a degree of consensus concerning the basis of legal authority of the state authorities, although the agreement was most marked in respect of the negative view about what it definitely could not be based upon. Further, there was a level of agreement that, insofar as there were to be structures for societal representation, it should fall to corporatist institutions, especially the corporation. What did unite the corporatists was their indifference to the concept of democracy and democratic norms. The foregoing discussion in the previous two chapters has revealed time and again that the theorists argued that the state authorities were to take decisions according to particular universal principles. Popular and particularistic demands could not be allowed to breach the taking or enforcement of such decisions and thereby override what were regarded as universal truths. The issue was not, however, so straightforward, because the theorists almost unanimously proffered that there would be a consensus about such principles, that is they would be popularly supported.

Whatever the different political and moral allegiances of the theorists, they were all not reticent in attacking majoritarian democracy: majorities could not determine truth, only those with the consummate capacity could. In revealing terms Othmar Spann captured the corporatist outlook: 'Using the ballot box to decide questions of truth and justice is the most ridiculous suggestion I have heard [...] Nobody can live by the majoritarian principle, but only on the basis of value and truth'.[1] The Viennese professor went on to complain that under democracies people were not organised in forms of common activity,[2] thus pointing the finger in the direction of the corporation as a representational structure. In fact Spann went further to provide an elitist critique of democracy's praxis, by

63

claiming that pure democracy had never existed because leaders and cliques and political parties always exercised the powers the people should have employed themselves.[3] Franz Hitze, likewise, did not see a true democracy as being one where the social and economic interests of real abiding functional groups did not receive expression and where legislative enactments resulted from 'accidental' and transitory verdicts of parliamentary majorities.[4] Along much the same lines, Ketteler deplored the lack of functional representation and condemned the present system 'in which one selected representative voices the opinions of an entire community'.[5] Not without significance, Ketteler was also concerned that the majority principle would lead inescapably to socialism.[6] Indeed, Ketteler was a severe critic of the majoritarian principle because he saw it, as it operated at the time in Germany on an indirect and three-class basis, as forming a basis for liberal majorities to attack the Church and prevent social progress,[7] while if the basis of elections became one of a direct and universal suffrage, the result would be disorder and a threat to private property.[8] The theorists, therefore, were concerned that democratic representation was not based upon permanent forces within society. There was, however, an additional side to their criticism. They also denigrated democracy because it assumed everybody was of equal capacity to decide the major political issues. La Tour gave vent to both lines of attack in outspoken fashion. To him where parliament did not represent permanent forces or interests, but represented nothing more than 'the favour of the mob and emanates from a suffrage more or less universal and unorganised, all is ephemeral as the impressions of the masses'.[9] Walther Rathenau, correspondingly, attacked the mechanical parliamentary system's omnicompetent character which made legislation 'a matter of chance', where those not competent to decide such matters, by virtue of their majority, were able to do so. Indeed, Rathenau went further and attacked the opportunism of politicans and the exertion of pressure by special interests which were also appended to the parliamentary system.[10] De La Rocque was more ambiguous in his criticisms of representative democracy but felt there was 'much to be said' for linking the suffrage with 'some sort of objective discrimination', which judges men according to 'their capacities, their functions and their responsibilities'.[11] In a technocratic tone Manoilesco argued that democracy was outdated in respect of the demands of the industrialised economy and its organisational needs. The state needed to lead and discipline, not serve popular interests.[12]

In the light of their attacks upon liberal democracy – which were very largely centred upon the twin issues of capacity and majoritarianism – the theorists moved on to outline an organic basis of representation that drew on the permanent forces of society. The underlying principle of such a

basis of representation is echoed in Vogelsang's criticism of liberal democracy and his proposals for change. He stated that: 'The basic fault is that
there is no inner relationship between the representative and those he
represents, no tie except the casual and superficial act of voting [. . .] The
representative must stand in a continuous and active relationship to his
constituents; he must be thoroughly familiar with their affairs and their
needs'.[13] Such familiarity, the theorists adjudged, would prevail in the corporations with their functional bases, and proposals for such a basis of
representation were prevalant in the literature. There was nonetheless a
degree of diversity in the schema set forth; differences existed over the
extent of representation, the basis for selecting representatives and the
form of representative bodies. Most favoured was the establishment of
chambers of representatives from the corporations, though several preferred a council of corporations rather than a chamber.

The proposals of Manoilesco reflect generally the views of those who
backed a chamber. In fact, he set out two different proposals, one with a
single chamber and the other a bicameral system. The unicameral system,
obviously enough, was to contain representatives from all the corporations. Under the two-chamber system, there would be a division between
one for social and cultural corporations and one for the economic corporations which it was held had not only different functions but also a difference in conception and mentality, although the demarcation was essentially functional. The dual system, it was argued, would realise equilibrium
and binding agreement (*l'accord obligatoire*) between these two groups by
giving each an expression of its independence, and equally neither group
would be able to take decisions contrary to the interests of the other.[14]
Interesting though such ideas of functional divisions between different
chambers are, the most important aspects of such chambers are their com-
position and method of operation. The representatives of a particular corporation were not to be selected by a form of 'universal suffrage' by all the
members, but were to be drawn from the various territorial and category
divisions of the corporation with parity between workers and employers,
and with each corporation getting a number of representatives according
to its 'national importance'. The representatives were to be appointed by
the general assembly of the corporation, which was itself to be elected by
the various categories within the function, with votes being distributed, not
proportionally to membership, but on the basis of the categories' importance relative to each other. The method of operation Manoilesco set out for
his corporative chamber was highly complicated. However, it is clear
enough that he envisaged legislative decisions being taken not by plenary
sessions but by the relevant sections, the full assembly simply ratifying the
decisions of the sections. Majority voting was to be avoided at all costs.[15]

Several other writers set out plans for chambers of corporations. Franz Hitze saw a Chamber of Estates as the pinnacle of the corporatist edifice, representatives being chosen by national electoral colleges of the various estates who would in turn have been chosen by regional and local assemblies respectively. In such an assembly, considerations other than the will of the arithmetical majority would prevail, and a true democracy where there was a national bond between government and people would exist.[16] La Tour for his part, however, was never consistently in favour of a national chamber, and by 1905 he was largely hostile to the idea because a single chamber 'would degenerate immediately into a closed field where no common interest would appear and where particular interests would be in perpetual conflict'.[17] Even when he had been favourably disposed he was uncertain as to whether representation would be proportional or according to national importance.[18] Rathenau similarly doubted the merits of a conglomerate chamber. Instead, he wished to see the 'ideal states'[19] of the nation being represented in a series of parliaments for each estate, thereby eradicating the 'desperate expedient' of an omnicompetent parliament.[20] On the other hand, Konstantin Frantz felt a functional parliament would generate harmony among the vocations.[21]

The Spanish writer Azpiazu sought to have both a national chamber and to ensure that the national interest would override vocational interests. He argued that a corporative chamber would authentically represent the country, with the representatives being elected by the corporations who would choose the most able men to obtain a 'favourable solution' of their interests.[22] Uncertain seemingly as to whether the national interest would not be lost in the cacophony of specific vocational interests, he proposed a further basis of representation for the corporations, namely, a Supreme Corporation Council drawn from the councils of the various corporations. This body was to be a means of ensuring that corporative interests were united with the general interests of the nation, and to this end the council members were to be endowed with public executive authority.[23] Azpiazu, therefore, saw corporative representation in both the 'legislature' and 'executive', although quite on what basis the system would operate, and how extensive an authority these bodies would enjoy, was left more to the reader's imagination than anything else.

French interbellum corporatists likewise discussed at length the issue of functional representation. Their ideas were influenced by Duguit, who suggested a professional senate;[24] Durkheim, who considered it legitimate that the corporation should become the fundamental political unit;[25] and La Tour (despite some belated hesitancy). Of course, ideas of professional representation within the political state, as in Germany, had a certain degree of popular currency in any case.[26] However, not all were willing to support the idea of a corporative chamber as a counterweight to the territorial Chamber of Deputies. Roger Bonnard, for example, saw the result of such an arrangement as being perpetual conflict 'due to their difference in origins'.[27] Those critical of the idea of a corporative chamber turned, instead, to the proposal of a national council of corporations. Such a body would be independent of the legislature and would be the apex of the corporative pyramid. It would be made up of the presidents or other delegates appointed from each corporation, often with a government minister as a presiding officer. Among the tasks suggested for the council were, most prominently, the general control and guidance over corporative activity, research and related tasks, assisting the minister of the national economy and, of course, representing corporative interests to the government.[28] Supporting the idea of a council of corporations, Georges Viance argued that this institution would be the only one adaptable enough to control the economy of France's organic and hierarchical society.[29] However, Firmin Bacconier of the *Action Française*, and a number of other theorists rejected both the idea of a chamber and of a council. Rather, Bacconnier put forward the proposal of organising a series of economic chambers, one each for industry, agriculture and the professions. Somewhat akin to La Tour's suggestions, these corporatively recruited chambers would be geographically located at the regional level which would, when required, appoint delegates for a national chamber.[30]

The suggestions for corporative representation, diverse though they were, all sought to give representation to what the corporatists regarded to be the enduring forces within society – the vocation or function. It was in this sense that they saw representation; not of individual members but of a function with its traditions and place within society. This emphasis on the place of the function within society was most explicitly recognised in the proposals which sought to allocate representation in proportion to national importance. The structure of representation can, therefore, be regarded as consensually-orientated, designed to allay conflict, particularly class conflict, through adopting a corporate[31] basis of representation that upheld the common good. Indeed, several writers quite openly admitted that corporate representation would stem the consequences of class conflict. For example, Albert Schäffle, the German Monarchical Socialist, wrote of the 'insane idolatory' that a mere numerical majority of individuals 'should reign supreme over the members and civilising agencies of the nation' and for the need to prevent 'class government'.[32] It might be surmised that doubts about the outright rejection of bodies encompassing collectivities of corporations is indicative of certain theorists' dubiousness about the practicality of generating a consensus. However, such vacillation probably is more to do with the writers' perspective of status, capacity and hierarchy: the corporations' leaders had the capacity and insight for that task, but simply bringing them together did not cut them out for national leadership – national leaders were the next rung up with their greater capacity and insight.

This point is fundamental to the discussion that follows. The corporatist case for functional representation was not the antecedent for functional democracy. The theorists did not regard it as desirable that representatives of the corporations should in some form hold the position of ultimate authority within the state, nor that those who held office would be responsible to their constituents. Of course, such a position is wholly consistent with what has been said so far about corporatist theory, but it still requires further development and analysis.

The best starting point for our analysis is to return to the statement already quoted from Othmar Spann's *Der Wahre Staat*. As was noted, Spann pointed out that 'truth' and 'justice' could not be determined through the ballot box. Spann was doing no more than reiterating the position of all corporatists, namely, that the ends of corporatism were not democracy and that democracy was not a particularly important or suitable means to achieving their ends. For Catholic corporatists, the end to which the whole corporatist system was directed was a 'just society'. Social justice was not something that could be decided through electoral choice of whatever form, but could be achieved only by invoking reason. Justice could not be the result of a competition over a number of choices, an essential element of democracy, but was given by those who were most fully acquainted with Christian teachings. In this context, it is hardly surprising that Ketteler argued that the various associations should be under the guidance of priests. The result would not be a government completely detached from the values of the people; but one in complete accord with these values because the assumption was held that all individuals and groups were fundamentally homogeneous and subscribed to a single belief system. Society was conceived as organic with a single purpose which requires only direction from the most enlightened and which can accept decentralisation of decision-making without fear of conflict. The same view is broadly true of nationalist corporatists. Their overriding goal was the national interest, somewhat variously defined, although justice remained an important element drawn from medieval concepts.[33] As with social justice, such an end was not something that could be determined by competition among conflicting interests but by someone or some persons who could reflect the national, organic will.

The organic premise of both the Catholics and the nationalists, therefore, made responsible government unnecessary, in that society was at one in reality, and at the same time created a 'true democracy' because the government reflected the true will or beliefs of society and not sectional interests or some 'artificial majority'. This position is well reflected by the statement of Franz Baader who asserted that: 'The state, the constitution, and society, in whatever form and shape, necessarily become onerous and unsupportable if they lack the community spirit of religion; for government without religion, which is despotism, can appear in the form of monarchy, aristocracy or democracy.'[34]

Upon this line of argument authority was to rest with those who had the necessary insight and capacity, not those who were representative. The role of representation became one of setting some relative limit to the authority of the state – in line with the notion of a hierarchy of authority – and to facilitate advice to the state authority – a consequence of differences in competence. La Tour's ideas capture the essence of this. For the *marquis*, the state was 'the ensemble of the powers and forces of a nation organised for the common good, which is called the national interest'.[35] His ideal form of government would be a monarchy. The monarch was to be assisted by councillors chosen by the monarch himself.[36] To him the exercise of public power remained distinct from that of representation in their respective roles;[37] the role of professional representation is 'essentially consultative' because 'it is not the expression of a sovereign will, but an appeal to the proper quarter'. If its role was not confined to one of consultation, then organised conflict would, he felt, prevail.[38] In short, the corporations' leadership had no national perspective; they were simply an agglomeration of different viewpoints. La Tour, therefore, saw the role of functional chambers, at whatever level, as one of deliberating and advising upon laws prepared by the executive which at the national level was the Council of State. Quite what this would add up to is not clear, because it was never made explicit what weight any recommendations would carry.[39] La Tour did not wish to see an absolutist monarchy established, but one that would govern according to custom, respecting the rights of corporative bodies.[40] Corporatist representation would act as a means of protecting associational rights rather than as a means of allowing interests to effectively influence, far less legislate, authoritative decisions.

Subsequent French theorists, writing after the First World War, maintained the position of functional representation at the consultative level; for example, Bacconnier's structure of economic chambers was to be such.[41] Those who favoured the notion of a corporative council, likewise, did not see fit to give these bodies any formal control over the governmental decision-making process. They too emphasised that such representation would guarantee the corporations some measure of protection against encroachment by the 'state' on their activities which was unjust, but they also indicated that the council would be able to represent its interests and desires to the relevant decision-making bodies.[42] Importantly, a number of theorists suggested keeping in existence the territorially based Chamber of Deputies, or at least they assumed its continued existence. Nevertheless, it is fully evident that its powers *vis-à-vis* the government were to be shorn. Those of more 'rightist' leanings were more virulent in curtailing its powers, some going as far as to suggest the complete abolition of any semblance of democratic, parliamentary government; however, explicit advocates of a one party state were a rarity.

The universal theme of the corporatists was, within the varying degrees of curtailment of the legislature's powers, to place the executive in a stronger position so it would be able to perform its tasks as coordinator of national activity and arbitrator of conflicts, and for it to remain above factional interests and party competition, to the extent that they would continue to prevail. De La Rocque, for example, suggested a family vote with the head of a family having as many votes as there are members.[43] More significantly, he put forward proposals for strengthening the power of the executive with the 'head of the Nation' being elected on a mandate of two successive parliaments and only removeable by a vote of two-thirds of the National Assembly. The 'head of the Nation' would have powers of dissolution of the National Assembly and ministerial choice.[44] Both the chambers of the Economic Council were to be given only restricted (although how restricted was far from clear) powers with regard to the executive.[45] Louis Baudin, who cared little for individual liberty, proposed a model of corporatism where the designated ministries of the government would not positively guard the public interest but would exercise hierarchical authority.[46]

The notion proffered by the French theorists that the state's executive authority should be severely restricted in its responsibility to institutions and individuals below it, and not draw its authority from them, was shared by other theorists. Hierarchical norms received much emphasis. The works of the Germans, Karl Marlo and Konstantin Frantz, gave expression to such proposals in terms of need to have a hierarchical system. The people could not be allowed to participate in legislation which required a greater degree of insight than they could give, although taxes, as La Tour likewise proposed, should be subject to some representative constraint from taxpayers. To them it was important that the principle of rank or status prevailed, with the more important affairs of state being the prerogative of the monarchy or those specifically chosen for their 'fitness'. Such a system would be counterbalanced by a 'federalistic' development, where lower groups would be granted greater freedom in their own affairs, if still ultimately under the control of the central authority. Under such a hierarchical system, elections would play only a very restricted role in selecting those suitable for higher levels of decision-making.[47] Manoilesco, for his part, returned to the need to have an ultimate source of authority to be able to arbitrate over conflicts that arose. He argued that it was necessary to have a strong head of government who had both the necessary authority and stability of office, with ministers aiding him, instead of holding the position of *primus inter pares* of cabinet government. The head of the government would be far from fully responsible to parliament. A simple majority would not oblige the head of government to resign; he would only be obliged to do so if parliament assembled an 'almost unanimous' opinion to that effect. And even given this strength of opinion, which Manoilesco saw as resulting only in times of crisis, the head of state would be able to continue the mandate of the head of government, whom he appointed, dissolve parliament and seek the opinions of a new parliament. Furthermore, despite the fact that his ideas owed less than most corporatists to medieval times, Manoilesco came out in favour of a monarchy as the form of head of state.[48] Again, like so many other theorists, it was emphasised that the government was not the sole source of public power, but was only the highest,[49] with the corporations enjoying their own 'autonomous' powers.

Albert Schäffle, apart from continuing some form of territorial representation, put forward similar proposals to those of Manoilesco with a monarchy and a Bismarkian form of government.[50] Othmar Spann was in favour of a high degree of 'decentralisation', but all levels would have to be strictly under the ultimate control of the one above. At the apex of the corporative system would be the corporative chamber where the *Stände* and the state were united, but it is clear that the political leaders in the *politische Stände* were the only ones who could speak for the entire nation and thus his system would be based on a completely irresponsible government.[51] *Völkisch* corporatists like Carl Schmitt argued along such lines as Spann, but the special occupational interests were not to be united by a political elite in the *politische Stände*, but by a national leader (*Führer*) who would be a (non-elected) representative member of the race of the *Volk*.[52] Hendrik de Man in his later corporatist years, similarly suggested that the 'new economic state' would have to be differently organised from the 'political state' to avoid internal bureaucratisation. In the new economic state 'representative institutions', that is, those based on the exercise of the right of individual suffrage, would have only the right of inspection and supervision; the exercise of the right to administer would be based on the *delegation* of power by the executive and through the representation of corporative interests.[53]

Whichever theorist is examined, whether his proposals for the political system were actually detailed, as Manoilesco's were, or whether a few basic principles were outlined as in Pirou's case,[54] the common theme in this area of the theory was that the hierarchical principle of the corporatist system could not be breached by territorial and/or functional representation. Thus the state's executive authority had to be both above and independent of those representing particular interests in whatever guise, insofar as these interests, even majority interests, might override the collective interests of society. The corporatists were in effect arguing for two political principles to be applied: (1) those who hold the office of the state's executive authority have to represent the collective interest, and none other in respect of economic and social affairs. The collective interest was, of course, the collective interest according to corporatist principles. And (2) those who held such office would hold ultimate authority and be responsible to no institution or collectivity of individuals that itself did not represent the collective interest.

The above two principles which guided the theorists amount to no more than the argument that a corporatist regime must have a corporatist government and nothing else. By definition a corporatist government could not be a democratic government in terms of the generally accepted conceptualisations of democracy, because it was higher principles – social justice or the national interest – not popular demands however articulated that would guide government. Popular government is only possible to the extent that it is held that such principles can be popularly determined, which in the case of Catholic theorists, who advocated following 'God's' will, is inconceivable. In respect of nationalist writers the general, but not exclusive view was taken that defining the national interest, reflecting the national will, was an activity which was not able to be served through popular participation but had to be conducted by the few (if not one) who had the commensurate insight. Therefore, both camps of corporatists held to the 'descending theory' of political authority which had predominated in medieval Europe under the influence of the Christian Church.[55] Authority descended either from 'God' or *via* some, often rather obscure, identification with the nation's past. Certainly, the predisposition towards a monarchy of numerous theorists is explainable in such terms.

However, the earlier discussion of the writers' prescriptions for the political and governmental system revealed a notable diversity. Further examination of other corporatists' views would have done nothing to de-emphasise this diversity. So the theorists provided a wide spectrum of ideas on political organisation, ranging from Othmar Spann's *politische Stände* or Carl Schmitt's *Führer*, seemingly representative of and responsible to nobody to Jules Romians' *Groupe du 9-ème Julliet* whose corporatist proposals included a stronger, but nevertheless elected executive.[56]

The question inevitably arises as to whether those who advocated a degree of popular government were in effect in breach of the two political principles mentioned above. The two principles presented were the logical position the corporatists had to adopt, that is corporatist principles over democratic principles. But what we are concerned with here is what prescriptions the writers actually put forward, not what views it would have been logically advisable for them to hold.

In practice, none of the writers adopted an illogical position on this fundamental point. There was never any suggestion that democracy should prevail over social justice or the national interest. What those writers who proposed some restricted form of popular government were arguing was that corporatism would induce a change within society whereby there would be acceptance of the hierarchical nature of society; those who chose office-holders would do so for their leadership, not representative, qualities; for their collective insight, not for holding particularistic interests; for their adherence to true corporatist principles rather than any other. In this sense, these writers were attempting to perform a marriage between the descending and ascending theses of representation. Executive office-holders had to have certain imperative qualities, but there could be some popular choice in respect of who most adequately displayed such qualities. It is worth remembering that it was very common for theorists to suggest some discrimination in favour of those held to be most competent to choose. Once chosen the authorities were not to be held in check, but be allowed to get on with exercising their powers.[57] In so far as procedures were laid down for the removal of office-holders from their position, the sole count of indictment mentioned by the theorists was that of exceeding the bounds of authority and 'interfering' with the authority of the corporations. Indeed, when the theorists discussed 'representation' they often as not were referring to such a check upon exceeding authority. Thus, for example, Vogelsang emphasised corporative representation to ensure local and occupational autonomy.[58]

The corporatists' ideas on the nature of the political system were clearly diverse. Cutting through the diversity, however, were two persistent themes – emphasis on social community and the centrality of higher moral principles transcending, and indeed above, the members of society. Society was collectivist, but collectively organised and governed in a form that was not collectively decided – or for that matter decided by a majority. In such a system of ideas democratic norms could only be granted honorary membership, and then in effect on terms of continued good conduct. Many theorists did not even consider it advisable to offer membership at all. Yet it would be wrong to regard corporatist ideology as purely authoritarian. Proximate to all their ideas was the notion of a moral transformation of society under corporatism. Such a transformation would create a society where there was an acceptance of a largely immutable hierarchy of authority. The acceptance of hierarchical authority not only conferred certain rights on those below, it also conferred upon them the duty to obey those above. In obeying those above, the subordinate was not just recognising the *legal authority* of the office, they were concomitantly acknowledging the *sociological authority* of the office-holder, his capacity and insight.

What the corporatists never considered, with a few exceptions, was the danger of falling head first into strident authoritarianism if moral transformation failed to materialise, particularly if those at the top remained morally suspect. This is not to suggest that economic and social theories should take on a contractual format with disclaimer clauses. But reading the theorists' deliberations a point that one continuously confronts is how close to the authoritarian winds they sailed, though they never breached them while holding to the promise of a harmonious society.

5

Corporatist thought: concluding thoughts and a model

At the end of the last chapter it was noted that the theorists overall view of political arrangements was at face value tantamount to being authoritarian except for the very important assumption of societal acceptance of the order established by the state under corporatism. State and society were viewed not only as hierarchical, but also as communitarian.[1] Nor were these two elements simply concomitant, they were interdependent: the community was best served by hierarchical organisation; society was communitarian, at one, when hierarchical. So, state and society under corporatism would be as one, they would be organic. There would be little in the way of dissent under corporatism, and those who did so attempt to breach the state's authority would be by definition acting against the community's interests, of which the state was guardian. Similarly, if the state ceased to act in the community's interests, checks – notably in the form of the corporation's constitutional authority – would pertain.

The organic conception of state and society was, therefore, fundamental to corporatist ideology. From this flowed notions of a society that had an ultimate single purpose and was united in that purpose. Moreover, the norms and values to be applied to serve this purpose were themselves widely accepted. This was particularly evident in Catholic writings, but nationalist corporatists (with the exception already noted) also viewed general approval to be the state of affairs. It is in this respect that corporatist ideology can be regarded as a *consensual* variety of corporatism. What hopefully was consistently evident throughout our examination of corporatist economic and social theory was that if there was no such consensus then corporatism would have been unable to operate in the form proposed. If the consensus did not prevail the result would, as Gaeton Pirou argued was inevitable,[2] be either chaos or a far more interventionist, and ultimately authoritiarian, state.

It is important to emphasise at this point that the centrality of a societal consensus to corporatist ideology does not undermine the component of a

75

dominant state set out in the General Model of Corporatism. Corporatist ideology did quite explicitly encompass a dominant state. This was reflected most evidently in the view that the state was at the head of the hierarchical organisation of society and economy. The corporatist notion was that it was an accepted domination, and accepted because the state – in line with medieval thought – had to reflect a single will to keep the various parts in harmony.[3] In other words, to draw the 'hierarchical' and 'community' parts together, only the state overseeing, dominating economic and social life could generate a harmonious and consensual society applying principles of justice and national interest. The role of the state emphasised many times over by the writers was to provide clear and unequivocal leadership – not to *run* the economy but to *guide* it. Such guidance was not to give overall direction to the popular will, it was to provide direction from 'above', that is from 'God' or the nation's past.

To summarise, therefore, the corporatists held to four basic premises: (1) The economic and social order would enjoy a degree of societal acceptance such that the state would not have to widely impose it; (2) the economic and social order could only be established and sustained by those with the commensurate capacity and insight to reflect the general interest, or, put another way, society itself could not establish and sustain the order; (3) society itself could not establish and sustain such an order because, while its members supported the general interest, they also held specific interests and so, where there was a conflict of interests that could not be resolved according to societal principles, it was essential to have an independent arbitrator above these interests; (4) societal groupings accepted the need to obey the commands of the state authorities, otherwise an economic and social order reflecting the general interests would not prevail.

So groups in society held that the state had to be dominant in generating and maintaining the economic and social order and, in consequence, as the theorists argued any significant attempt to popularly determine the order, despite general support for it, would be bound to fail. On this point it is worth quoting Max Weber that 'every genuine form of domination implies a minimum voluntary compliance, that is, an interest (based on ulterior motives or genuine acceptance) in obedience'.[4] The corporatists' general outlook was that there would be substantially more than a 'minimum voluntary compliance'. That there should be such extensive voluntary compliance to a corporatist order ultimately rested on particular metaphysical premises about the nature of man in society, particularly his inherent desire to be governed according to certain principles and his acceptance of a relatively rigid and ordered social structure clearly set out in differential rights of status. Not all corporatists, though certainly the overwhelming majority of them, regarded the basis of voluntary compliance as one of genuine acceptance of corporatism as a natural or historically true ordering of society. Writers like Manoilesco and Rathenau made concessions to ulterior motives by arguing that corporatism was the most effective means for national economic well-being and thus would gain acceptance on the grounds of material interests.

In addition to proposing that corporatist ideology be regarded as a consensual variety, it was also suggested that it was a *licenced* variety. By licenced it was meant that the authority of the corporation to regulate the function and of producer groups to regulate members was granted from above. The consequence of the licencing system was that no other individual or organisation had the authority to enforce decisions within the remit of the powers granted and that if the powers were exceeded or abused then the state had the right to intervene to prevent this. It is valuable to reiterate here that the regulatory powers granted to the corporation were not only to apply to those actors who were members, but generally to all actors within the relevant category with the force of public law. Obviously licencing was the means by which the state was able to achieve the twin imperatives of delegation to private actors and ultimate control. The reasons the corporatists did not advocate encompassing regulatory powers within state agencies proper was their notion of different levels of competence which held that the state was incompetent in the productive process. The need for an intermediary between state and socio-economic actors was, therefore, paramount.

The two factors that most clearly represent the nature of corporatist ideology are the socio-economic consensus and state licencing – *consensual-licenced corporatism*. From the examination of what the corporatists thought in the previous three chapters it is possible to extrapolate certain generalised but commonly prescribed views about socio-economic organisation. These common views can, in effect, provide the components of a model of consensual-licenced corporatism. Such a model can be used to examine and analyse politico-economic systems along a number of dimensions to determine to what extent and in what ways they conform to consensual-licenced corporatism. Indeed, it is with the aid of this model that we will analyse Italy and Portugal, employing it in conjunction with the General Model of Corporatism to ensure that whatever is discovered it remains some variant of corporatism. The model of consensual-licenced corporatism is not essential to the analysis of corporatist regimes, but given the claims of the leaders of the regimes to be following the ideologies' prescriptions and the persistent confusions that continue to exist over the differences between corporatist ideology and practice it will significantly enhance analysis. Our concern is not just to establish a model of authoritarian-licenced corporatism but to elaborate upon the differences between it and the consensual variant. However, before any of this can proceed it is necessary to set out the model. The components of the model will be set out under the headings employed in Chs. 2–4.

Model of consensual-licenced corporatism

(1) *The state, the economy and the market*
    (a)   The state has ultimate responsibility to ensure that economic and social conditions conform to certain collective principles and the state, or its agents, will intervene into markets (including international markets) when and to the extent that the market fails to create the desired conditions.

(2) *The role of capital*
    (b)   The means of production are predominantly privately owned, and public appropriation is only carried out on strict functional grounds.
    (c)   Private capital has a social, as well as individual function, and therefore is subject to legally enforceable social obligations to both its employees and the national economy.
    (d)   Profits are considered a legitimate and necessary form of income so long as they are not earned from what is held to be a position of monopoly.

(3) *The role of labour*
    (e)   Wages are to be determined with reference to the basic needs of the worker and his dependents and according to the requirements of the national economy.
    (f)   Employees have the right to a minimum provision of welfare.
    (g)   Employees of a certain designated status are afforded particular 'property rights' or protection in respect of employment.

(4) *State licenced intermediaries*
    (h)   The state sponsors and licences a comprehensive system of functional bodies, bringing together representatives of all members of a particular function (notably capital and labour), to act as an intermediary between itself and economic actors.
    (i)   The intermediary bodies are separate legal entities from the state, but of a quasi-public status, enjoying powers of public regulation set within a framework laid down by the state.

(5) *The intermediaries membership*
    (j)   Membership of the intermediary organisations is compulsory for all organisations who wish to engage in a particular activity covered by the function over which the intermediary exercises a public monopoly.

(k) Membership of the intermediary body is organised into a number of producers' associations, and these associations are licenced by and granted a monopoly by the intermediary.

(6) *The intermediaries' functions*

(l) The intermediaries exercise regulatory powers over prices, production, wages and other labour conditions, vocational qualifications and welfare provision.

(m) The intermediaries compulsorily arbitrate, assisted where appropriate by the state, all disputes between capital and labour, completely or nearly completely rendering industrial action illegal.

(7) *The nature of the political system*

(n) Representative government is curtailed at least to the extent that it does not preclude authority resting exclusively with those with the capacity and insight to represent the general corporatist interest.

(o) Government responsibility to any institution which does not fully have the capacity and insight to represent the general corporatist interest is curtailed at least to the extent that no such institution can change or overturn a decision of the authorities or remove the authorities while acting within their jurisdiction.

(p) The state licenced intermediaries will perform a representative role to the state authorities.

The above represents the areas of agreement amongst the corporatist ideologues. Throughout the examination of corporatist economic and social theory the emphasis has been placed upon the areas of agreement amongst the writers. The result has been to possibly create a picture of greater unity and coherence than was the actual case. There were clear differences among them. Probably the most significant were not to do with the structure and functions that we have largely focussed upon, but in their conception of what corporatist society would be. Manoilesco and Rathenau's concern for national productivity stands in contrast to Ketteler's central interest in the plight of the proletariat or La Tour's desire to return France to the glory that was the *ancien régime*. For all their suggestion of latent societal harmony, there was a good deal of discord amongst the theorists themselves as to what corporatism would ultimately mean for society. Furthermore, one cannot detect much recognition in their writings that such divergences were significant politically in terms of who, and with what values and ideas, would assume on a largely unaccountable basis ultimate authority in the corporatist state. Such a question certainly gains greater poignancy when one considers how corporatism actually ended up in practice. The conception of corporatist society was not the only area of difference between them, though many others were probably subsequent upon it such as the division of jurisdiction among the corporations. Differences also reflected the divergent national and historical contexts within which the authors formulated their ideas – aspects which unfortunately we did not have the time to pursue further. Indeed, such a study of corporatist thought remains to be conducted, particularly one that draws together the diverse influences and linkages – the wider context – in detail.[5]

Part III

Fascist Italy and Portugal 1933–74: authoritarian-licenced corporatism

6

Corporatism and Fascist Italy (1922–39)

Our attention is now turned to an analysis of corporatism in practice – in this case Italy under Fascist rule. As previously mentioned the analysis will be conducted by utilising the model of consensual-licenced corporatism, and the chapter will be divided under the same headings. Under the ever-present imperative of space it will not be possible to detail the origins of Fascism or enter into lengthy assessments of the regime. Such matters are nonetheless of importance to consideration of Italian corporatism and, as we proceed, mention of these two interrelated topics will frequently emerge onto the surface of the discussion.[1]

So, rather than enter into some potted, and inevitably misleading, history of Italian fascism, a number of themes relating to the regime and its corporatist structures will be laid down. (Readers who wish some more substantial evidence are referred to the texts listed throughout.) These themes are (1) While corporatism in Italy was in some respects a paper empire, a facade of propaganda, it was ultimately an integral and substantial part of the regime. (2) The seizure of power with the famous 'March on Rome' in 1922 brought Mussolini to power, but the acquiescence of the old political elites was given at a price of their combined security. (3) The Fascist regime was an uneasy alliance between the new, Fascist political masters and the traditional elites – the monarchy, military, state bureaucracy, Church, large industry and finance, and major agrarian interests. (4) The life of the regime was characterised by continual tension – indeed often downright distrust[2] – between the traditional elites and the new political masters, but the accommodation never broke down because of the fundamental interdependence. (5) This tense, but enduring accommodation gave the regime a curious flavour of both being at one and the same time – as the tensions worked themselves out – dynamic, radical and revolutionary *and* static, supportive of the *status quo* and anti-revolutionary.

The state, the economy and the market

Mussolini's corporate state, like Rome, was not built in a day, but was developed and matured throughout most of the regime's life. It is, however, the case that the general characteristics of the corporate state became evident from the early days of the establishment of the corporatist structure in 1926. Concomitant with the period that saw the foundation of the corporatist edifice was a definitive move to extend the degree, indeed the whole scale, of state intervention in the economy such that during the 1930s Italy was the most extensively regulated economy amongst the major capitalist countries.[3] In fact, during the first four years or so of the regime, under the influence of Finance Minister De Stefani, the Fascist government had pursued an economic strategy of state withdrawal and economic liberalisation. The tenor of the strategy was fascist responsibility, capital accumulation and development led by private capital. In part De Stefani was continuing the process of economic demobilisation after the Great War, and in part giving reassurance to those major interests upon whose support Mussolini depended. De Stefani policies,[4] however, did not prove wholly successful. Certainly production increased but inflationary and, more ominously, balance of payments problems persisted. On top of this the Finance Minister courted the opposition of many leading industrialists because of a stock market crash and his opposition to protectionism. Under pressure from these industrialists Mussolini engineered De Stefani's resignation in July 1925.[5] The demise of De Stefani marked the beginning of the end of the Fascist flirtation with liberalism. Thereafter, intervention on the economic front increased so that by the middle and late 1930s, wages, prices, industrial investment and structure, production, employment and hours, and foreign trade and exchange were all subject to some form of regulation. In addition, there was an extension of state supported welfare schemes, though, in part, such developments must be regarded as a response to the recession of the 1930s.

The doctrinal thinking behind the interventionist strategy came not directly from the original Fascists, but from the conservative Italian Nationalist Association whose principal ideologue, Alfredo Rocco, had outlined a plan to develop the Italian economy by means of a regimented corporatist system to free Italy from dependence on the 'plutocratically controlled' international economy. The nationalists expressed themes and ideas that can be seen as implicit and explicit in Fascist thought from the movement's outset and, indeed, beyond to its political precursors, the national syndicalists and the interventionalists, but importantly they did so with much greater coherence.[6] So with the accession of the Nationalists to positions of prominence in the regime in 1925 (the Fascist Party and the

Nationalist Association having agreed to unite in February 1923),[7] Fascist Italy set off in a conservative-nationalist, corporatist direction. Much of the Fascist economic policy must in some significant proportion be viewed from the perspective held by the regime's ideologues of the need to free the Italian economy from foreign dependence to bring about national development. Thus along with increased regulation – and often as the direct cause of such regulations – went a sustained process to insulate the economy from the international market. In short, the rapidly effected and dramatic moves towards economic isolation generated an inevitable slide towards an extensively regulative economy. Only Italy's extreme dependence on imported raw materials possibly prevented the drive towards insulation going forward more rapidly and more rigorously.

The first significant example of international disengagement began in June 1925 with the announcement of the *battaglia del grano*, designed to achieve self-sufficiency in grain production, and so free Italy from 'the slavery of foreign bread'. The scheme entailed high tariff protection, raised prices and projects to raise yields.[8] Of even greater import was the next of Mussolini's great 'battles' – that of the lira – inaugurated in July 1926. In an act of national economic virility Mussolini pushed the value of the lira up to *quota novanta* (90 lira to the pound), the rate pertaining when he took power. The fall in the lira's external value reflected no more than movements in external payments and prices, and so by any standards the lira was thus greatly over-valued. The impact on the economy was dramatic as depression set in. However, there is some validity in the argument that the attendent deflation had as its *raison d'être* the creation of an environment for the extension of state controls[9].

The advent of world-wide depression in the 1930s and a continually precarious balance of payments saw protectionism inevitably spread beyond the reasonably extensive, but somewhat *ad hoc*, increases in tariff protection introduced in the late 1920s.[10] At first, Italy raised tariffs on a *quid pro quo* basis in retaliation to other countries' action.[11] However, the pressure on the reserves continued to increase, in part because Italy followed neither sterling (1931) nor the dollar (1933) in devaluing, and in May 1934 the government initiated a strict system of control over foreign exchange and proceeded to establish a system of import licences, covering some 1500 products in due course. In addition tariffs continued to be raised, such that by 1935 Italy had one of the highest tariff barriers in the world, while trade was conducted through barter arrangements.[12] So, when in November 1935, the League of Nations applied sanctions on Italy for her invasion of Ethiopia, she could not have been much better prepared to resist them.[13] After the sanctions were lifted in May 1936 Mussolini's drive towards autarchy was reversed with a devaluation of the lira back to quota 90[14] and a relaxation of restriction to trade.[15] Nonetheless, there was no dramatic swing away from protectionism. For one thing the trade deficit in 1937 stood at a dangerous 3.7 million lira.[16]

It was behind this wall of economic insulation that the corporate state operated. In large part protectionism and its consequences set the terms of reference of the corporate state's operation – adjusting to recession, restructuring industry and agriculture, trying to develop import substitutes and – most prominently – allocating the share of the burden of recession and restructuring. This is not to argue that the intervention under corporatism was all the result of the drive for economic insulation. For one thing the state had always played an active economic role from Cavour onwards; the state had been a key factor in economic development under the liberal regime, where there had been an absence of a substantial entrepreneureal class.[17] Additionally, the Italian economy consisted of a relatively small number of concentrated, powerful economic entities who developed close links with the state. The experience of the war helped to strengthen these relationships between the state and private entities.[18] Also the world recession itself pushed all states to varying degrees towards greater intervention; Italy the more so because she was affected longer than most other nations.[19] Finally, it is evident that any political dictatorship will not remain in business long if independent sources of economic power remain unchecked by the state; a degree of state control over the economy was necessary to sustain, and in some respects fuel, the engine of the dictatorship.

The process of increasing intervention under Fascism from 1926 onwards was, therefore, a major consequence of the doctrinal premiss of Italy as a proletarian nation that had to insulate itself from the world economy to bring about national development,[20] but was also a result of the structural development of the Italian economy prior to the advent of Fascism and the prevailing international economic climate, as well as being a necessary concomitant to political dictatorship. The reasons such an interventionist regime was placed firmly in a corporatist structure are less clear cut, but again one can trace the ideas back to the doctrines of the nationalists. It should be remembered that the conception of corporatism held by nationalists like Rocco[21] was far more regimented and statist than the corporatist writers' prescriptions discussed earlier in Part 2. Italian Fascism, particularly once the nationalists entered into positions of prominence, therefore, incorporated corporatism centrally into its doctrine. But it was a different brand of corporatism, one that held no assumption of a harmonious society, instead imposing the new order – the imposition being justified on grounds of external threat. Corporatism, however, had more than a nationalist appeal to the Fascists. The corporate state provided the major basis to Fascism's revolutionary appeal; it was the substance of the radical dimension of Mussolini's regime. The fact that it was never as radical as the propaganda suggested should not detract from its significance in this respect. Finally, corporatism provided a useful piece of ballast to relations with the Catholic Church, a prominent social and political force that Mussolini could not ignore and often had to prudently court.[22]

How this imposed and ultimately highly dirigiste corporatism operated in practice is what we now proceed to examine. The analysis will commence with the corporate structures, the licenced intermediaries, because they illustrate vividly the overall character and bias of Italian corporatism compared to consensual-licenced corporatism.

State-licenced intermediaries

To corporatist theorists the notion of an integrated functional intermediary – the corporation – reflecting the consensus and harmony among all of those engaged in the function was paramount, because it would engender feelings of solidarity in place of conflict. For the Fascist leaders in Italy seeking to impose their will on what was presumed to be, and evidently was, an economy of disparate and conflicting interests, the corporation held no such central appeal. So under the Italian corporate state the corporations played a belated and peripheral role.

The possibility of there being corporations was first referred to in the basic law of the corporate state (on Syndicates and Collective Relations of Labour) in April 1926.[23] A further law of July the same year reiterated that they would incorporate all groupings, or syndicates, within the branch of production[24] and added that the corporation was to be 'an organ of the State Administration'.[25] Thus the corporation was not to be the quasi-public, separate legal entity of corporatist ideology. Despite the case that such state bodies would pose no serious threat to the government's regulation of the economy, the corporations were not inaugurated until some eight years later. In fact, the regime from 1926 onwards had been so successful in presenting itself at home and abroad as a *stato corporativismo* that, to give some tangible evidence that the well-publicised corporations actually existed, 'expedient corporations' made up of sections of the National Council of Corporations had to be established in 1930. These makeshift corporations, of which they were seven, were based on broad economic categories and, reflecting the lack of weight attributed to the corporations, no more than sub-committees of a previously inoperative advisory committee to the Ministry of Corporations – the National Council of Corporations.[26]

When the corporations proper did finally appear in 1934 they had some more substance to them than the National Council's sections. The lengthy debate on the corporations form and structure that preceeded the 1934 law[27] was confined, however, to the terms of the 1926 law, and so they proved to be state bodies *per se*. Nevertheless, unlike the sections of the National Council the twenty-two corporations were based on a particular function as understood in corporatist theory, and they did cover almost every area of the economy. Furthermore, the representatives of the employers' syndicates and employee syndicates were given equal representation on the council of the corporation, although all members were subject to ratification by the head of government. The membership of the council, in addition, however, included three representatives of the Fascist Party and the President in every case was to be the Minister of Corporations.[28] Finally, the Corporations were to enjoy a number of regulatory powers but exercising such powers was to be subject to government approval.[29]

In spite of the Mussolinian fanfare that surrounded the arrival of the corporations[30] they never operated as the linchpin intermediary organisations of the corporatist system. Although the corporations were heralded as constituting 'the unifying organisation of all elements of production [...]',[31] it was a means of control, not unification, which the Fascist government sought. The significant channel of control, and hence central structure of the corporatist system, were the member associations of the corporations, the syndical associations.

The intermediaries' membership

The syndical system (proffered as the first stage in the development of corporatism) was established in 1926 by decree-laws. Under the law, syndical associations (trade unions or employers' organisations) could be given official recognition through a process that amounted to licencing. Any such syndical organisation thus recognised acquired the exclusive right of representing all workers or employers, as the case was, within the prescribed occupational and territorial jurisdiction with regard to the collective relations of labour. A number of conditions had to be fulfilled before recognition was granted including that 'the directors of the association shall give proof of their competence, good moral behaviour and sound national loyalty'. Recognition could similarly be granted to federations and confederations.[32] Thus for each side of industry there was created a single representative body for collective bargaining within a designated constituency, with a reciprocal organisation for the other factor alongside it.[33] In reality, all the Fascists had done in licencing the syndicates was, on the labour side, to recognise the existing Fascist syndicates which had risen to a position of dominance by violence and state oppression[34] and, on the employers' side, to recognise the principal trade associations.[35] While the unions were clearly a guaranteed source of considerable conformity, it must be noted that employers' organisations themselves underwent a process of 'Fascistisation'. This process was only partial and did not involve a take-over of the organisations; instead there were internal purges and the ascendency of those who were willing to conform to and deal with the Fascist leaders.

Membership of the syndicates was not compulsory, and figures suggest that at the time the corporations were formed, large numbers of employers and workers chose not to join, or were not allowed to join.[36] The syndical law of April 1926 had also allowed for the existence of non-recognised *de facto* associations,[37] but they were of little significance and, in the case of workers' associations, subject to continual harassment.[38] Membership of recognised syndicates was not of itself particularly significant. The only concrete benefit was the right to participate in elections,[39] a right that we shall see was severely circumscribed. Otherwise members and non-members alike paid the appropriate fees[40] and, more importantly, were bound by collective labour contracts agreed among the syndicates.[41]

The corporations being part of the state bureaucracy did not conform very readily to the idea of state licenced intermediaries. The syndicates in comparison, did much more closely approximate to corporatist intermediaries, at least in respect of labour relations. However, until there is further consideration of the nature of these syndical associations the picture must remain partial.

In terms of the letter of the law, the bye-laws of the syndical organisations did contain provisions for the election of officers and committees by the members or by persons elected as representatives of the members. But the value of such elections was nullified because each election result had to be ratified by an officer at a higher level, with the outcome that officials were *de facto* appointed from above, which in the last resort was the Ministry of Corporations. Indeed, in a number of cases, notably with labour syndicates, the electoral procedures were openly ignored. On top of this, many members of committees were simply coopted on from higher bodies and Fascist Party organisations. Finally, just to ensure a tight rein, any officer could be removed from his position if 'rendering himself unsuitable for the position held' and any 'election' of officers could at any time be subject to dissolution. Control was not, however, the only objective of such an appointments scheme, and many safe bureaucratic jobs were available for political patronage. To complete the centre's grip, the decisions taken by the officials were likewise subject to this higher approval, creating an excessively bureaucratic structure.[42]

It is necessary, nonetheless, to draw a distinction between the operation of the process in the case of capital and that of labour. On the employers' side there was a bias in the appointment of officials usually in favour of the larger, and hence politically more influential, entities, but they were evidently representative in some general sense.[43] In the case of industrial representation, the leadership personnel of the *Confederazione Generale Dell' Industria Italiana* (CGII) remained largely unchanged from pre-syndical days.[44] This is not to suggest that the employers' organisations enjoyed great autonomy – they did not – but capital did have a voice and was close enough to the centre of things to modify many decisions. The same was not true in labour's case. The employees' 'representatives' for the most part were party members who had little or no connection with those whom they purported to represent. Instead the officials, certainly above provincial level, came from young middle-class party faithfuls anxious to get safe bureaucratic jobs, and whose principal loyalty lay with their benefactor, the *Partito Nazionale Fascista* (PNF)[45].

The syndical associations represented a form of licenced intermediary, though in the case of labour associations, as control was so paramount, they enjoyed very little autonomy. In contrast, employer syndicates did enjoy a degree of autonomy (at least those that continued to operate under the corporate state, the smaller associations having been dissolved), but the evidence suggests that, while they were able to use such autonomy to good effect, the licencing system, and the potential for its extension, did place significant constraints upon their behaviour. However, before making any final assessments it is necessary to probe further, beginning with an examination of the intermediaries' functions.

The intermediaries' functions

The twenty-two corporations, though state bodies under the clear authority of the Head of Government rather than proper corporatist intermediaries, were given *de jure* a number of important economic functions. The corporations' general powers included authority to issue rules for the collective regulation of economic relations and for the unitary discipline of production subject to the consent of the Head of Government and, after a proposal by one of the syndical associations[46], on labour matters and on collective economic relations. Apart from these broad areas for rule making, or ratifying and possibly amending agreements between syndical associations, the corporations were legally empowered to: fix salary scales for work and services (though subject to approval by the National Council of Corporations);[47] promote, encourage and subsidise all initiatives aimed at the coordination and improvement of production; set up labour exchanges wherever necessary;[48] regulate apprenticeships by issuing general compulsory rules;[49] and give advice when requested by 'Public Administrations concerned'.[50]

In actual practice the principal function of the corporations was to act as a legal showpiece; the regulatory functions were given little credence. Some indication of the minor regulatory role of the corporations can be gleaned from the fact that during their first year of operation each corporation met only once for a session of four to five days. Nor is there any evidence that during these few days the corporations were centres of regulatory activity. During the first series of sessions the twenty-two corporations between them could only adopt six regulations of economic relations and one tariff of professional fees under their rule-making powers. In addition, some eight collective economic agreements were passed and transmitted for final action to the Central Corporative Committee. A majority of corporations had no recourse to any rule-making. Instead, most of the corporations acted as arenas to lobby with numerous resolutions being passed, import substitutions being the favourite theme. There is, however, no evidence to suggest that these resolutions induced direct action. The second cycle of corporation meetings in 1936–7 did not mark any radical departure in the extent or nature of business transacted.[51] Yet despite their largely uninspiring start, further functions were granted to the corporations. The decree of 14 January 1937 entrusted to the corporations the task of commenting upon applications for the building of new industrial plants or the enlargement of existing ones, and the Royal Decree of April that same year gave them an advisory role to the Central Corporative Committee in respect of commodity price control.[52] Ironically, because the Ministry had neither the staff nor competence to take such decisions, the advice became in effect binding. The result was that the industrialists' representatives, the CGII, who were well placed in the corporative machinery, were able to make numerous decisions in their own private interests, the ministry being unable to provide any check.[53]

These two examples of assumed regulatory powers apart, the corporations were never regarded as structures suitable for regulating the economy. Indeed, the corporations with their 'self-government', or *auto-disciplina delle categorie*, which gave certain interests a measure of decisional autonomy, and their complicated machinery, were viewed by government officials as not providing the necessary direct control for the coordination of their economic and politico-military strategy. Instead, the 1930s, with increased intervention as a result of the depression, protectionism and later mobilisation, saw a more familiar pattern of the continued existence and creation of state and parastate regulatory agencies paralleling the supposed work of the corporations.[54] Thus economic regulation within the corporate state was conducted through a vast and bureaucratic network of agencies.

In addition to these economic functions, the corporations had as far back as 1926 been endowed with powers in the area of labour relations, notably 'to conciliate disputes that may arise between the affiliated organisations'.[55] The 1934 law did indeed set up special machinery to perform this task – Boards of Conciliation[56] – but by the time the corporations were under way the syndical machinery was already well-established in regulating labour relations, and there is no evidence of the corporations acting as conciliators. Under the 1926 legislation the wages and conditions of labour had to be set out in a collective labour contract negotiated between, and only between, the two appropriate officially recognised syndicates. A quasi-legislative character was given to such contracts because they were binding upon all members of the category, whether syndical members or not.[57] The contract, which had to follow certain legal procedures, had to be approved by the inspection service of the Ministry of Corporations.

However, the protaganists to any industrial dispute could not draw on the usual sanctions to further their cause. The 1926 law expressly forbade the use of strikes, lock-outs and other forms of action, all being subject to sanctions of fines and imprisonment.[58] In spite of the rigid legal position a number of strikes (under thirty a year 1926–33)[59] did occur involving on average around 50 workers. Not surprisingly, the number of convictions for a lock-out were minimal, though the law was easily circumnavigated in any case.[60] Devoid of any sanctions to wield as a means of settling disputes, an alternative method had to be provided for reaching a settlement; more accurately the alternative to be effective needed industrial action to be illegal. The alternative provided was the judicial settlement of disputes through a series of labour courts, which were also responsible for enforcing existing contracts.[61] It need hardly be added that only officially recognised syndicates could take action before the court.[62] The courts were not, however, to be brought into the drama at the first appearance of a dispute. An action could not be brought in a collective labour controversy by a syndical organisation belonging to a federation or confederation or linked with the other party in a corporation unless the federation, confederation and corporation had attempted and failed to achieve a friendly settlement.[63] There was, in theory at least, a hierarchy – with the corporation at the pinnacle – of bodies which first had to attempt to conciliate the dispute. Even the court itself was to attempt conciliation before hearing the case.[64] Such a chain of conciliation was in part, it is worth noting, a response to pressures from employers who were concerned about the possible consequences for themselves of judicial arbitration.[65]

In the event, few collective labour controversies actually reached the court. By 1937, only 41 had got as far as the labour courts, and of these only sixteen were settled by court decisions.[66] The scarcity of actions being taken to the court was not indicative of a new corporative harmony between employers and employees. Instead, it reflected the great inequality between employer and employee syndicates because the officials of employee associations, accountable to Party leaders and the governmental bureaucracy, were willing to be more conciliatory and accept less favourable conditions than would have been acceded by proper labour organisations.[67] Furthermore, the Ministry of Corporations itself was engaged in a reasonable number of cases of arbitration and mediation,[68] thereby usurping the labour courts. In any case, employees had very little to gain from pushing their case up to the heights of the labour court because its political independence was only noted for its absence;[69] this reflects why the quicker expedient of using ministerial offices was so frequently employed as an alternative. The hopelessness of the workers' position was doubly so because in the court their syndical officials continued to be over-zealous in their conciliatory approach.[70]

To summarise, therefore, the intermediary bodies under Mussolini's corporate state never were the regulatory linchpins implied in Fascist propaganda or prescribed in corporatist theory. The only significant exception to this was the syndical associations which regulated wages and other labour conditions. This regulatory function, as we shall see in the section on labour, was a crucial element in the achievement of the state's economic goals. The corporations, for their part, never effectively performed any regulatory functions, except the two by default – licencing new plants and price controls: rather they were grandiose ministerial advisory bodies. This is not to argue that licenced intermediaries played no significant function under Italian corporatism – they did – and this is a point we will develop more fully later on. Next, however, there needs to be a consideration of the nature of the political system that developed and sustained Italian corporatism.

The nature of the political system

Corporatism in Italy was an instrument of, and only sustainable by, a political dictatorship. The 1928 Royal Decree on Approval of the Electoral Law had ended any vestiges of free elections with the substitution of the electoral system by one of accepting or rejecting a single national list of candidates chosen by the Fascist Grand Council, aided by the syndicates and other organisations under party supervision.[71] Thus from 1928 onwards the dictatorship nominated its own choice of deputies and put them to a plebiscite of a limited suffrage. The Chamber of Deputies was guaranteed to be free of any opposition. In reality, the Fascist leadership had guaranteed their election to government with the passing of the Acerbo bill in 1923 which stipulated that two-thirds of all seats should go to the list with the highest number of votes.[72] Even with the odds weighted in their favour, the Fascists had to embark on a wide range of illegal and violent tactics during the election in April 1926.[73] So, from the beginning of the corporatist system in 1926, representative government was severely circumscribed, and by 1928 it had been effectively eradicated.

Moreover, governmental responsibility to any representative body, even one that was handpicked, was ended by the decree on the Powers of the Head of Government of December 1925 which had been passed in the wake of the Matteotti crisis and the collapse of the opposition.[74] Indeed, the decree did much to bolster Mussolini's personal position by making the President of the Council of Ministers *Capo del Governo*; the Statuto of 1848 had not envisaged the existence of a Head of Government as distinct from the rest of the Council of Ministers with a legal, rather than conventional, primacy. The law ended responsible parliamentary government by rendering the Head of Government responsible to the King, while the ministers the Head of Government proposed to the King were responsible to himself and the monarch.[75] The Head of Government had virtually total control over the Council of Ministers, and the ministers can best be regarded as his aids.[76]

In constitutional terms, therefore, only the monarch could act as a check on Mussolini and his government's ambition. This was in some respects an important check because, although Victor Emmanuel had been compromised from the outset of Fascist rule, he provided an important source of legitimacy to the regime. Thus the constitutional diarchy had some practical significance despite Mussolini's attempts to undermine the monarch's position. By the late 1930s Mussolini's frustrations with the cautious King were beginning to show when he reportedly made it clear to his foreign minister and son-in-law, Count Galleazzo Ciano, that he intended to 'liquidate'[77] that 'acid and untrustworthy little man'[78] at the first possible opportunity. Nevertheless, despite the conflict between the two men, the monarch does not appear to have been a serious impediment to the regime's leaders in their corporatist ambitions. But the notion of an independent, ultimately authoritative state committed to corporatist goals proposed by the ideologues was never the case in Fascist Italy.

While it is true that the Fascists came to power by means of force, it was not the only basis, and indeed, at the time was not a sufficient basis, upon which to take over the government. As Giuseppe Rossoni states: 'Although the March on Rome was the most visible part [...], the decisions that won Mussolini the king's invitation to form the government were made in Mussolini's headquarters in Milan where the future Duce negotiated with the country's business and political notables. Coercion and compromise were thus from the beginning inseparable traits of Fascist government in Italy.'[79] The Fascist government, itself a heterogeneous grouping, was also dependent upon outside powerful interests, who managed to operate within and around it with the intention of deflecting Fascist efforts from their stated goals.[80] The regime may have removed the pressures from the electorate, political parties (including the mass of the Fascist party) and numerous groups, notably trade unions, but it had still to mediate between and compromise with powerful interests including the army, the Church, big business and landowners, officials of the party and the civil administration.[81] Indeed, as Lyttleton points out, it is generally accepted that from 1926 onwards Mussolini consolidated his dictatorship by strengthening the old administrative apparatus, rather than destroying it, because it had been in pre-fascist days strongly authoritarian and hence was amenable to such developments.[82] Fascism, therefore, never developed its own cadres, a new elite to run the corporate state.[83] In the case of all the new corporatist and other regulatory agencies they drew their staff groups from outside the Party, notably from business.[84]

The concern of corporatist ideologues about the ultimate feasibility of their proposals centred around the development of a consensus within society – the 'corporatisation of society'. The theorists never gave much consideration to the corporatisation of the state, only its ultimate autonomy from societal interests. In Italy, the state was never corporatised. Even if one accepts that the regime's leaders were fully committed to corporatist objectives[85] – and this is difficult to accept without qualification given their cynical abuse of power – Mussolini and his political allies were forced to trade with traditional elite groupings esconsed within the state machinery. The state was not, therefore, the community's guardian but an amalgam of cliques of private interests and Fascist politicians who themselves did not often seem blessed with a community spirit. Usually, the Fascists appeared in the driving seat, taking the strategic initiatives, but concessions had to be given (e.g. over revaluation of the lira)[86] and control over the pursuit of these initiatives often had to be partially relinquished. Such constraints clearly frustrated Mussolini,[87] but the unsteady foundation of his authority never enabled him to free himself of them. Likewise, the other elite groups were constantly suspicious and wary of the Duce's intentions. There was, therefore, a good deal of behind-the-scenes jockeying and the inevitable compromises. This is not evidence that the corporate state was not a dominant state, though it was clearly an amalgam of dominant groups. Such a view is reflected in the literature of Fascist Italy – even of liberal writers – which acknowledges the existence of the dominant elites and subordinate groupings. Further evidence of this division was the extreme centralisation of decision-making. So the national corporative bodies – the National Council of Corporations and its executive the Central Corporative Committee – and from 1939 onwards the Chamber of Fasces and Corporations – were never allowed to take any decisions, despite the strict controls of their memberships, agendas and procedures.[88] It was decision-making by a handful of insiders, the corporative bodies being there to add some *ex post facto* approval to the irreversible. One grouping without any foothold in the decision-making process was labour. It remained completely subordinated, stripped of any political or industrial bases.

Labour under Italian corporatism

The establishment of state licenced labour organisations, the syndicates, in the wake of the destruction of the free trade unions left the defence of workers' rights not with themselves, but in effect with the state. The Charter of Labour promulgated the year after the syndical law suggested workers' rights were in safe hands, arguing that the Labour Court guaranteed that wages correspond 'to the normal demands of life, to the possibilities of production, and the output of labour'.[89] In fact the Charter, which was not a legal document, being promulgated by the Grand Council of Fascism appeared on the eve of severe wage reductions in the wake of the revaluation crisis. It was not a guarantee of labour rights but a cynical piece of propaganda. The syndical machinery was, therefore, used as an effective instrument to keep wage levels in check.[90] The first round of cuts announced as part of the drive to revalue the lira were of the order of 10–20%, despite there having been a fall in real wages over the period 1922–6 resulting from the dissolution of free trade unions. Further rounds of cuts occurred in December 1930 (8–20%) and May 1936 (7%).[91] The reduction in wages emanating from the lire revaluation were supposed to be compensated for by reductions in monetary prices but this was not the case, though the world depression 1929–33 did see prices fall more than wages and hence real wages regained some ground. (However, this was not the full picture because, in absence of effective labour organisations, a number of 'unofficial' reductions were implemented by employers.)[92] From the mid 1930s onwards there was a series of increases in money wages, but they were for most of the time outstripped by rises in the cost of living, so that by 1939 real monthly wages (a better indicator than hourly rates because of reduced hours) were at the same level they had been in 1928 for industrial workers. Overall the index of real wages showed them to be a fifth lower than when Fascism came to power.[93]

In contrast over the period 1920–39 the annual average growth rate was 1.82%,[94] while during the period 1929–39 – one of at best wage standstill – national income had grown 16%.[95] Nor was it the case that these figures reflected an attempt to transfer resources from consumption to (enforced) saving to provide investment funds for national economic development. The basic statistics show that gross investment as a percentage of G.N.P. never rose under the regime and actually fell in 1933.[96] Further, there does not appear to have been any economic rationale to the pattern of industries that benefited under Fascism; rather it appears largely to have been shorter-term political considerations that were the determining factor. There is virtually no evidence, contrary to what James Gregor has proposed, that Fascism was a modernising developmental dictatorship.[97] Instead, the enforced saving appears to have involved the transfer of resources to the public administration,[98] to certain employers, and, lately into military expenditure.[99] Italian Nationalism under Fascism was primarily directed towards cultural and political, not economic, ends.[100] So the workers paid for the apparatus and mythology of the regime that oppressed them.

It would be inaccurate to lay the blame for wage-cuts solely on the government; the syndical system created major opportunities for employers to extract reductions. But this qualification itself needs to be balanced by the evidence that the government imposed large cuts on its own employees, the state sector in many respects leading the way for the private sector,[101] despite the publicly acknowledged low level of public sector pay.[102] In addition, the recession that prevailed during a good part of the regime's life would – syndical system or not – have created a downward pressure on wages. This still left the corporate state with the opportunity to redeem itself in terms of its own oft-propounded criteria,[103] through the provision of welfare and security of employment. Indeed, still to many people today, Fascist Italy was regarded as a 'benevolent dictatorship', providing social welfare and public works programmes. Without doubt the regime did extend welfare provision. The most notable aspect was the introduction of family subsidies in October 1934 to compensate for short-time working and fewer wives in employment. Also the provision was designed to secure a high birth-rate, population increase being part of the regime's goals 'to justify territorial expansion and to provide the bayonet-wielding hordes appropriate to his [Mussolini's] 1914–18 vision of warfare'.[104] The family subsidies scheme was extended from 1934 onwards; for one thing, the subsidies were consolidated into wages when reduced hours were ended. They were further extended to the first child (1935), granted to white collar workers and extended to cover wives (1939), and increased in amount over the regime's final years. But the allowances, while an advance, were never very generous and scarcely met the needs they were supposed to.[105]

Family allowances apart, social security was subject to piecemeal developments. Sickness insurance was included in most Labour contracts after 1928, but only incorporated into legislation in 1943. It provided insurance only (50% of worker's salary) to the worker and did not cover medical expenses (until 1930), or medical assistance to family members (until 1940). One other innovation was the introduction of insurance against tuberculosis on a compulsory basis in 1928.[106] However, no improvement was made in the nation's modest unemployment insurance,[107] while only in 1939 was old age insurance moderately improved.[108] The most successful of Fascist schemes was in the provision of leisure activities to workers through the *Opera Nazionale Dopolavoro* which by 1939 had 4 million members, who were entitled to reduced rates for recreation and popular entertainment.[109] It hardly was, however, a substitute for higher wages and adequate welfare benefits. The regime can also take some credit for developing public health and hygiene programmes and improving education provision, although claims for such schemes should not be over-emphasised.[110]

Thus, while welfare provision did advance under Fascism from the inauspicious base of the Liberal regime, the practical and financial benefits were modest. Mussolini's claim that 'in the field of social legislation Italy leads the vanguard of all the nations', made in 1928,[111] was never true.[112] Furthermore, while employers paid more than double what employees contributed to insurance funds they in all probability were able to recompense themselves in part through lower wages, and workers themselves were paying out on average 9% (by 1939) of their already low wages to the funds. Therefore, the schemes cannot completely be regarded as a net gain. It is also worth mentioning that not all the schemes were linked to the corporatist structures through the syndicates,[113] employers wishing such credit there was to be gained falling to themselves.[114]

Of course, one of the major costs labour had to bear during the periods of recession was unemployment and short-time working. The government did take certain action to alleviate the problem. Cheapest and most effective among the methods utilised was doctoring the figures by excluding certain categories from the statistics,[115] which had the added bonus that they were not entitled to unemployment benefit.[116] Tannenbaum suggests, therefore, that approximately 75% be added to official figures to get a more accurate picture.[117] Of more practical effect was the programmes of public works, of which land reclamation was the most notable. The land reclamation schemes, which were not novel in Italy, were far from an unqualified success. Carried out under the *consorzi di bonifica* on a joint public/private basis there was evidence of serious inefficiency – launched in 1928, by 1938 less than 20% of the designated land had been reclaimed – and private profiteering.[118] Moreover, around one-third of the finance went into the Pontine Marshes near Rome, although there were more fruitful locations elsewhere, because being close to Rome they offered easier access to foreign journalists. Although some 2000 million lira a year was put into public works programmes – as a proportion of national income no greater effort than occurred in Britain, France or the USA – only some 15% to 20% of all unemployed were absorbed by such projects.[119] By 1935 military expenditures were reducing the funds available for public works.

In industry the main prong of attack was the encouragement of work sharing, but government initiatives were introduced rather late in the day, and only some 130 000 men benefited with part-time work, at reduced wage rates of course.[120] A more direct approach was adopted in agriculture, where minimum quotas of workers were prescribed to firms through collective constraints, thereby guaranteeing work-sharing.[121] It should also be noted that unemployment was disguised by controls placed on the movement of labour from 1934 onwards through the *libretto de lavoro*. This 'workers' passport', which a worker needed to gain a job through an employment exchange,[122] was an effective instrument to discipline labour. In particular, it was used to clear urban areas of unemployed and send them back to rural ones, following Mussolini's idea of ruralisation and to dissipate urban unrest.[123]

Capital under Italian corporatism

Despite the rather limited efforts to improve the conditions of labour, which were squeezed dry of their propaganda value, Italian corporatism clearly had as a principle objective controlling and disciplining labour. The maintenance of the labour order was one of the more successfully achieved objectives of the regime. Some analysts have, therefore, presented Fascism as simply a tool of capitalist domination, an alliance of big business.[124] Without doubt the disciplining of labour was of universal benefit to employers. But it would be inadvisable to see the relationship between capital and the Fascist regime in too instrumental terms. The regime drew its support from a range of established interests, previously mentioned, none of which could be regarded as anti-capitalist. Even the PNF itself had from 1923 onwards, with its merger with the Nationalists, had its radicalism diluted. The old guard that had initially given Fascism a radical, revolutionary side were, in typical Italian fashion, squeezed out by state servants and parasitic functionaries.[125] So, the Party became an organisation not for the pursuit of ideological ambitions, but one of cliques and individuals seeking self advancement. Radicalism remained necessary to Mussolini's and the regime's legitimacy, presenting a picture of a movement of change rather than a personal dictatorship based on a network of *clientelismo*; however, creating such an image did not always necessitate a great deal of substance.

In this hospitable climate private capital was safe. But life under Fascism was not relaxed for capital, never being a period of total security. The syndical structures, although the means for disciplining labour, always posed a threat that they might be extended to similarly regiment employers. Captial therefore had to act continuously to sustain the autonomy it held within the corporate state. From the battle of the lira onwards Mussolini had made it clear that their wishes would not stand in the way of his grandiose schemes and the same was true of his military expansionism in the late 1930s and early 1940s.[126] Part of the autonomy capital enjoyed appears in part to have been the consequence of the state's indifference. The syndical structures and the labour courts allowed employers to reduce wages unofficially,[127] to breach contracts on hours[128] and welfare provision[129] and illegally to employ children.[130] The high declarations of the equal positions of capital and labour and the protection of labour's rights under Fascism set out in the Pacts of the Chigi Palace (1923) and the Vidoni Palace,[131] and the Labour Charter had a very hollow ring in practice.

The autonomy enjoyed by capital in respect of production, however, was not a matter of indifference. Mussolini in the 1930s, when his military ambitions were growing, clearly became more impatient with the degree of state control over production and the continued independence of capital.[132] In particular, as Knox states 'the dictator found the industrialists' preference for financial stability and modest profits over aggrandizement increasingly irritating'.[133] However, the 1930s do appear to have been a period when the industrialists' position was weakened and their autonomy reduced. The recession in the early 1930s hit private capital severely because the large deposit banks, which held sizeable blocs of industrial shares, were in financial difficulties, thereby creating a severe shortage of investment funds. By 1931 the government was facing not simply a rash of bankruptcies but collapse of the financial system. The response forthcoming was to establish the *Istituto Mobiliare Italiano* (IMI) which was authorised to collect private and public funds to take up securities the banks were unable to, and hence rescue industry. However, IMI's endowment proved inadequate and so it was superseded by a new agency, the *Istituto per la Ricostruzione Industriale* (IRI),[134] in January 1933. The remit of IRI was to provide long-term finance to private firms and to relieve the banks of their commitment by taking holdings. In effect IRI became the means whereby the state took over the banks' role of financing industry. With the end of the recession IRI's role changed but it did not turn out to be the temporary body expected and was declared permanent in June 1937. More significantly its asset sales which had been a feature of the period 1935–6 were cut back, and investment became directed to specifically chosen sectors, most notably shipping, steel and engineering.[135]

It should be emphasised that IRI's holdings were in certain sectors substantial. In terms of output it held 90% in shipping, 80% in shipbuilding, 75% in metal tubes, 45% in steel, 67% in iron ore production and had major holdings in cars, telephones, aircraft production and armaments.[136] Without doubt IRI's role from 1937 onwards was closely linked to the foreign policy ambitions of the regime with its autarkistic and militaristic aims; indeed, the preamble to the legislation making it a permanent body stated this and it is significant that holdings in non-military industries like textiles and electricals were largely sold off. There is the further argument, bolstered by the fact that around 80% of credit available was directly or indirectly controlled by the state,[137] that IRI was part of a more general strategy to control the economy and guide its development. There is some validity in this line of argument; after all the Italian state had always sought to perform a guiding role in the economy. But general economic well-being, like so much else, emphatically played second-fiddle to the Fascists' foreign-policy ambitions in the second half of the 1930s. Finally, it cannot be ignored that to some extent, while the state sought to gain control over industry through financial means, the state finance did relieve private capital of certain unprofitable and high risk sectors.[138]

Despite the financial purse-strings the state pulled over the private sector and the various agencies of intervention which sprang up, the evidence does not suggest that such dependence made the private sector beholden to the state. They continued to enjoy a fair degree of autonomy. What did happen was that particular sectors and firms which were regarded as important to the regime benefited from finance, government contracts and guarantees – in some cases simply gifts – but others did not so benefit and had to survive in a none too auspicious economic environment. What did not emerge was any extensive control by the state over the internal decision making of the firms. In some cases, industrialists were able to turn the machinery of public regulation to private advantage. A good example of this was the system of licencing industrial investment introduced in 1933 which was designed to prevent wasteful duplication, but which ended up being a means whereby powerful industrialists regulated competition, established *de facto* monopolies and curtailed production to raise prices.[139] Likewise, the *consorzi obligatori* introduced by the government in 1932 to rationalise production were rendered a dead letter by the industrialists who ensured there was no interference with their own private cartels.[140]

What in effect happened with attempts at regulation, which from the evidence appeared genuine, was that the government bureaucracy did not have the expertise or information to carry out the regulations effectively and so it was handed over to politico-industrialists who were able to supplant public with private goals, if to varying degrees. Even in those firms where the state took substantial holdings, the management remained largely intact. In large part the delegation of regulation to those who were the target of the regulation was both out of necessity because of the incapacity of the usual state bureaucracy. It also reflected in part, though, Mussolini and his colleagues' disposition to apolitical functionaries – 'the experts'.

So private capital had an ambiguous relationship with the Fascist regime. It benefited from a disciplined labour force but had little influence over the direction the government pulled the economy in. Industry was in a position of reacting to, but not setting the framework. In reacting the industrialists were able to bring to bear considerable influence. However, the costs and benefits were not equally shared. From 1927 onwards export industries suffered from the moves towards economic isolation, while the recession allowed larger firms to consolidate their position at the expense of the smaller. The ability to pursue private ends under public guise through *autodisciplina* fell to those firms with political influence inside the syndical associations. Sometimes the government itself showed clear favouritism to the largest entities as for example, when it assigned favourable import-quotas to a select group of thirty of the largest firms, leaving the rest severely short of necessary imported raw materials.[141] The government, moreover, was able in the liquidity crisis of the 1930s to channel funds to the chosen sectors, but it was never capable of effectively regulating private firms. Thus price controls were applied with some stringency to prevent exploitation in an insulated economy, but because the employers held the sole source of statistical information existing distortions were never checked.[142] In terms of profits the regime provided a period of modest return, though the larger entities did fare much better than their smaller counterparts,[143] many of whom fell by the wayside. No doubt the industrialists were happy with these unexciting, but secure, industrial circumstances. Set against this, however, was the less tranquil political environment and the Duce's ever-growing imperial ambitions. During the final years of the regime a rift clearly emerged between the Duce and the industrialists who were none too enamoured with his foreign adventurism, which *inter alia* they were having to make a financial contribution towards through much resented taxes and capital levies.[144]

Much of what has been said about industry could similarly be applied to agricultural landowners, though their power was largely locally based *via* the Party. Again they all benefited from labour legislation – possibly more so – and it was the larger landowners who gained the most from the regime's policies. There does, however, appear to have been much less conflict between the interests of the landowners and the regime's goals.[145]

It may appear that corporatist licencing was irrelevant to state regulation of capital, unlike labour, under Italian corporatism. Certainly in a positive sense, this was mainly the case but, as will be argued in the chapter assessing authoritarian-licensed corporatism, it was significant in negative terms. However, before drawing any conclusions on the general nature of corporatism in Italy 1922–39, which will be done in Chapter 8, we shall examine another example of authoritarian-licenced corporatism, Portugal 1933–74.

7

Corporatism and the Portuguese
Estado Novo 1933–74

Antonio de Oliveira Salazar, the professor of political economy who ruled his country for over four decades came to power in circumstances different to those that swept Mussolini into government. Salazar did not lead a mass movement nor require political violence to secure his position. Instead, he was invited by the military leaders, who had seized power in an essentially nationalist coup in 1926 against the widely discredited republican regime,[1] to take on the job of finance minister in 1928 on a permanent basis (he having held it briefly in 1926). Thus Salazar's appointment was initially a straightforward example of a military government appointing civilian experts to conduct specialised areas of government, which in this particular case involved remedying Portugal's precarious financial position. Yet within four short years Salazar had so enhanced his prestige and developed his political power that he was nominated prime minister. The army had no desire to govern, and no plan for government anyway, so they handed power back to civilians whom they regarded trustworthy enough to protect their honour and keep this position secure. Therefore, while the military had brought Salazar to power, the regime that he moulded – the *Estado Novo* – after the 'return to barracks' was very largely civilian. Not surprising though, 'The New State civilian elite, dominated by the person of Salazar, demonstrated that in governing, and in surviving threats pragmatism, opportunism, and the art of ruling took precedence over doctrine and ideology.'[2] Nevertheless, the year 1933 – just one after Salazar[3] was appointed prime minister – proved to be the *annus mirabilis* of Portuguese corporatism with the establishment of a corporatist constitution, the passing of a Labour Statute and a plethora of decrees establishing the corporatist structures.

The state, the economy and the market

The Political Constitution of the Portuguese Republic, ratified by a suspect and limited plebiscite in March 1933,[4] which stated that 'the Portuguese

State is a unitary and corporative republic',[5] gave the state on paper at least wide socio-economic responsibilities. Most notably, it was the duty of the state 'to coordinate, stimulate and direct all social activities in order to promote a proper harmony of interests within the lawful substitution of private interests to the general good'[6] and to strive to assist the 'least favoured classes'.[7] There were also references to fair remuneration, balancing profits with social benefit, to intervene in private enterprises for a larger social benefit and so on.[8] In September of the same year the Labour Statute was promulgated by decree-law. The Statute which was a Portuguese hybrid of the Italian Charter of Labour and the papal encyclical *Quadragesimo Anno*, spelt out in far more detail the state's obligations including guaranteeing the right to work,[9] minimum wages and conditions for employees,[10] regulation of prices, production[11] and several references to achieving social ends.[12] The Statute also set down the basic structure and function of the corporatist system.[13]

There are several reasons why Salazar and his colleagues chose to take Portugal in a corporatist direction, and indeed were allowed to by the military, though the exact processes involved remain under-researched. Firstly, the state in Portugal had always performed a significant role in the economy. The Portuguese economy had never experienced a liberal capitalistic revolution or anything approaching it. Instead, it had remained dominated by a historic tradition of monopoly mercantalism and state 'enterprise' with the owners of business dependent on governmental access for contracts and privileges. Private capital developed not in a liberal competitive environment but in a close relationship with the state that was quasi-medieval in character.[14] Corporatism was not a departure, but more of a development. Second the period during which Salazar established his position was that of the 1929 crash and world depression; the indicators in many countries were pointing in an interventionist direction. Thirdly, the international climate with Mussolini's experiments, *Quadragesimo Anno* and the plethora of works by corporatist ideologues made the 1930s the decade of corporatism and gave such ideas great prominence. Fourthly, a significant element in the army were sympathetic to general corporatist notions, and many were Catholics and aware of the Church's social teachings. Finally, there was Salazar himself who was able to forcefully articulate his corporatist ideas and, importantly, sell them effectively to key political constituents. His powerful personality as much as anything helped to mould the new corporatist regime.[15]

Until the regime was toppled in 1974 the Portuguese corporatist state comprehensively regulated the economy, controlling wages and working conditions, prices, investment, production and foreign trade. Further, as we shall see, there was probably a greater degree of effectiveness in the regulation than had been the case in Italy, though the regime's economic aspirations were concomitantly lower. Even in the post-war era when virtually all West European countries found a formula for economic success, Portugal stayed with her highly *dirigiste* approach established in the 1930s.[16] In distinction to Mussolini's drive to insulate the Italian economy and reduce its dependency on 'plutocratic nations' which did so much to determine economic developments at home, Salazar never sought to turn international dependency into the overriding consideration. The Portuguese leader was far more pragmatic in approach. In 1931 he stated that, while Portugal could not be left standing in the spread of protectionism, 'we sincerely hope that conditions abroad may enable us to abstain from methods of narrow nationalism'.[17] Nonetheless, although Salazar did not pursue full-blown protectionism, the very weak international position of the economy and balance of payments deficits necessitated a degree of protectionism. The most accurate description of commercial policy in this period was one of 'relative economic autarky'.[18] In the 1950s, however, Portugal clearly eschewed international trends and continued to maintain 'relative economic autarky', though pragmaticism remained an element of the approach.[19]

In 1960, however, the nation's external economic policy began to change direction when Portugal became one of the original members of the European Free Trade Area (EFTA). Nevertheless, Portugal entered on preferential terms, EFTA recognised Portugal's relative economic underdevelopment and permitted her to keep protective tariffs for her new industries, with a gradual reduction taking place up to 1980.[20] Thus, Portugal was set on a slow, but inevitable course of trade liberalisation, despite the implication which this had for Portuguese corporatism. But two factors had forced Portugal's hand. Firstly, many of those countries which joined EFTA, including Britain, were the major consumers of Portugal's and her colonies' basic products. If she remained outside, the markets were at serious risk. Secondly, with agriculture in stagnation (which in the final years of the regime necessitated increasing food imports),[21] the growth of industry was the only route to development, but the sector required a market far larger than that provided by the integrated market of Portugal and her colonies.[22] This increasing pressure to develop the industrial sector was further emphasised when in 1965 a decree was passed which greatly liberalised the law concerning foreign investment.[23] Again it was necessity rather than desirability that was the key factor; foreign resources were needed for the home economy because large amounts of domestic resources were being channelled into the colonial wars.[24] So despite the threat it posed to domestic capital, Portugal ended up with one of the most liberal foreign investment laws in Europe.

The moves in the 1960s towards a more open economy reflected the increasing tensions that existed within the Portuguese economy, intensified by costly colonial wars. But even prior to this, domestic economic considerations, not international isolation for its own sake, had determined the nature and direction of the Portuguese corporatist economy. The primary concern of economic control, as far as one can generalise, was directed to determining the form and pace of economic development. Salazar's actions largely appeared designed to maintain the existing social order at the expense of economic development; rapid and relatively unfettered development appeared to the regime's leaders to pose such a threat. With this point in mind we turn to examine the structures of the corporatist system.

State-licenced intermediaries

The Portuguese corporatist system was largely mapped out in a massive flurry of activity in the period 1933–5, and, apart from some appendages in the 1950s and 1960s, never reached any further peaks of creativity, but fell into 'lethargic evolution'.[25] Given that the establishment of state control over the economy was paramount, not the generation of class harmony, the corporations were a belated and very half-hearted addition to the machinery. Instead, as imposition, not consensus, was the tenor of the system, the corporatist structure was fundamentally based upon the syndical associations. On the same day that the Labour Statute was enacted, several decree-laws were passed establishing most of the syndical structure of licenced organisations for a particular branch of production or occupation. The decrees, reflecting the peculiarities of preregime associability, established the following complex structure: a national system of *gremios* which were associations of employers' interests in industry and commerce, based according to branch of production;[26] a national system of *sindicatos*, or worker organisations which paralleled the *gremios*' structure, except they were more strictly classified according to job;[27] a number of *ordens* to give members of the liberal professions their own agencies;[28] a nationwide system of *casas do povo* which were organisations in all rural *frequeisa* (parishes) consisting of both rural workers and landowners in a two-tier system of membership;[29] and a structure of *casas dos pescadores*, initiated somewhat later in March 1937, which were similarly mixed organisations of workers and owners, based on fishing centres.[30]

The *casas* represented an attempt to have integrated intermediaries. It was, however, a false dawn. The *casas do povo* were not in the first few years anything more than local mutual aid societies. More importantly, the mixed formula did not prove successful and in 1937 owners and workers were given separate organisations, the landowners being organised in specially constituted *gremios da lavoura*. The new *gremios da lavoura* and the *casas do povo*, once the latter had their regulations changed in 1940, came to parallel the syndical bodies in industrial sectors.[31] Likewise, in due course, the fishing organisations were also divided despite genuine senses of solidarity in such communities.[32] The idea of the integrated intermediaries certainly did not get off to an auspicious start – even in the most fertile sectors.

Nevertheless, the urge to complete the corporatist edifice with the establishment of corporations proper was there, and in 1938 legislation for their creation was drafted. But the war and the general need to consolidate the already existing structures intervened, and it was not until the mid 1950s, when there was an attempt to inject some life into the flagging system, that legislation was actually enacted.[33] Even once the legal go-ahead had been given, though, urgency was not a prominent feature: the decree was passed in 1956 but it was not until a decade later that the final one of the eleven corporations was established. The corporations were not, however, based upon a function or trade, but instead drew their constituences from broad economic sectors like agriculture, industry, trade and fishing and canning.[34] Further, formally they were supposed to be composed equally of representatives from worker and employer organisations, but the workers were represented by professionals and business managers whom the Portuguese perversely categorised as workers.[35] Business and bureaucratic elites dominated the governing councils. In addition, the state had its own 'observers' on the governing councils. The so-called observers, however, were not only empowered to attend all meetings and consult all documents, but also to veto any proposals and, even, to halt all deliberations whenever they judged it to be necessary.[36] Thus, although the corporations were separate legal entities, having the juridical status of 'collective persons', they were kept under near-obsessively rigid state control.

In the absence of corporations to perform regulatory activities Salazar emulated Mussolini and created a series of bodies *en attendent*. The organisations were, however, not designed to paper over embarrassing gaps for propaganda considerations, but were effective regulatory agencies. These Organisations of Economic Co-ordination (OECs) were of three types: Regulatory Commissions to control imports of certain nationally important productions; National Juntas for developing and regulating exports; and Institutes designed to coordinate production. The OECs were designated 'pre-corporative' to indicate that in due course their functions would be assumed by the corporations,[37] but from an early stage the OECs became well-entrenched agencies of the regime, becoming the machinery through which the state extended its control over almost every area of the economy. By the mid 1950s the regime's leaders were not willing to put at risk the grasp they had over the economy.[38] Throughout the regime the OECs were, in consequence, the effective corporations in terms of performance of functions. Moreover, while it was severely circumscribed and biased, representation was granted to syndical units on the appropriate OEC and probably provided the most effective arena of participation for them.[39] The whole issue of membership of the intermediaries, and the consequences this had for representation, nonetheless, requires further investigation because it reveals much about Portuguese corporatism.

The intermediaries' membership

With the syndical structures forming the basic units of the corporatist system it was the membership and jurisdictional attributes of these bodies that was pertinent, because they were the effective intermediary organisations. Although the regime had placed considerable emphasis on spontaneous development, the syndical associations were largely created by government fiat. In the case of organisations of industrial workers, membership of the *sindicatos* was left on a voluntary basis. However, as only one *sindicato* was officially recognised per category and that once recognised that *sindicato* represented all workers in the designated constituency, membership was not of primary significance. In any case, in 1939 a law was passed that allowed the government to make mandatory contributions from all workers in the category; such powers were increasingly exercised, usually on 'a discretionary basis to reward compliant *sindicatos* and punish recalcitrant ones'.[40] Most importantly, the *sindicatos*' charters, elections and decisions were under constant supervision by the state.[41] The *sindicatos* were, therefore, first and foremost agencies for controlling the workforce; there did not appear to be any serious effort to offer them a means of participating. Not unexpectedly, the statistics reveal that by 1945 almost all categories of urban worker were organised into *sindicatos*, though some do not appear to have actually operated.[42]

Turning to agricultural workers and their organisations, the *casas do povo*, the case was somewhat different. Like the *sindicatos* (at least after 1938 when they became simply workers' bodies), they had the advantage of representational monopoly, but though there was supposed to be a *casa* in every parish, in practice coverage was limited.[43] Despite the marked increase in numbers between 1955 and 1965, in the mid-1960s only 625 out of nearly 3600 parishes could boast a *casa*.[44] Such a low level of coverage it should be noted was not through lack of potential members, because membership of these state sponsored bodies was compulsory.[45] Instead, it largely reflected that the *casas* system existed largely to stultify any pressure on the public authorities, and in many areas, with the absence of other forms of organisation, the need for a *casa* was not pressing. Just to rub salt into the rural workers' wounds, through the regime's life landowners remained compulsory members of the *casas*, because of their role in social assistance, and in the South the *latifundistas* (large landowners) played a prominant part in these supposed workers' organisations.[46] Indeed, the predominent position of *latifundistas* is well illustrated by the fact that several men who headed the *casas* were also leaders of the *gremios da lavoura*.[47]

Turning to the *gremios* themselves a further twist to the corporatist system is revealed. To facilitate an institutional structure for economic regulation that was corporatist in character, Decree Law No. 23049 allowed the state on its own initiative to command the creation of employer guilds in any industrial, commercial or agricultural sector. All those operating in the sector were required to join and abide by its decisions. Voluntary establishment of *gremios* was also permitted from 1934 onwards but they still had to be licenced by the state and abide by certain regulations and subordinate their interests to those of the state.[48] The *gremios* were originally conceived of as being monopolistic, with the sole power to speak for a particular sector, but the regime left a loophole in the original decree as a palliative to employers that provided for the continued existence of previously constituted 'class associations'. Such compensation was not afforded to workers' organisations; rather it forcibly closed down and seized the property of over 750 workers' organisations. In the event the concessionary approach to employers continued throughout the regime's existence. The number of obligatory *gremios* created was relatively small; by 1967 only 91 out of 559 employers' *gremios* had been obligatorily formed. This tendency to rely on voluntary formation, however, did not hit the state authorities regulatory ambitions as they simply turned to the para-ministerial OECs.[49] One consequence of the voluntarist approach (50% of businesses had to approve a *gremio* before it gained a representational monopoly) was that many sectors, including important ones like cork and metal working, remained for years 'non-corporatised' with many businessmen in these sectors utilising their old industrial associations to express their views. By the end of the regime in 1974 certainly not all sectors could claim a *gremio*. Likewise, the spread of *gremios da lavoura* on a largely voluntary basis never extended to anything approaching its full complement. So the syndical associations, the grass-roots of the corporatist system, presented a miscellany of bodies. Despite the point that the charters of all these syndicates clearly reflected corporatist notions of an intermediary providing the state with a means of regulating economic actors – their charters explicitly stating that interests had to be subordinated to the state – the coverage of the economy was very far from complete. Thus the corporations when they finally appeared could not be the great, integrative capstones of the corporatist system, even although organisations could be compelled to join.[50] That apart, as already mentioned, the formal equality between employers and employees masked the relative predominance of business interests on the governing councils. Such bias was a feature of Italian corporatism, but the limited development of a syndical structure was not.

Only in the case of urban industrial and service workers was coverage anything near comprehensive. The *sindicatos* tended to be small and localised, and there was no effective organisational structure of federations worth talking about. Organisational fragmentation of the urban workforce was the key feature.[51] This had led Hermino Martins to describe the corporatist system in essence as one of control over the industrial working class.[52] This was undoubtedly a prime function. But even where organisations did not exist corporatist licencing had an impact – it prevented any other organisation from existing and hence completely blocked potential channels of influence. It was very much part of a strategy of control by the dominant groups: unorganised workers were of benefit to business and land elites. The reasonably widespread development of urban workers' organisations probably reflected the need to have organisations of control where workers were fairly concentrated in numbers. Without doubt the policing role of the *sindicatos* is well-documented. Moreover, the greater threat the urban workforce posed necessitated greater palliative welfare provision which the *sindicatos* were involved in administering. The issue of control would not, however, appear to explain the incompleteness of the *gremios* system given the position of economic elites in the system. The *gremios* that existed were a means of control in the marginal and less-powerful sectors, they also acted as a placating and buffer institution for the industrialists who were excluded from the national arena. Where they did not exist or were otherwise redundant, corporatist licencing was still relevant because they left the field clear for the dominant industrial elites to use the channels they commanded without fear of challenge.[53] In short, licencing allowed channels of influence and arenas of decision-making to be kept within a tight, centralised bureaucratic structure.

The intermediaries' functions

The corporations under the 1956 decree had been given broad economic, social and political (i.e. representative) functions.[54] In actual operation though the regime sought to seriously debilitate their creations. For one thing they were all but starved of financial resources.[55] Additionally, they were never effectively integrated into the rest of the corporatist system.

Quite literally, they ended up as small offices up back streets, far from the centres of power; they did not even have the standing of Mussolinian grandeur. With a tight-knit, bureaucratic system initiated in the 1930s, now tried and tested as an effective instrument of state control, Salazar had no intention of weakening this command structure that just moderately significant corporations would have entailed. Even in an advisory capacity, the corporations' role was limited; occasionally they gave technical advice, but more usually they were not even consulted. The corporations became essentially research bodies, supplying information of interest only to the business community.[56]

The functions of regulating prices, production, wages, investment and trade were the remit of the ministerial agencies, the OECs. This plethora of juntas, institutes and commissions provided by all accounts a very effective machine for state regulation over production. Further the controls were extensive, regulating the creation of new and the expansion of old industries, and giving the government virtually all the necessary power to set wages, prices, production quotas, exports and imports.[57] Such representation as was granted to outside interests[58] interfered little with governmental control;[59] the bureaucracy created by Salazar in the 1930s reigned supreme.[60]

Extensive centralisation also resulted in a limited and subservient role for the lower corporative bodies, the syndicates. The *sindicatos* never had any real influence on events. Only in the final years of the regime, when Marcello Caetano succeeded Salazar as Prime Minister, did the *sindicatos* come to participate seriously in wage determination, though in a circumscribed manner.[61] The *sindicatos* also received a fillip from the development of the social security system in the 1960s as they had been granted powers over administering funds and benefits. Likewise, the *casas do povo*,[62] until these developments in the 1960s, performed virtually no functions except collecting membership fees. The *casas* were in fact revised under Caetano to become agencies for administering social assistance schemes, and it is suggested that there was also a consequent increase in their numbers so that by 1973 on paper 80% of parishes were covered.[63] Overall the social security improvements provided a much-needed lift to the flagging corporatist system.[64] Turning to the *gremios* the picture is clearly one of more substantial institutions though, ironically, they appeared to go into decline in the final years of the regime. The business organisations did enjoy a degree of discretion in implementing decisions taken higher up, although tight controls did not allow them to 'bend' the decisions. It would be wrong, however, to imply that the *gremios* ever breached the principle of central control – delegation was always limited. The main function of the *gremios*, in addition to being administrative arms of central government, was as a representative body for business. But for those entities for whom this was the only channel of influence, the *gremios* do not appear to have provided a particularly resonant voice or a direct line to centres of decision-making.[65]

If the example of Italian corporatism was to be taken as indicative it would be anticipated that the syndical associations of the corporatist system, at least where they were developed, would have played a direct role in relations between employers and employees. The National Labour Statute envisaged collective bargaining between the monopoly *sindicatos* and *gremios* to achieve 'social justice'. But if the parties failed in their attempts to get a just resolution, it was the exclusive function of the state to step in to enforce it.[66] To make such procedures operationally effective, strikes, lockouts and other disturbances to production were made illegal;[67] indeed strikers were classified as criminals.[68] In place of the outlawed methods for settling disputes a series of *Tribunais do Trabalho* (Labour Courts) was established to arbitrate over collective, and also individual, labour disputes.[69]

The proposals to bring capital and labour together in an *espirito de justiça* were not, however, seriously pursued. Instead from the outset the state stepped in. The first round of collective contracts was negotiated with active participation of ministerial officials acting as conciliators and arbitrators. Such events were indicative of what was to come. Under Salazar, the predominant pattern quickly became that the subordinate *sindicatos* and *gremios* did not in fact negotiate with each other over conditions and wages. Rather, the Subsecretariat (after 1950, Ministry of) Corporations, through the *Tribunais* and other of its agencies settled all aspects of labour conditions.[70] Indeed, the ministry often just ignored legal requests to renegotiate contracts. Thus influence over wage determination and conditions was dependent upon influence at ministerial level. Centralisation in this extreme form remained the norm until Salazar gave way to Caetano. The changes announced in June 1969 most significantly involved making it mandatory that labour contracts be formulated by direct negotiation betwen employer and employee associations, with a few exceptions, rather than by state administration. Other attempts at introducing greater decentralisation, including some involvement of the corporations, were also pursued, but the changes were not always successfully accomplished.[71] One serious obstacle to reform was Caetano's weak political base, and reform of industrial relations remained only partial.[72]

On top of this the participants, the *sindicatos* and the *gremios* remained evidently subordinated,[73] and the state was not averse to stepping into the breach whenever appropriate, as for example when in 1971 one-year contracts were automatically increased to two years by the government.[74]

Overall, even making allowances for belated developments in the 1960s and early 1970s the corporatist structures – both syndicates and corporations – did not provide a network of regulatory agencies; their regulatory functions were in terms of regulation conducted by the state small scale and marginal. Often the state took positive action to ensure such organisations could not operate effectively. The tight grip of the central state bureaucracy was not easily loosened. It is to the politics of this state structure that we now must turn.

The nature of the political system

Salazar was brought into government at the request of Portugal's military leaders, who had seized power in 1926, for his technical abilities, and, as was mentioned in the introductory section, from this base he moved on to consolidate his position, building up a strong personal dictatorship, and to shape Portugal's corporatist constitution.[75] The Constitution itself reversed the power arrangements for the Republic, giving supreme authority to the executive and limited functions to Parliament, although this reflected the *de facto* situation that had emerged after 1926. There were certain elements of a compromise with liberal democratic forms, but these were all on the surface and lacked any substance. At the top of the state structure was the President whose only important function, the rest being merely ceremonial, was to appoint and dismiss the Prime Minister. In constitutional terms the President was to be elected 'by the Nation' for a term of seven years.[76] But in practice there never was a free and fair election for President. In the first place, all elections were based on a legally restricted franchise which was further subject itself to interference to disenfranchise certain people and generally discourage registration. Until after the Second World War, no 'opposition' candidates presented themselves at either presidential or National Assembly elections. Instead, the presidential elections took on a plebiscitary nature with only one candidate (nominated by the governmental 'anti-party', the *União Nacional*) standing.[77] After the war, candidates from opposition groups did stand, but restrictions on electioneering resulted in candidates withdrawing before the poll in a last ditch protest. In 1958, however, General Delago, with some obvious popular support behind him, did not stand down, and, despite the bias of the electoral system, took 31% of the vote against the União candidate, Admiral Tomas.[78] Given the problems caused by

Delago's candidacy and its side-effects for the regime, 1959 saw the system of presidential elections changed to one based upon an electoral college of both houses of parliament, plus some delegates from districts and overseas provinces.[79]

To all intents and purposes Salazar's rule was a self-perpetuating dictatorship. The prime minister was constitutionally responsible to the President[80] but the head of state's powers of appointment and dismissal were in practice of little real significance. Nor did the two legislative assemblies place any marked constraint upon the executive. On major issues, including the legislation of the corporatist system, they were by-passed through the use of decrees. The National Assembly was empowered formally to advise on and consent to, and even occasionally modify, laws emanating from the executive.[81] In reality, these powers meant very little. The elections for the Assembly were of the same type as those for the president prior to 1959, with the result that Portugal was a one-party state (even if a few hardy opposition candidates stood against all the odds), Salazar himself handpicking the *União Nacional* candidates.[82]

The other assembly, the Corporative Chamber was likewise given a limited role in political decision-making. It was 'composed of representatives of local autonomous bodies and social interests, the latter being those of an administrative, moral, cultural and economic order'.[83] Until 1960 the Chamber was exclusively government appointed, although thereafter the one-third from corporatist bodies were selected by the corporations themselves – if still under government supervision. The function the Chamber was granted was to issue advisory opinions (*pareceres*) on pending legislation. Such advice, which was not without its impact on decisions, usually pertained solely to technical matters. But it was always the case that in the last resort the advice could be ignored. Nor was the Chamber in any real sense representative of interests – even selectively so – within society. Instead as Schmitter states the Chamber 'more closely resembled a sort of National Honours Society or functional-administrative College of Cardinals who had been anointed for their service to the State'[84] – a feature that the Assembly in part shared.[85]

In corporatist Portugal, therefore, power rested with the executive, representative of nobody and responsible to a political figurehead, with Salazar, to whom ministers owed their appointments and were responsible, dominant.[86] The Constitution recognised and to some degree protected this state of affairs. Salazar's power base was not, however, the paper upon which the Constitution was written. The near personal dictatorship he built up rested upon his control of the bureaucracy, which he reformed and regularised by strict fiscal accountability and purges. To all practical purposes the bureaucracy became the arena for making and overseeing policies. Indeed, so effective became this bureaucratic machine that in the 1960s it began to usurp the power of its creator. However, while Salazar was in complete control of this administrative state, any policy decision could be his personal prerogative. Obviously, Salazar could not manage or control everything and he formed around himself a governing team of like-minded ministers, secretaries and under-secretaries who in their relations to the Premier acted somewhat like White House aides.[87]

Interestingly, like Salazar many of the chief architects and early administrators of the corporatist system – men such as Caetano, Pereira, Costa Leite, Augusto da Costa and Castro Fernandes – were not professional politicans but were academics-cum-corporatist ideologues.[88] Despite the fact that the regime's leadership was steeped in corporatist doctrine, there was never any attempt to apply principles of self-regulation for producers. Salazar's foremost reason for establishing such a centralised state was clearly to consolidate his own political base by removing autonomous sources of resistance. The crisis of the Spanish Civil War and the Second World War reinforced, but certainly did not initiate, these tendencies. Justification of the *étatiste* system from the dictator was in terms of the state, in the absence of a strong corporatist consciousness, having to assume control 'as the representative and custodian of the people's interests'.[89] No doubt this was true, but the paternalistic state also was a screen for Salazar's near obsessive concern never to lose control.

Salazar and his colleagues never faced until into the 1960s any real challenge to their consolidated position, though power at the centre did undergo change. As already mentioned, the bureaucratic machine that Salazar established as the basis of his dictatorship latterly began to usurp him (though partially this was the result of his own withdrawal from *affaires d'état*). Further, Caetano, when he became Prime Minister found the bureaucracy so well entrenched that he failed to make a dramatic mark on events. Thus it appears that while power remained consolidated within the top echelons of the central bureaucracy, the power within that arena became more widely diffused.

Evidently other interests were not without some influence. One obvious grouping was the military and secret police who did so much to maintain the regime in power after 1945. The military did not, however, interfere in the operation of the corporatist system itself; the military's objectives were safeguarding its honour and ensuring order and stability. Until the outbreak of colonial wars in the 1960s, it was not the case that the regime bought military support through healthy expenditure on armaments and pay. Instead, many officers were coopted into the domestic and colonial administrations as a reward for loyalty. Thus much of the military was compromised and became a part, rather than an overseer, of the regime.[90]

The Church also represented a major source of potential influence within society. Like the Army it was closely bounded to the state structure, but while it shared in numerous, if not exorbitant, benefits, its wide espousal of the corporatist ethic did much to reinforce the regime. Nonetheless, the regime was never 'clerico-fascist' in character. Latterly, the Church began to dissociate itself from the regime and stand on the side of change, but its influence in this respect was never extensive in face of the established regime.[91]

The leading source of power within the regime, in spite of certain outside groups wielding a degree of influence, lay in the hands of the personnel of the state administration. With the exception of certain economic elites, the personnel of the bureaucracy was largely an autonomous grouping drafted in under the regime: 'the Estado Novo was founded and staffed in large measure by a new generation composed mainly of civil servants, technicians and professors of fairly provincial origins who, with the important exception of the financial sector, do not appear to *initially* have been controlled by or held accountable to either a liberal, internationally linked, modern industrial-commercial bourgeoisie or a conservative, provincially bounded, feudal-landed aristocracy [...]'.[92] This is not to deny that in the course of time this new elite began to penetrate the major economic interests, such that the elites of the polity became extensively fused with those of the economy. The bureaucracy itself became riddled with elaborate patronage patterns and systems of access whereby private interests could be pursued and public officials share in private spoils. This was all the more significant because the civil service was the main area of recruitment to the governing team and because each ministry enjoyed some degree of autonomy.[93] The channels of patronage and influence were, however, strictly restricted, and outsider groups such as workers, peasants, small businesses and all but a few landowners had scant other effective routes of influence. Thus the *Estado Novo*, unlike the Italian corporate state, created its own ruling cadres composed largely of self-made men who through a mixture of technical/ professional education and ideological commitment worked their way up to considerable power and rewards. Large private capital, guardian of the nation's economic hardware in an economy that was always in a precarious state, had its strategic position recognised and safeguarded, though it was absorbed into the state system, merging very directly its interests with those of state personnel. The new elite of the Portuguese state, however, were not particularly radical or reformist in inclination. Here Salazar's influence and his concern to carefully check the rate and direction of development appears to have been the crucial factor, though a process of osmosis resulting from the rigid character of the structures is also widely mentioned by authors. In this respect the takeover of the state did not mark a break with the traditional patrimonialist mercantilist-bureaucratic state.

Stability and order became the *raison d'être* of the regime; corporatist notions of justice remained confined to ideological debates and never really surfaced in day-to-day life. There was never even any serious attempt to 'corporatise' society, to develop a new moral order. In the final years of the regime, the rigid bureaucracy appeared to be more and more devoid of any clear direction, unable to respond to the developmental process it was supposed to control. It is not surprising that Caetano's rule swayed without apparent direction between reformism and the *status quo*.[94] In the end, the corporatist regime did not fall to 'outside' opposition, which was limited and weak,[95] but collapsed from within because of the state's inability to respond to changing circumstances with regard to both Portuguese society[96] and a bureaucratic pillar of the regime, the army.[97]

Labour under Portuguese corporatism

In the previous sections we have already seen that labour was devoid of any independent organisational base and a politically impotent outsider. To all intents and purposes the workforce was dependent upon the state and its agencies for the level of their wages and standards of working conditions and opportunities. In constitutional terms at least the workers were reasonably well-protected. The Constitution made it the duty of the state to ensure the 'highest wage consistent with fair remuneration for other factors of production',[98] while the Labour Statute made references to the right to 'humanely sufficient' and subsistence wages.[99] The state through the highly effective OECs were certainly not without the means to fulfil the promise.

The first contracts negotiated under the *Estado Novo*, regularising employment conditions for the first time in many industries, did see some modest increases in remuneration levels for workers, although these limited gains had been preceeded by a period of wage freezes and austerity.[100] Such increases as there were appear to have been more of a palliative than an attempt to implement the minimum wage legislation, and at best over the early years of the regime real wages only just managed to maintain their level.[101] But the events of 1934–6 were not indicative of the future and, despite the continual promulgation of new laws governing minimum wages by the National Institute of Labour and Social Security, legal theory began to diverge markedly from actual practice.[102] The corporatist arrangements for 'collective negotiations' instead of becoming a means to social justice, became simply a machine for holding down general wage levels. Given the grip Salazar had, such events could not have occurred without his positive support. With the crises of the Spanish Civil War and the Second World War there was a tightening-up of state control over wages, most notably through a decree in April 1934 which gave the government the legal right to regulate all wages and conditions of work.[103]

It was during the period of the war that the real nature of the system fully manifested itself. In July 1942 a group of *sindicato* representatives presented a petition to Salazar concerning the fall in real wages, although many firms were earning huge profits.[104] The prime minister, however, ignored the appeals to social justice, but blamed employers *and* employees for their selfishness having an adverse effect on productivity, while related strikes and protests were dealt with by harsh repression.[105] More significantly, wages continued to be allowed to fall behind prices, and in cases money wages were cut.[106]

After the crisis of the World War the state did not move to take up the objective of social justice. Thus, in the 1960s, after thirty years or so of corporatism, the average earned income was around £90 a year, with some particular wage rates being abysmally low, especially as certain prices of basic necessities were not correspondingly low.[107] These low wages in part reflected the low level of development of the Portuguese economy, but also was a consequence of the returns to property: in 1950 labour took only 39% of the national product, leaving 61% to interest, rent and profits; by 1965 labour's share rose to 47%, and in 1971 it reached 52%. So over the post-war period real industrial wages grew faster than real per capita income, though agricultural wages only kept pace with per capita growth.[108] This relative improvement in returns to labour, however, needs to be put into the context of continuing extremes of poverty – one writer described the condition of Portuguese workers and peasants as 'highly deprived'[109] – compared with high and secure profits and a very wealthy elite, including one of the wealthiest aristocracies in Europe. Part of labour's plight resulted from Salazar's intention to check development resulting in low productivity, but as figures on profits show (see below p. 124) the regime's pretentions to be guardians of justice were vacuous. In the late 1960s, even under pressure of labour militancy and labour shortages caused by massive emigration,[110] the wage concessions granted did not include acceptance of the idea of a national minimum wage proposed by labour leaders.[111] The legislation of the 1930s was left with a very hollow ring to it.

Nor were labour's sacrifices made to allow for increased funds for investment to develop the economy. Some writers have indeed argued that the regime deliberately fostered stagnation,[112] fearful of the social dislocation development would engender. With not untypical arrogance Salazar held to the view that betterment would be morally corrupting,[113] a view widespread amongst the Portuguese upper class. Moreover Salazar was pessimistic about Portugal's economic potential.[114] But more substantially the resultant social change would have broken the grip of the dominant politico-economic group that held the majority in a near feudal social structure.[115] In the end, the strategy proved unworkable: even a 'guided development' brought forth economic[116] and social[117] changes which the political structures of the state begun to lose their grip on in the 1960s.

The regime, therefore, can be seen as attempting to try to freeze the subservient position of labour, even against a historical background of constant change. Moreover this was conceived as a strategy that was sustainable with the minimum granting of concessions. This is reflected by the point that up to the early 1960s Portugal had virtually no social security system. Only those workers – essentially the skilled urban workers – covered by *caixas de previdência* attached to *sindicatos* enjoyed any benefits. The *casas* which were to provide for the rest of the country, of course, were few in number. In the 1960s a new generation of somewhat more enlightened elements began to find themselves in prominent positions in the regime and in consequence the Ministry of Corporations became a hive of activity to improve welfare provision. Behind these moves was a growing awareness of the endemic poverty in Portugal, combined with concern about the threat this potentially posed to the regime's existence and the lack of credence it gave Portugal with her increasingly important European allies.[118] In typical manner the promise of legislation, of new agencies, programmes and funds, was not translated into practice. So throughout the 1960s a smaller proportion of G.D.P. was spent on welfare than had been the case in the 1940s and 1950s.[119] The system, moreover, remained concentrated on the 'urban elite' by-passing the rest, while the new spending often simply increased the public payroll, and provided funds for corrupt officials and a financially constrained government to tap.[120] The general lethargy, indifference of the Salazar period remained ever resilient. Under Caetano, a concerted effort was made to try to implement the array of legislation with the intention of creating a genuine *Estado Social*,[121] but it was a case of too little, too late. Indeed, the growing worker militancy and its attendent economic disruption undermined the effort and created further paralysis,[122] while the colonial wars proved a serious drain on funds.[123]

The generally low level of wages in Portugal and the paltry provision of welfare which depressed labour costs, however, did not even provide the compensation of high levels of employment for the workforce. The generally retarded development of the economy was the major factor explaining this. Underemployment, rather than unemployment, was the form the problem took. An official survey of the economy carried out in 1964 stated that, although unemployment was only 2.4 to 2.8% of the active population, there was an 'appreciable margin of underemployment difficult to measure'.[124] The difficulties apart, others did put forward estimates of 40% or above of the working population.[125] Despite the severe situation the thrust of governmental policy was not channelled primarily at job creation. Instead, much was directed towards developing the nation's infrastructure at the expense of long-term jobs. As Pintado pointed out in 1964: 'Some grounds exist for the suspicion that employment has not been a major consideration governing decisions on investment in Portuguese industry in recent years.'[126]

The period 1960 to 1973 was, nonetheless, a period of high growth-rates, between 6.1% and 7.1% per annum. But such developments, which owed much to foreign influence of investment and trade, had little impact on employment opportunities *per se*, because labour productivity grew at the same rate.[127] Over the period 1960–73 the number of workers in manufacturing increased only by 8.1%.[128] Nonethless economic growth did help to reduce underemployment as the primary sector declined relative to the secondary and tertiary ones.

Economic growth, however, was not the sole cause of change. Probably a more prominent factor restructuring employment during this period was brought about by emigration. Net emigration over the period exceeded one million, which was greater than the natural increase in the Portuguese population. Such an outflow, which reduced the global size of the working population, manifestly acted as an important safety-valve on underemployment, and reduced the need to take remedial action, i.e. develop the economy more rapidly. It further had the benefit in the 1970s of supplying a very high level of income from abroad through remittances to migrants' families (in 1972/73 it was equivalent to 10% of national income). However, as part of the emigration consisted of skilled workers seeking to escape from the comparatively low wage-rates, it latterly caused problems of labour shortages.[129]

Over the era of corporatist Portugal the position of labour undoubtedly improved. But this has to be contrasted with what might or could have been. Often the benefits that were gained resulted from a fortuitous side-effect of governmental intentions elsewhere, e.g. to expand the economy to finance the colonial wars. Labour seemed to count for little in the authorities' eyes. An elite of urban workers did make certain gains latterly, but for the rest it was a story of very low wages, insecure employment and inadequate or non-existent welfare provision.

Capital under Portuguese corporatism

'Property, capital [...] have a social function in the field of economic cooperation and common interests, and the law may determine the conditions of their use on exploitation in accordance with the community aim in view [...]'.[130] Thus the *Estado Novo*'s Constitution explicitly recognised the social function private capital was to perform under corporatism. The Statute of Labour added more directly that: 'The State recognises the right to property' which was explained in Catholic terms as 'a rational imposition of human nature',[131] though property's social obligations were also elaborated.[132] Under the regime the principle of private property was indeed protected, full state ownership pertaining only in a number of defence industries and public utilities. It should be added that Government shareholding was a reasonably common practice, designed to bolster sectors that were weak.[133] The protection was not, all the same, universal. Despite Salazar's pledge 'to create the largest number of small proprietors',[134] between 1933 and 1950 many peasant proprietors were evicted from or pressurised to leave their land. Similarly, small and medium businesses were often ousted because they lacked access to government funds and assistance from which the larger concerns benefited, while in other cases legally enforced mergers were pushed through.[135] Referring to these biases, Pintado in the mid 1960s, pointed out: 'There remain two [other] fields in which almost everything has still to be done in Portugal. These are control of economic concentration and the provision of aid for medium- and small-sized businesses'.[136]

Throughout the regime's life it was the handful of dominant companies that gained not only at the expense of labour but also smaller entities. Portugal's private sector was dominated by 40 great families whose dynasties were often linked through marriage to the great southern arable estates.[137] As Harry Makler has so well exposed, these entities not only escaped the effective, rigid grip of control of the Salazarian bureaucracy, they went one better by being integrated into its command structure. The new political and administrative elite of the regime which, as we saw, emerged independently from other societal elites, became impregnated by these exceedingly wealthy sectors of Portuguese society; and not surprisingly the process was not all one way. Makler's studies reveal that the various state regulatory agencies, most significantly the Organisations of Economic Coordination, but also *gremios* and other public bodies, were substantially taken over by the industrial elite. In his survey Makler found that nearly half (46%) of the industrial elite held some corporative or public office simultaneously. The interlocking between the elite of wealth and the elite of the polity was well established by the 1960s, but was a process that had begun in the 1930s when the state first began to exercise direct control over the economy. The *gremio* system itself was recognised by most industrialists as being an unsatisfactory means of getting their demands met and even of articulating their interests. Only the top national industrialists saw it of being beneficial to their interests, not it appears for any positive reasons, but because, by dominating the *gremios*, the large concerns were able to block the only channel open to their smaller competitors. The *gremio* system was too cumbersome to be effective even for the top industrialists and so they turned to other channels. They circumvented the system by directly contacting high officials and government personnel, by recruiting top civil servants for executive posts with their *consortia* and by gaining public positions themselves. Smaller entities could also practice such tactics but, as a general rule, they had to set their sights lower down the state hierarchy; some remained complete outsiders.[138]

Thus regulator and regulated became inexorably interlinked through various networks. It would be wrong, however, to simplify the state of affairs. As far as one can tell the most significant process of interlocking would be reasonably complex. It would take the following form: the most educated (sons of businessmen and professionals) are recruited into state bureaucracy as technocrats and work way up to senior position in state; they then move into newer more dynamic industrial sectors where merit rather than familial connections are basis of recruitment; and thence use knowledge of state machine and laws, and connections with state officials and family business to further own business interests.[139] Of course it must be reiterated that numerous industrialists retained both their public and managerial positions simultaneously. Further it needs to be said that latterly the smaller, more traditional propertied elite began to be eased out by the larger, newer and more dynamic entities from positions of dominance. So, while there was during the regime a dominant position held by the industrial elite *per se*, the character of this elite underwent a process of change over the period. The regime became, or more accurately was moulded into, the protector of the newly emergent modern capitalist entities who were only just emerging in the 1930s. This is not to argue that the old families who previously dominated were ousted; many of them moved into these new sectors. But what clearly did happen was that with the opening up to foreign capital and trade in the 1960s, the old traditional quasi-feudal companies became increasingly less viable, and so the newer more dynamic entities superseded them. Some capitalists were no doubt able to swim with the tide, others began to sink slowly.[140]

The Portuguese *Estado Novo* was from its early days onwards protector of dominant bourgeois interests. While the regime performed this function it has to be acknowledged that over the period of its life the character of dominant capitalist entities was changing with resultant tensions, and it was not until the 1970s that the ascendency of the modern capitalist was clearly discernible.[141] The emergence of modern capitalist entities, in addition to its costs on other sectors of society, had a generally adverse affect on the Portuguese economy. The nature of their advance was not of long-term advantage to the Portuguese economy, because it resulted in not only economic growth but also a process of distorted development such that Portugal grew both richer and more underdeveloped (i.e. more dependent upon external factors and less able to provide economically for the majority of its population).[142]

While the Portuguese economy was being guided down the path of restrained and latterly distorted development, the accumulation of large capital was healthy. With such a high level of concentration and low wages this was hardly surprising. Pride of place went to the conglomerate *Companhia União Fabril* which was responsible for 20% of all Portuguese industry and 10% of national production.[143] By the beginning of the 1970s it was calculated that 168 companies, many of them interlinked or part of the same *grupos*, despite accounting for only 0.4% of the companies in Metropolitan Portugal, held 5.3% of total capital. In the 1960s, furthermore, many of these *grupos* developed foreign connections. Thus several important sectors had effectively a very few suppliers, and in some cases only one.[144] These favourable positions were protected and sustained by the state.[145] Many sectors it should be added, notably textiles reflected the opposite extreme – a high degree of fragmentation.[146] In landholding a picture of extremes was also found: 1% of operators with farms over 50 hectares had 5.1% of crop land under their control, while 78% of holdings accounted for only 15% of total crop land.[147] While exact information about profit levels is not widely available, a study in the early 1960s is very revealing and supports the conclusions of many observers. Working from official figures Ramos demonstrated that in industries where concentration was high, the average profit per worker's week was always well in excess of the average weekly wage. Often it was of the order of two to nine times higher.[148] Such returns were not the result of capital's super-high productivity; in fact it was particularly low.[149] Nor were they, once earned, clawed back through tax. In the period 1967–9, indirect taxes accounted for nearly half of government revenues, while tax on corporations was only 17.6% of revenue.[150] Additionally, a range of generous tax concessions were available to encourage investment[151] and tax assessments were weighted in favour of large enterprises.[152]

Overall, it is difficult to escape the conclusion that, whatever its other features, Portuguese corporatism was a decidedly benevolent guardian of big capital in a manner that was not the case under Mussolini's corporate state. It is to a comparison of these two corporatist systems, and a wider assessment of authoritarian-licenced corporatism that the next chapter is directed.

8

Authoritarian-licenced corporatism: an assessment

It is the objective of this chapter to make a comparison of corporatism in Italy and Portugal and to develop a model of authoritarian-licenced corporatism, drawing upon studies of other corporatist states to give supportive evidence. In making a comparison the emphasis will be on the areas of commonality, but it has to be recognised that there were differences. At a basic level the difference between them was that Italy was Fascist and Portugal was not, being instead a traditional-conservative authoritarian state.[1] However, it is possible to list a number of common elements, while recognising that corporatism can be imbedded in a number of regime types. Before setting out these common features it is worth outlining the attendant features corporatism in both countries shared as a basis for explaining the overall character of authoritarian-licenced corporatism.

These features are as follows:

1) A limited and insecure establishment of liberal democracy, with states that were significantly authoritarian in character.
2) A political system characterised by a dominant ruling elite or grouping and very limited mass participation.
3) At time of initiation of corporatism industry was not extensively established, and agriculture (often non-commercial) was predominant. (In 1926 agriculture accounted for c.40% of national income in Italy, the primary sector c.55% of employment in Portugal at time Salazar came to power.)
4) The industrial sectors displayed marked tendencies of structural dualism, with at one extreme marked fragmentation and at the other high concentration. Moreover, the large capitalists, despite their predominant place in the national economy, were 'immature' being dependent upon state support, internationally uncompetitive and were backward in terms of industrial organisation and labour relations.

5) Corporatism emerged at what can be regarded as a crucial phase in the development of the national economy with the emergence of the predominance of modern large-scale industrial capital.

Corporatism it may, therefore, be hypothesised was a means for bringing about the transition from a relatively backward agrarian economy[2] to an essentially modern industrial capitalist one. The operative word here is 'guide'. Such a process was not going to be extrapolated by the free play of domestic and international markets. In Italy there was concern to avoid dependence upon other stronger national economies. Nor was such a view simply just a reflection of Mussolini's eye for the main chance in propaganda or the extravagant ideas of nationalist ideologues. It reflected the outlook of major capitalist interests with their preference for protection. Portuguese corporatism on the other hand, was concerned to check the rate of development. The ostensive ideological reason behind this stratagem was to prevent the allegedly corrupting influence of affluence upon the masses. In practice controlled development allowed for a very effective discipline to be placed upon labour thereby allowing inefficient and internationally uncompetitive capital to earn not unhealthy profits. Of course, the disciplining of labour was a central facet of Italian corporatism also. The essentially unsophisticated capitalists of both countries were concerned that the process of changing from a rural-agricultural to an urban-industrial economy would produce a well-organised labour force with which they would be unable to cope.

It would be inaccurate, nonetheless, to see corporatism simply as a structure to subdue the workers. Industrial development wrought its own tensions and conflicts between sectors of capital and between industry and agriculture. Corporatist structures were employed to resolve these in a manner largely beneficial to large capital and land. The state assisted in a restructuring of capital that certainly would not have been a foregone conclusion under a more liberal regime. There is no doubt that the evidence indicates that smaller entities – both industrial and agricultural – suffered, sometimes to the point of extinction, under corporatism.

The key to state control under corporatism was the system of licenced associations. However, as we saw in the case of Portugal this on occasion meant that no associations for a particular section of the economy existed at all. This reflected the very essence of the licencing system – it controlled the organisation of economic actors. Such controls evidently operated in a differential manner, according varying degrees of autonomy to the constituents. The non-existence of any organisation as per the Portuguese example, demonstrated the importance of the licencing system in preventing independent organisation of producers, which in some cases was all that the state required. Beyond that particular case the licenced associations were afforded different degrees of independence on a basis that was largely dependent upon their influence over and importance to the regime's leaders. Furthermore, the state licenced associations did not enjoy any exclusivity in performing regulatory functions though they did perform such tasks in the areas of production, labour relations and welfare – much important regulation being conducted through state and parastate agencies. Significantly, the licencing system curtailed the organisational capacity of producers thus creating an environment where more effective regulation by these state agencies was possible than might otherwise have been the case. And one might add that the threat of extending the grip of licencing may itself have been a further instrument of control. Likewise the representational role of the licenced associations was restricted, but nevertheless it was part of their activities – if severely distorted in some cases.

Thus, while the licenced associations acted as intermediaries between state and producers, other significant channels existed that in several instances overshadowed the corporatist institutions proper. It would not be beneficial, however, to see Italy and Portugal as examples of incomplete or underdeveloped corporatist systems. There never was among the state authorities any serious intention either to delegate regulatory authority or to respect jurisdictional independence – two central tenets of corporatist ideology. Bureaucratic centralisation was the very foundation of the system. However, even if the notion of a structure of intermediaries was underdeveloped and in part usurped this should not be regarded as not in conformity with the General Model of Corporatism. The intermediary bodies did provide a link between state and society, but it was not in a manner akin to the 'natural estates' of corporatist ideology. Instead, the intermediaries were more negative in character, the licencing system providing the state with a very extensive degree of control over the behaviour of producers. Economic actors were integrated into a network of control that extensively limited their autonomy and thereby ensured their amenability to some effective form of regulation by either the intermediaries themselves or some other agencies. The licenced intermediaries performed a crucial, but not exclusive, role in shaping the forms of articulation and regulation. Therefore, it would be unwise to apply a criterion of 'extent of intermediary functions performed' as indicative of the degree of corporatist development. It misrepresents the fundamental nature of the regimes.

The fundamental nature of these regimes was an imposed order determined by certain dominant interests. Those at the centre could not readily afford to let their grip loosen, fearing there was scant legitimacy for their

rule and decisions. Devoid of the societal consensus that was the linchpin
of corporatist ideology, authoritarian rule was the only possibility. There
are nonetheless limits to and costs of rule by force – authoritarian rulers
need a measure of justification for their exercise of power – and the wider
corporatist system provided a means for legitimising the regime with the
emphasis upon class collaboration, justice, the national interest and so on.
This in itself was a major function of the corporatist system, facilitating an
institutional and doctrinal level of disguise to the regime's true nature.
How successful it was at this is another matter, but it is hard to believe it
had no impact at all. Certainly the respective state authorities regarded the
'trappings' of corporatism as a source of legitimacy, while in these
Catholic countries corporatist ideas, if not the way they were misused,
would have had a wide appeal.[3]

Before going on to set out a model of authoritarian-licenced corporatism, one aspect of Fascist Italy requires further consideration. Unlike the
Portuguese case where there was a notable degree of cohesiveness between
the politico-administrative elite of the state machine and dominant
members of the economy, the dominant groupings of the Italian corporate
state enjoyed no such cohesion. This alone does not pose any serious
problem for our General Model of Corporatism; there is nothing to
exclude the existence of an accommodation of elites sharing a dominant
role within the state machine so long as they remain limited and the vast
majority of the citizenry is excluded. Certainly there is no need to have
recourse to simplistic notions of class rule, though certain sections of
capital were able to consolidate their positions during a period when they
were potentially vulnerable, and capital generally benefited from a disciplined workforce. Nor is it particularly fruitful to argue that at some
deeper level these various elite groupings were a cohesive entity – a single
elite. There was undoubtedly a recognition of their mutual interdependence in securing and maintaining their position but, while this placed
constraints upon conflict among them, there were persistent strains of the
conflict of interests.

Instead, the Italian corporatist system can best be regarded as one where
there was a dominant state composed of a *relatively cohesive* accommodation of a limited number of dominant interests – what might be termed a
shared dominance. This reflects more accurately the stage of development
of industrial capitalism in Italy over the period of the 1920s and 1930s
when important landed interests were still influential, if receding, *and* the
central place held by the upper state bureaucracy in the politico-economic
system throughout the history of the Italian nation. The balance within
this shared dominance was not surprisingly subject to change over the
regime's life.

A further point that follows on from the above was evidence of the industrialists ability to usurp government economic policy ambitions through self-regulation. Again this need not be regarded as a question-mark aginst the 'dominant state' thesis. Rather it illustrates the conflicts between the dominant groups within the state machine and how these were played out. The power of self-regulation did not fall to or benefit all businesses, but were administered by the few dominant politico-industrialists heading the CGII. These exercises in self-regulation to private ends were not a breach of the centre's dominance, but a reflection of disaggregated interests at the top. So the dominant centre-subordinate periphery remains the most accurate approximation of Italian corporatism.

It is now appropriate to establish a model of authoritarian-licenced corporatism. Much will obviously be drawn from the two studies presently conducted, but it is necessary to have a model that is sure of applicability beyond the specific instances of these two examples. Therefore, in constructing the model I have paid particular attention to the practice in a number of other developed corporatist regimes, particularly those more recently inaugurated ones in Latin America. It is not possible to furnish any description of these examples, instead what the literature has to reveal on these corporatist systems has been checked against the Italian and Portuguese experiences. One important point that is illuminated by such an exercise is a variation in experience of these regimes around the key components extrapolated. Thus the components of the model will be set down as variables, not absolutes of an ideal type.

The model is as follows:

Table 8.1 *Model of authoritarian-licenced corporatism*

(1)	Authoritarian state imposes a particular socio-economic order upon society for which there is no major consensual support within society.
(2)	Control of the state machinery can rest with a single coherent dominant group or may be shared among a few disparate groupings in an accommodation of mutual interdependence.
(3)	Control over the behaviour of socio-economic actors is achieved through a system of monopolistic, state-licenced intermediary associations.
(4)	Membership of the licenced intermediary associations need not be compulsory, but the associations exercise comprehensive jurisdiction over all those within their constituencies.
(5)	The level of control afforded to the state can vary significantly over different categories of actors.
(6)	The intermediary associations will perform regulatory functions in the areas of labour relations, production and welfare, but such functions will also be performed by non-licenced state agencies.

(7)   The intermediary associations will perform a representative function, but this will be subjected to varying degrees of distortion by the state.

(8)   Industrial disputes will be settled through compulsory arbitration procedures backed by the state, the normal forms of industrial action being rendered illegal.

(9)   Around the licenced associations will be established institutional structures that by purporting to encapsulate certain ideological premisses – such as social solidarity, justice and the national interest – are designed to legitimise the order, particularly the disciplining of labour.

One can detect such components embedded in the practice of corporatism in Franco's Spain,[4] Brazil since 1964, with generous helpings before the military seized power,[5] Peru under the Revolutionary Government of the Armed Forces,[6] Mexico under the *Partido Revolutionario-Institucional*[7] and other Latin American states.[8] There have nonetheless been important national variations and changes of note over time within these countries such that some have eased away from being purely corporatist systems. However, the majority of Latin American corporatist systems can trace their legislative origins to the 'crowning era of corporatism' – the 1930s and 1940s – and the examples current at the time, most notably Salazar's *Estado Novo*.[9]

The Latin American corporatist systems, as mentioned, revealed variations in their form around the components of the model. Not surprisingly there were differences in the nature of the dominant group or groupings within the corporatist state. Further different categories were subject to varying degrees of integration into the control by the state authorities, though the constant objective was state direction over associational organisation as a means to securing more effective regulation of the economy. As in Italy and Portugal a secure grip on labour organisations was of paramount importance, though in particular instances, for example Brazil in the 1950s, the grip was broken[10] or labour was able to utilise strikes and demonstrations in political bargaining.[11] But without doubt disciplining the emerging workforce was the principal, though by no means only, intention behind such initiatives. The illegality of strikes was an important instrument in helping to maintain that state of affairs. Furthermore, as the more limited examples of Portugal and Italy hinted, there were variations in the regulatory and representative functions performed by the licenced associations both across states and over time.

Overall extending the study to Latin America and possibly Spain reveal one significant trend in the *modus operandi* of corporatism not found in the case of our two examples, with the partial exception of Portugal in the 1960s. This trend was one of genuine, if limited, labour reforms that extended for a variety of reasons the benefits accruing to labour, often against employer interests.[12] Such reforms, concrete though they were, undoubtedly helped to generate support for the wider system and reflected a more 'flexible' authoritarian-licenced corporatism than either Mussolini or Salazar had adopted; there was a greater use of the carrot and less of the stick. One further point also comes out of an examination of certain Latin American countries, particularly Peru under the Revolutionary Government of the Armed Forces. In both Italy and Portugal the licenced corporatist associations largely operated to exclude, to freeze out producers from the politico-economic process. However, certainly in Peru[13] and elsewhere one can see attempts to integrate and mobilise producers towards national goals, making them participants in, rather than recipients of, the nation's development programme. Undoubtedly there are limits to such strategies, but it is nonetheless suggestive of two possible sub-types of authoritarian-licenced corporatism – exclusionist and integrative. The detailed form of such sub-types, however, must await further investigation.[14]

Whether authoritarian-licenced corporatism is a declining force in the contemporary world is open to conjecture. In Latin American countries it has displayed both adaptability and resilience. Whatever the stresses and pressures, corporatist properties have displayed a remarkable persistence, reflecting that corporatist norms are well-embedded in the culture of such countries. Portugal post-1974 probably represents another example of this buoyancy. It is unlikely that out of such corporatist regimes will emerge in the foreseeable future any system that conforms more readily to a liberal-pluralist model than to the corporatist one. The general weight of opinion of analysts is that the corporatist 'paradigm' reflects the bounds of development in the Latin American world, and probably in the Iberian one too. Nonetheless, it is recognised that these polities cannot be seen solely in terms of the corporatist model, there are other layers and strands producing a 'mixed' system.

It was hypothesised earlier in this chapter that corporatism emerged to manage the stresses of transition from a backward agrarian economy to a more advanced, largely industrialised one. Once such as transition has been nearly completed it is probable that pressures will exist to at least ease the rigid bureaucratic form of authoritarian-licenced corporatism. But with development of an industrial capitalist economy by state guidance and with a regimented labour force, the corporatist route may not be easily abandoned. This is particularly true if national capital remains internationally weak. Therefore, corporatism may evolve, if irregularly, into a more flexible, less rigid form, but remain predominant. After all the next part of this book examines the issue of the applicability of a variety of corporatism to some of the most advanced capitalist nations in the world. Hopefully, the model set out above will prove both precise enough to identify and describe the authoritarian variant, and be adaptable enough to trade the evolution of such systems.

Part IV

Neo-corporatism: the development of contract corporatism

9

Neo-corporatism and contemporary pluralism

In the introductory chapter it was mentioned that neo-corporatism presents a disparate and somewhat incoherent conceptual and theoretical face. Diversity may be no unusual attendent aspect of political theory, but within the canon of neo-corporatist literature inconsistencies can readily be detected – a point given much exposure by critics of neo-corporatism.[1] Until such inconsistencies are resolved it is inevitable that the utility of corporatism in analysing advanced industrial, ostensible liberal-democratic polities must remain constrained. One particularly important inconsistency across the range of writers – important at least in its resultant confusion – has been the general conceptualisation of the 'state–societal interests dichotomy'. On the one hand neo-corporatism (for brevity's sake from now on just 'corporatism') has been characterised as a model of societal interests dominating the state[2] such that it appears to be a developed form of pluralism. On the other hand, the concept has been characterised as the antithesis, state domination over societal interests[3] such that it is an unequivocal alternative to pluralism. In fact, many writers place their view of corporatism somewhere in the middle (some indeed might be accused of placing it nowhere), but this does not help clarify the corporatist relationship to the state, and hence corporatism's relationship with pluralism.

That 'state–societal interests dichotomy' and the relationship with pluralism is not the only conceptual issue that corporatist theorists have to grapple with. More importantly, even for those who are reasonably clear in respect of the above dimension, there remain major conceptual difficulties in developing a testable theory of corporatism. Indeed, it will be a theme of this present discussion that distinctiveness from pluralism and developing theoretical propositions within a general conceptualisation are interrelated problems facing the advancement of neo-corporatism. Further, it will be argued that by seeking to distinguish between corporatism and pluralism a clarification of the route to theoretical enhancement

137

of corporatism will result, and *vice versa*. This part of the book is concerned to determine the general distinguishing traits between corporatism and pluralism and from that basis suggest what framework corporatist theory could be developed within before finally going on to consider what outstanding theoretical issues remain. In particular, the development of the framework of what will come to be termed in due course *contract corporatism* will centre around the twin conceptual issues of power and the state. It has to be emphasised that our discussion will proceed only to outline a means of conceptualising corporatism theoretically but will not develop a testable theory of corporatism. For this reason I have chosen to talk in terms of a *theoretical framework* rather than a *theory*.

Our starting point must be the General Model of Corporatism set out in Chapter 1. The first component of the model suggests that corporatism be viewed – at least in a pure form – as one of state domination where the state sustains a particular socio-economic order and overrides any popular or particular demands which conflict with the maintenance of that order. This is, as we have already seen, the basis upon which corporatism can be viewed historically. However, historical precedent need not be the sole ground for viewing neo-corporatism in such terms. Many of the major theorists of neo-corporatism have themselves worked within the bounds of such a general conceptual remit as we shall see presently. In fact, contemporary discussions of corporatism, although having developed along divergent routes, can be evidently seen as a riposte to pluralism.[4] In addition, one can argue that there is a demand for corporatism in this form. Pluralism is not only a political model, it is more fundamentally an approach to political analysis.[5] Given that the utility of the pluralist approach and, therefore, of the pluralist model is being subjected to increasing criticism as 'radical political science' advances,[6] the case for a model of state-organised interest relations that is based upon an alternative approach to political analysis is a strong one. In short, there is an identifiable 'demand' for corporatism in this form. In any case, while accepting that pluralism is a broad church based upon the notion of significant dispersion of power in the political system, it is hard to see what serious benefits will accrue from treating corporatism as a denomination, a variant of the pluralist church, because that church already covers a nomenclature and set of models which encompass the same phenomena as corporatism. The pluralist–corporatist debate should be – and at its best is – more than semantic discourse and a skirmish over conceptual territory.

In this chapter the central issue will be to illuminate and begin to clarify what has been argued to be the general conceptual differences between pluralism and corporatism. The exercise will commence with a brief discussion of contemporary pluralist theory that seeks to highlight the two central deficiencies to which corporatism needs to respond. Following on from that particular discussion we will proceed to examine a number of pluralist and 'in-house' critiques of corporatism to argue both that pluralists have not effectively invalidated the corporatist theorists' attempts to provide an alternative model to pluralism *and* that corporatism should not fundamentally be concerned with institutional structure as argued by Schmitter. Finally, the chapter will set out what general phenomena corporatism should encompass and upon what basis it therefore needs to develop as a distinctive model to that of pluralism. Overall the chapter is concerned to argue, by reference to contemporary writings and debates, the case for a particular, and hopefully precise, foundation upon which to develop corporatist theory that both resolves current difficulties *and* also stays within our historical perspective of corporatism.

Contemporary pluralism: still leaving the door wide open?

Traditional pluralist theory in the United States has been granted its democratic credentials through what Playford terms the balance of power theory,[7] with the emphasis being on countervailing power of what are presumed to be near co-equal units. This line of reasoning had a degree of validity so long as it was assumed that the power of the units rested significantly in mobilising electoral support[8] or lay in a range of power resources to which the individual has access,[9] and that potential groups and overlapping membership were effective mechanisms, not theoretical pieties, for keeping in check tendencies to domination.[10] In the early 1960s, however, such assumptions came in for marked criticism, notably from Bachrach and Baratz's argument that non-decision making meant that 'pluralist political systems' were not as open as pluralist theorists suggested.[11] Consequent upon these criticisms, pluralist theorists began to revise their theoretical propositions in such a way as to both answer the criticisms and remain reasonably true to pluralism's democratic credentials.

One line adopted in the defence was an increasingly wide acknowledgement that within pluralist democracies there was an imbalance of power amongst different societal groupings. The mentor of modern pluralism Robert Dahl clearly has revised his ideas from the late 1960s onward, re-emphasising the concept of polyarchy that argued there was a range of elites taking political decisions, but these elites were fragmented across issue areas, were competitive, not cohesive, and government decisions were indirectly constrained to a significant degree by the majority through electoral competition. It was recognised, however, that certain powerful interests were proving a current threat to the democratic dimension of polyarchy, but importantly the elite–mass dichotomy was still held to be false.[12] In his most recent works Dahl has made it very explicit that he never adhered to the balance of power thesis,[13] aided by quotes from his early works, but there seems little doubt that he is now giving the distorted aspect of pluralism far greater prominence than previously.[14] Perhaps an even more marked transformation has occurred in the position of Dahl's one-time associate, Charles Lindblom, who in his work *Politics and Markets* recognises the structurally privileged position of business and questions whether there is not a significant influence by business over the volitions of the mass of citizenry.[15] Lindblom now suggests that his commitment to pluralist theory is of the order of '.4'.[16]

Such revisionism of pluralist theory towards greater power imbalance, which is widely diffused through the pluralist literature,[17] while clearly making concessions to radical critiques, does not free pluralism from important criticism from that quarter.[18] In particular, although the power imbalance is acknowledged, there is little serious theoretical consideration given to the fundamental nature of the imbalance. There is a tendency to treat the imbalance as some unfortunate 'fact of life', the inevitable failure of reality to conform to the ideal. While it is admitted that the imbalance means 'government decisions reflect and reinforce a structure of inequalities',[19] there is no predilection to follow the logical path and pursue the consequence of the cumulative impact of unequal influence over the decades. There is no inquiry as to whether such inequality is not so much a variable effect of the system, but in fact is the very structure of the system.[20] Relatedly, there is no consideration of how far power can be imbalanced such that it is still dispersed among an adequate range of interests to continue to conform to pluralism. As Manley notes: 'But if it is true that pluralism has always recognised that not all groups are equal, it is also true that pluralism seems to require the assumption of at least some rough equality among groups for a system to be a polyarchy [...] So far pluralism has not specified the parameters or levels of power distribution necessary for a system to be judged a pluralist democracy.'[21]

A second area of censorship for contemporary pluralism is one of methodology. Briefly, it is argued that the imbalance of power is discussed within a conceptual framework that, despite some allowances being made to detractors, remains open to fundamental challenge as a method of analysis of the political process. This methodological criticism centres upon the extent to which the political process in 'pluralist systems' excludes, through organisational and ideological processes, 'key issues' so that pluralist politics is limited to those of prime interest to an elite or dominant class.[22] A final criticism placed at the pluralist door is that the state is largely treated as a non-issue,[23] attention instead being focussed upon the role of elected governments to arbitrate between conflicting group demands and to strive to pursue their party political goals. Certainly other state institutions, notably administrative ones, are regarded as significant and influential, but they are treated solely as a series of disaggregated self-seeking interests[24] and never considered from the perspective of a coherent power structure of domination.

The above arguments suggest that pluralist theory, while trying to answer criticisms raised in the early 1960s, though giving far more prominence to power imbalance, can legitimately be regarded as having failed to answer adequately these adverse judgements, and indeed to appropriately respond to subsequent theoretical challenges.[25]

There was, however, another distinctive case for the defence of pluralism that a number of writers drew upon in the 1960s. This sought to acknowledge the imbalance of power within society but also drew the state into a more positive role as guardian of the common good. The proposition was put forward that the state acts as a source of countervailing power; it partakes the role of umpire ensuring fair play.[26] The influences suggested as being at work to ensure the state maintains a balance are often complex and the result of sophisticated analysis. For example, it is argued that the increased professionalisation of the public sector and the attendant extension of the professional ethic towards the public interest act as a counterweight to other sources of power.[27] Similarly, the state will seek to limit the power of the over-mighty, for example by placing checks on monopolies. While there is a series of specific criticisms of the approaches under the umpire umbrella,[28] the core flaw is the assumption that the rules applied or the balance achieved reflects the general or communal interest. But this assumption rests on a very suspect line of argument: that is that the 'over-powerful' are only influential in respect of policy decisions (if the state was not thus influenced, then it would not be possible to talk of the 'over-powerful'), but that the state is immune from any excessive influence from such sources in determining the framework within which groups operate. Therefore, we are asked to believe that the state has some pure, undistorted view of the general interest in respect of the framework of influence processes and that it has the power to maintain that condition, but in respect of the outcome of influence processes – policy decisions – the opposite is the case. The state always loses battles, but manages to win the war. This strand of neo-pluralism, therefore, has offered a means of overcoming the charge of societel imbalance – though how conclusively is a matter of debate – but it has certainly not disposed of the twin issues of the nature of political power and the nature of the state.

Despite the evolution of pluralist theory over the past two decades or so, it remains open to considerable theoretical challenge. Corporatism represents a more recent body of theory to pick up the gauntlet, though the critique of pluralism – whether explicit or implicit – has not been unified from this quarter. Nevertheless, the challenge by any standards has been a substantial one, providing explicit alternatives in the wake of growing dissatisfaction with pluralism. Not surprisingly, corporatist theory itself has been subject to a pluralist retort. One element in the reproach of corporatist theory, as already mentioned, has been the fact that corporatism provides alternatives in the plural to the conventional model. Diversity however has not been the sole basis of criticism, and we now turn to look at some of the more prominent critiques from pluralist writers. These critiques hopefully will, when combined with a broader discussion of current problems in corporatist theorising, provide a clearer picture of the central differences between pluralism and corporatism and thereby establish a securer basis for the theoretical evaluation of corporatism.

Critiques of corporatism: valid and invalid judgements

The criticism set against corporatist theory by pluralist writers significantly is conducted from a perspective that acknowledges no reference to the major criticisms laid against pluralism in the past 25 years, especially those concerning method. Probably one of the severest attacks on corporatist theory has come from Martin Heisler. His criticisms pertain to three of the major theorists of neo-corporatism – Schmitter, Gerhard Lehmbruch and Leo Panitch. Heisler's central point is to question the constructs as political theories *per se*. Noting that the constructs are based on certain premises, he argues that the theory represents 'a set of almost organically linked, mutually reinforcing hypotheses – to be proved, rather less to be tested', adding that 'it is difficult to anticipate any empirical or theoretical findings that do not support the premises'.[29] Such a denouncement is valid. The theories of the three authors do encompass some fundamental in-built assumptions – such as the nature of the state and 'diachronically consistent motives to all or most classes of actors' – that leads inevitably to the desired conclusions. It remains questionable, nonetheless, to what extent Heisler has placed too much emphasis upon these premises, while giving the constructs themselves little consideration. However, because he clearly does not adhere to such premises it is not regarded by him as necessary to consider any means of developing the theory of neo-corporatism. Yet the basis upon which he rejects going any further, that of empirical findings of complexity and disorder compared to corporatist order, reflects adherence to certain other premises. These premises, essentially those based on the pluralist one-dimensional view of power[30] are not valid grounds alone

upon which to dismiss corporatist constructs, whatever their other de-
merits. The political phenomena Heisler with his pluralist approach may
consider significant, need not be the same as those by non-pluralists.
Ostensible liberal democratic systems with extensive state intervention will
inevitably display a complex myriad of arenas of conflict, but the bounds
of conflict, and hence the structures which set these bounds, it could be
argued are of greater significance. If Heisler wishes to dismiss the corporatist thesis on grounds of its approach to political analysis, then he should
provide some further grounds for accepting his own approach.

Grant Jordan similarly has outlined why he has no sympathy for
corporatist theory. His central line of complaint is that corporatism as
applied has consistently been watered down by its sponsors so that it is
virtually indistinguishable from pluralism in all but name. Corporatism is
employed as a label of dissent. The refining or revising of corporatism is
seen by Jordan as the result of it having to accommodate a 'fragmented
policy making process'. So, we have Heisler dismissing corporatism for
being too parsimonious in relation to other (i.e. pluralist) models, while
Jordan discounts corporatism for being ambiguously similar to pluralist
models.[31] There can be no denying that the distinction between pluralism
and corporatism is unclear, but Jordan's claim is not consistent with his
own line of argument. On the one hand, he criticises Schmitter's model
empirically for its emphasis on a 'limited number' of arenas where modern
societies 'have an excessive number of problem areas each with its own
system of groups'.[32] There is a plausible suggestion of a mis-match of
images. But on the other hand, Jordan then goes on to discount Schmitter's
societal corporatism for being the 'brand leader' of revised corporatism
(which it is not as Jordan mentioned (pp. 109–10)), that has led to a
'softening' of corporatism, whereby 'essentially pluralistic descriptions
have been able to conveniently borrow Schmitter's corporatism label'.[33]
Yet, if Schmiter leads the way in the qualifying of the model 'to improve
the match' the question arises as to why he can so readily be dismissed on
empirical grounds. The only answer is to reconsider the empirical applicability, as Jordan does on the same page: 'If "revised corporatism" fails to
discover a dominant structure of interest relations [. . .], it seems unwise to
be quite so dismissive of pluralism.'

Thus Jordan ends up in a seemingly untenable position in respect of
Schmitter: on the one count his model is dismissed for being empirically
found wanting; on another he is implicated, *via* his societal sub-type, of
being the leader of revised corporatisms which are empirically sound being
'essentially pluralistic descriptions'. At face value it appears that Schmitter
has been found guilty on two mutually exclusive grounds. In any case, it is
unwise to indict him on the second charge because his societal corporatism

is not a revised version at all, but is a sub-type in terms of processes leading to the emergence of corporatism.[34] Furthermore, as will presently be discussed, few writers have directly followed Schmitter's primarily institutional model, but instead have concentrated on group–state bargaining. This is true of Gerhard Lehmbruch's liberal corporatism which Jordan criticises for being qualified, rendering it no more than a variant of pluralism. Ignoring for the moment that Lehmbruch is the softest target on the corporatist range, the main theoretical slant against him by Jordan is that liberal corporatism regards 'policy as a bargain struck between groups and the state'.[35] Bargaining, however, cannot be regarded as the exclusive property of pluralism, as Jordan appears to be suggesting, but is generally accepted as being a means of resolving conflict within a wide range of power structures. Indeed the division between corporatism and pluralism over bargaining is reinforced by Jordan's counter-assertion that corporatism incorporates 'command' and 'imposition' if a consensus does not exist. Jordan is claiming bargaining for pluralism and contesting any corporatist pretension to encompass the same phenomenon.[36] In effect, Jordan is attempting to squeeze corporatism out of any serious analysis of modern interest organisations. But it must be added that the grandiose claims made for corporatism by Schmitter, combined with his carefree readiness to tolerate any theoretical laxity so long as it is corporatist in persuasion, which Jordan effectively highlights in a drollish manner,[37] do nothing to enhance corporatism's claim to be taken seriously.

Perhaps a more sympathetic criticism of corporatism from the pluralist perspective is supplied in a more recent article by Ross Martin. This work has the merit of focussing upon the two major 'conceptual deficiencies' of corporatism, viz the role of the state and the structuring of group–state bargaining. However, Martin's concern is to argue that the claims of distinctiveness by corporatist writers for their concept is exaggerated and that in consequence corporatism should be treated as an 'outgrowth' or variant of pluralism placed on a continuum. On this continuum the 'corporatist pole would signify a situation, broadly speaking, in which groups have a formalised and substantial share in formulating and administering government policy [...] The opposite extreme then translates (at least in the British context) into a "parliamentary" pole signifying a situation in which parliamentary channels provide the only means of contact between office-holders and organized interest groups.'[38]

The result of employing such a continuum will be without doubt to please neither pluralists nor corporatists – and add further to the confusion. More importantly, it is only by seriously misrepresenting corporatist writings that the above prescriptions can be made. Firstly, Martin argues that because corporatists hold that pluralism assumes a passive state they draw a rather false distinction between themselves and contemporary pluralist theory. This criticism does not, however, appear to hold much water: in the first place, my reading of the various writings cited would not suggest this was a prominent or decisive fault with corporatists; in the second place, Martin misrepresents the corporatists by suggesting their conception of the *state* as non-neutral is very close to the pluralist conception of active and initiative-taking *government*. To suggest that Leo Panitch, for example, has a similar view of the state to those of Professors Beer, Walkland and Wooten[39] is to court fantasy in support of one's argument.

Martin's second ground for suggesting that neo-corporatism be regarded as a close relation of pluralism is the corporatist proposition that bargaining entails non-competitive collaboration – for Martin 'a contradiction in terms'.[40] This argument appears to rest on an over-zealous exploitation of ambiguity and diversity in corporatist writings. What the corporatists are propounding is not that there is no genuine bargaining,[41] but that it is not based on competition among equals and that it is structurally constrained. Again the case for emphasising the similarities, over the differences, between pluralism and corporatism looks to be rather suspect. In addition, the question must be raised as to where this fusion leaves the concept of corporatism. The answer is in a position devoid of much analytic utility and distinctiveness, being a more 'formalised' and 'developed' variant of pluralism.[42] Moreover, we do not appear to be very much further beyond the position expounded by Samuel Beer in the mid 1950s, when he labelled formalised group-government relations as 'quasi-corporatism'.[43]

The benefit of Martin's study is that he does clearly centre his attention upon the two key analytic deficiencies present in corporatism as it currently stands, and additionally suggests a possible path to follow to alleviate them. That said, the proposed line of development may not be so novel and does not seem likely to satisfy the desire by both corporatists and pluralists to maintain their analytic distinctiveness, which is itself in a large part symptomatic of diverse normative attachments. More generally, looking at these examples of pluralist critiques of corporatist theory, one can detect a combination of legitimate questioning of the present constructs which highlights concrete problems to be overcome, with suggestions, based upon an adherence to certain analytic premises, that corporatism will never be amenable to development as a valid alternative to pluralism (at least in Western polities). Thus, at best, corporatism may become some limited variant of pluralism, or, at worst, be dropped altogether from the conceptual language of contemporary political analysis. Such judgements about the future of corporatism, however, only gain validity insofar as pluralist premisses are valid. But as already noted such premisses are under increasing assault. Part of the problem here is clearly that analysts employing a particular theoretical model tend to argue in terms of constructs, not premisses or in-built assumptions. Yet it is the premisses that remain the fundamental basis of difference between competing models. Without reference to underlying premisses it looks very much that the pluralist–corporatist debate will retain an air of protracted irresolution.

The tendency to criticise corporatism at face value is not just, however, the preserve of pluralists. Charles Sable, for example, who is a neo-Marxist, provides a critique of corporatism that is very close to a liberal-pluralist one.[44] Sable's argument basically stated is that neo-corporatist theory takes for granted that the rules of procedures within which the corporatist compromise are bargained will remain unchallenged, but in practice such stability is unlikely to prevail. For Sable neo-corporatist theory is not 'very far from Michels' theory of the Iron Law of Oligarchy',[45] but in reality various forces work against such oligarchic tendencies which challenge the theorising; both between and within groups actors will successfully seek to change the rules. He in fact goes on to argue that reciprocal recognition of the temptation to change the rules of bargaining will 'make it very difficult to establish a self-perpetuating bargaining regime'.[46] Similarly, within corporate groups organisational power structures will not be accepted as irreformable and organisational politics will be a persistent feature because of factionalism.[47] Sable has pinpointed a key doubt surrounding corporatist theory – the preponderance of oligarchic assumptions – but his own quasi-pluralist perspective prevents him from addressing how corporatist theory can legitimately move away from its rigid, oligarchic stance. He fails, in other words, to examine the key issues of whether the rules can be subject to reasonably continuous change, but remain within the bounds of some overall pattern: Sable is treating power at 'surface level' only, and not probing underneath to see what underlies the manifestly fluid rules and procedures.

What the above criticisms of corporatism in various ways illustrate is that a substantial element in corporatism – if it is to enjoy distinctiveness from pluralism – must be a distinctive theoretical treatment of power. Without such a treatment corporatism is, therefore, not going to be able to develop an adequate answer to empirical evidence of complexity and fluidity in state-organised interest interactions. This in turn raises another issue at the heart of corporatist theorising, namely the question of state power and hence the matter of what interests the state encompasses or is shaped by. Again on this separate issue corporatism remains open to challenge, not just from the pluralist camp, but also from those more sympathetically disposed to corporatism. As Andrew Cox has argued there remain serious analytic limitations to corporatism because its treatment of the state has been reductionist. In many writers' theoretical deliberations there is an underlying assumption that 'the role of the state is monolithic with definite goals and interests'.[48] The 'politics of the state' cannot be ignored without restricting severely the explanatory capacity of corporatism. But Cox further illustrates the point that several writers who have incorporated the perspective of the state responding to definite pressures and interests have nonetheless indulged in 'monocausal and reductionist (if not to say economist) explanations of state behaviour'.[49] More recently Wyn Grant, a strong adherent of corporatism has acknowledged that the concept is still in need of developing a theory of the state.[50] How so to develop a theory of the state is a matter of intense debate within the corporatist camp, itself being part of a wider configuration of state theory discussions. Corporatist theory has indeed been advancing along with no serious resolution of the problems inherent in providing propositions re state behaviour and form. Birnbaum rightly points out that corporatist writers have treated the state to reification which makes it impossible to gain satisfactory explanations of the incidence of corporatism[51] and therefore, one must conclude, state behaviour under corporatism. Although the problematic nature of theorising about the state has largely been debated internally amongst corporatist protagonists, it has additionally provided further ammunition for pluralist critics. Heisler for one has gone for the 'Corporatist Internationale's'[52] jugular by condemning their 'state-centric' approach with imputed roles for the key classes of actors.[53] Again Heisler has only exploited present weaknesses, but not conclusively won the argument because he has failed to follow through on the issue of structural constraints upon political behaviour that his pluralist approach explicitly excludes.

To summarise thus far: it has been argued that corporatist theory's utility and distinctiveness rests, as illustrated by a range of critics with varying degrees of sympathy, upon the incorporation and refinement of macro-theories of power and the state. This standpoint can hardly be regarded as advocating an exit through the most accessible door; theorising about power and the state are areas of protracted and controversial discourse in political analysis. Leo Panitch is correct in this respect to suggest that the future of corporatist theory's development is problematic because 'the debate over definitions is really a debate betwen different theoretical frameworks, in which normative and ideological preferences play their part'.[54] To be sure, the heat of the debate within the corporatist camp is nearly in the same temperature range as that between themselves and the pluralists. Nonetheless, one need not be so pessimistic as Panitch who feels the best that can be hoped for is a 'minimal descriptive definition which would be so formal as to be of little use in substantive social and political analysis'.[55] Corporatism, like any other concept in the social sciences, need not be subjected to a drive to reach a definitional consensus requested by Panitch; within a broad framework competing models and theories provide the greatest guarantee of more insightful analysis. It is with the development of such a general framework that, of course, we are presently concerned. The question that inevitably has to be addressed at this point is whether or not Schmitter's 1974 model provides us with the very framework needed? There can be no denying that Schmitter's ideal-type model has provided at least a reference point for a host of writers on corporatism.

In practice, it appears that Schmitter's descriptive-institutional model of corporatism has done much to obfuscate the corporatist issue by providing a highly quotable, but nevertheless false, basis for discussion. Nedelman and Meier correctly point out that, like all descriptive models, Schmitter's ideal-typical model 'seems rather arbitrary in its selection of the types and range of structural elements included'.[56] More importantly, Schmitter's model overtly poses questions about the political behaviour of the state and interest organisations, but being descriptive it does not supply the answers by filling in the power relationships within the structure. Yet, without tackling the theoretical need to answer these questions, the descriptive models of corporatism remain virtually valueless, unable by themselves to relate the structure to any other political or socio-economic phenomena[57] except by highly generalised hypothesising. It is not just the arbitrariness of his components that limit the utility of Schmitter's model, but also that he encompasses a range of closely related variables which are not of central relevance to state-group power relationships. The components contained in his definitions of 'a limited number of singular, compulsory, noncompetitive, hierarchically ordered and functionally differentiated categories [...]' set out an institutional arrangement compatible with both highly effectively organised groups able to bring extensive pressure to bear on the state authorities *and* a means for domination or control by the state over groups: it is a structure compatible with either powerful articulation of interests or of state domination of interests, or indeed anything in between. The crucial factors are the 'balance of power' between the state and groups and the degree of autonomy groups enjoy from the state. In the second part of his ideal-typical definition, Schmitter begins to deal with such factors: he adds that the constituent units are '[...] recognized or licensed (if not created) by the state and granted a deliberate representational monopoly within their respective categories in exchange for observing certain controls on their selection of leaders and articulation of demands and supports'.[58]

This latter section of the model, however, does not take us very far. Certainly there is a suggestion of curtailment of group autonomy, but being recognised or licensed or created by the state have different (if imprecisely so) implications. Schmitter's elaboration of this point focuses on 'recognition' which can either be 'granted as a matter of political necessity imposed from below upon public officials' (societal) or be 'granted from above by the state as a condition for association formation and continuous operation' (state).[59] This does not explain what 'recognition' actually entails; it only hints that it may be enigmatic, given that it can come about out of necessity or fief. Moreover, we are told that ideal pluralism does not entail 'specially recognising' the units of the system.[60] To say the least, it is very vague because the terms remain under-defined. Indeed, this is a general criticism that can be laid against the Schmitter model *in toto*. To operationalise it the analyst will have to clarify what is meant by the terminology of the various components, but there is little or no guidance about how to remain true to ideal-typical corporatism. In more recent essays Schmitter has dropped 'recognition' from the schema and has instead talked of the 'coercive intervention of the modern bureaucratic state subsidising organisational existence', 'licensing respective jurisdictions', 'granting monopolistic access'[61] and 'defining, distorting, encouraging, regulating, licensing and/or repressing the activities of associations'.[62] One should also note that this all applies to the 'societal' sub-type and is not simply allied to authoritarian 'state' variants. In extending the range of state actions on interest associations Schmitter is adopting distinctive contributions from other neo-corporatist theorists and, it appears, in consequence, is moving away from the circumscriptions of his own model.

The link between Schmitter's model and many other contributions lies in the final segment of his definition where he posits the granting of a 'representational monopoly' by the state to associations in exchange for their observing 'certain controls' on leadership selection and articulation. The question, of course, that is begged is what are these controls? All that is outlined is that under the 'societal' sub-type, which is of central concern to us here, it is 'the product of a reciprocal consensus on procedure and/or goals',[63] but this does not specify the scope and the subject-matter. (It is the case, anyhow, that such a consensus is usually incorporated into pluralist models in that there is acceptance of the 'democratic creed',[64] except that there is no suggestion in the pluralist model that this affords the state 'control'.) The implication of the suggestion that the exchange results from a 'reciprocal consensus' (what forces generate this?) is that the terms of the exchange favour neither one party nor the other; it is not a power relationship. Moreover, one is left to assume that different consensuses will produce different exchanges in terms of controls enjoyed by the state, and, therefore, 'consensus' may be the key variable.

The more one weaves through the components of Schmitter's model the more one can trace the germ of an idea, lost bcause he has started from the wrong perspective of the centrality of institutional arrangements. The central place given to institutional arrangements can be the result of one or two intentions. One is that they relate to the significant variables of group–state relations. This does not appear particularly plausible. The contending model of pluralism is defined more prominently (except by Schmitter himself) in terms of 'power relationships' and processes.[65] Further, the 'pre-corporatist critiques' of pluralism have similarly focussed on these aspects.[66] Even Wright Mill's widely influential institutional approach was, of course, concerned with institutional power, not institutional structure.[67] Most damning of all has been the fact that the main proponents of neo-corporatism have not markedly themselves taken the institutional line, but have focussed on power relationships and decision-making processes. Schmitter's own predilection for the institutional is that it is 'relatively directly observable', compared, that is, to the other approaches mentioned. This does not, however, confirm the case for the institutional approach.

According to the second, the institutional approach could be justified on the grounds that historically corporatism has been concerned centrally with institutional arrangements. In discussing the normative theorists of corporatism, Schmitter points out that they converge 'upon the advocacy of an institutional relationship between the systems of authoritative decision-making and interest representation which can be considered generically corporatist by my praxiological definition'. So Schmitter has distilled a number of common institutional traits out of a range of normative theorists (many of whom did not call themselves corporatist) and constructed these into a model. However, Schmitter adds that these theorists 'conceived of this arrangement as involving radically different structures of power and influence, as benefiting quite distinctive social classes, and as promoting diametrically opposite public policies'.[68] Yet, before we know where we are Schmitter is telling us that 'corporatisation of interest representation is related to certain basic imperatives or needs of capitalism to reproduce the conditions for its existence and continually to accumulate further resources'. So, 'in a nutshall, the decay of pluralism and its gradual displacement by societal corporatism can be traced primarily to the imperative necessity for a stable, bourgeois-dominant regime'.[69] Therefore Schmitter empirically places corporatist institutional arrangements into a specific socio-economic 'power structure'. The outcome of this hypothesis should be a clear indication of how corporatist institutional arrangement can serve this particular 'power structure', but Schmitter has not to date, beyond the odd hint,[70] actually tied the two together. Instead, as Leo Panitch has observed, Schmitter's 'group-theoretical' model of corporatism sits uncomfortably alongside his 'class-theoretical' approach to the origins of societal corporatism.[71] Indeed, Schmitter's more recent writings tend to further cloud the wider political and social context of neo-corporatism.[72]

There must remain – to date at least – a serious question-mark over whether Schmitter's model provides a framework for the development of neo-corporatist theory. The model may well come to provide a useful adjunct to analysis, but at the moment it needs a general framework of corporatism to make it operationally viable. The question is 'where to turn to?'

Corporatism, pluralism and bargaining

To begin to answer the question just posed we need to step back a pace or two and fundamentally examine what phenomena corporatism is concerned with. Throughout the discussion however, the premiss that corporatism entails state domination, in line with arguments developed earlier in this book, will be adhered to. It will also be valuable to retain cognisance of the points made earlier about the necessity of corporatist theory to develop macro or attendant theories of power and the state.

If one sifts through the corporatist literature the writers' common concern, with the exception of J. T. Winkler's proposals, is the general phenomenon of continuous, structured participation of interest organisations in the policy-making process and other stages of the policy process, especially policy implementation. In the main, such organisations convey particularistic demands, usually dealing with an economic or producer subject-matter. Thus, interest organisations are incorporated into the policy process in the sense that their access is more or less assured, and often institutionalised, rather than that they are seekers of intermittent influence and access.[73] True, corporatist writers have variously focussed upon attendent features, but the core element has been the symbiotic relationship between ostensively private organised interests and the state authorities, or more laconically incorporation. However, this phenomenon does not of itself merit the label corporatist, though some writers appear to use 'incorporation' and 'corporatism' synonomously.[74] That key producer groups are incorporated does not of itself give a theoretical explanation of the balance of political forces. Traditional pluralist views were concerned with intermittent access, or lobbying as it is known in Britain and the United States, but since the early 1960s, if not before, pluralist analysis has readily moved on to encompass group incorporation. Indeed, group incorporation has added much to the pluralist case because, at one level of analysis, it very explicitly shows government as an arena where groups 'fight it out';[75] the very fact that governments have to 'accommodate' so many groups and are severely constrained by these groups in what they can achieve is taken as evidence that pluralism is alive and well. Yet, as was pointed out, several times in the previous section, corporatist analysis has offered quite distinctive explanations, or more precisely has reached different conclusions about, the same phenomena.

What both pluralists and corporatists recognise – indeed they can hardly fail to – is that the extension of state responsibilities in Western societies in the post-war era into economic and social affairs has left the state authorities dependent upon private actors in respect of policy making, and more crucially in policy implementation, such that the nature of governing (or if one prefers ruling) has fundamentally changed. The reverse side of the authorities' dependence is the potential power it affords private actors over the authoritative decision-making process. To continue to govern by relying on the traditional sources of legitimacy for authoritative decisions is not possible as a general principle,[76] nor is it possible for the state to return to an era of general rule-making because of the needs of managing a capitalist economy either for popular or class interests. So, the authorities cannot ignore these private interests and the political constraints they present. Instead, the state authorities have to 'accommodate' these interests, preferably mediated through some representative organisation. And private interests for their part recognise the benefits of organising to exploit their potential power. Without doubt the context of state–group relations has changed; but the consequence of a contextual change for the state remains uncertain.

A probing pluralist analysis of such developments has been provided by Professor Ionescu, although he places his analysis outside the context of the role of the state in managing modern capitalism. For Ionescu, the focus is the impact that corporate forces have on society: 'The industrial-technological revolution has meant that within a given country the corporate forces [...] have accrued sufficient power and autonomy to impose their sectional decisions on the rest of the community'.[77] Therefore, to combat the threat of increasing 'ungovernability', 'the representative governments relinquish their positions as unique national policy-makers and seek "partnerships" or "contracts" with each of those corporate forces in modern society without which that society would cease to function'.[78] Not surprisingly, it is suggested that the result of government seeking 'partnerships' with opposing forces is that 'government may often sink in the difficult role of go-between, or re-emerge in its classic role of umpire'.[79]

Significantly, Schmitter describes the usage of the term 'corporatism' when employed in respect of 'a mode of policy formation' in a very similar manner. He states that corporatism is regarded

as a mode of policy formation, in which formally designated interest associations are incorporated within the process of authoritative decision making and implementation. As such, they are officially recognized by the state not merely as interest intermediaries but as co-responsible 'parties' in governance and societal guidance. Ostensibly private and autonomous associations are not just consulted and their pressures weighed. Rather, they are negotiated with on a regular, predictable basis. Their consent becomes necessary for policies to be adoped; their collaboration becomes essential for policies to be implemented.[80]

Thus, we find pluralists and corporatists talking in a similar language and evoking the same images with notions of group-government 'partnerships', 'contracts' and 'communities'. The emphasis on both sides is of continuity of the relationship and that there is an exchange.[81] What is of even more crucial importance than a similarity of language and imagery, is the fact that they regard the same phenomena as significant, and thus direct their attention towards them. Such a convergence of attention on particular phenomena being significant is far more marked than occurred in the debate prevalent in the 1950s and 1960s between the pluralist and elitist theorists. This factor may go a good part of the way to explain why there has been such ambiguity concerning where the boundary between corporatism and pluralism lies. The boundary lies not in the political phenomena regarded as significant in explaining power and influence within the political system, but in the attendent theories of power and the state. Yet, it is these attendant theories that remain rather unexplicit, ambiguous and contentious. Similarly, it is in this domain that the pluralist repost has been most wanting.

At a basic level what both pluralists and corporatists are concerned with is the development of negotiation or bargaining between private groups and the state authorities. Eckstein has sought to define 'negotiations' as taking place 'when a governmental body makes a decision hinged upon the actual approval of organisations interested in it, giving the organisations a veto over the decision'. This stands in contrast to consultations which occur when 'the views of the organisations are solicited and taken into account but not considered to be in any sense decisive'. Eckstein's 'polar extreme' definition of negotiation[82], however, is not of any serious utility because it ignores the crucial 'exchange process' in negotiations or bargains and assumes that those negotiated with have or are granted superior influence compared with those consulted. Eckstein, therefore, seeks to define negotiation and consultation in terms of an outcome – influence over a decision – rather than in terms of a process – how influence is brought to bear. It is probably more analytically sound to see bargaining and negotiation in terms of trading. Furthermore, in actual practice it is possible that many interests consulted may wield as much influence as (possibly more than) those bargained with.[83] Indeed, in certain of its forms consultation may merge into a form of trading and in many cases will involve an exchange as commonly defined in organisational analysis.[84]

It appears, in consequence, more valid to regard structured participation by organised interests in state decision-making in terms of exchange, and the related concepts of power and dependence, rather than in terms of particular types of activities.[85] The emphasis is on power relationships and organised interests, not on the form through which influence is brought to bear within the general context of structured participation. This approach of centring analysis upon exchanges reflects the predominant concern of both pluralists and corporatists with power and its distribution. (For convenience's sake we will continue to employ the term 'bargaining' alone as a generic term for activities whereby some form of trading takes place.)[86]

In summary, therefore, both pluralists and corporatists focus on bargaining between the state authorities and groups as a process whereby an exchange is made, the terms of which are in some form binding on the participants. On the one hand, the state authorities have principally authoritative allocations (extractions, regulations of behaviour, distributions and symbolic outputs) to offer groups that can be more or less accommodating to the interests of the organisations and their members. On the other hand, groups can offer the state authorities enhanced legitimacy for their policies and facilitative and supportive action for implementing policy decisions. Yet, the pluralists and corporatists differ markedly in their view of the fundamental nature of the bargaining process or processes. To the pluralist, the exchange is on an equal basis in the sense that the bargaining process is regarded as one where there is no constraint upon the terms of exchange other than the power resources participants can mobilise in their interests and possibly the strategies pursued. The framework within which bargaining takes place is to all intents and purposes neutral as between one party and another, in much the same way as liberals regard exchanges in the market between capital and labour. Just as the market is based upon legal equality so political bargaining is based upon a 'set of rules' that is equally applied; there is no questioning of what interests the law or rules serve. Instead analysis operates along one dimension, at one level – that of observable behaviour.[87] Within this paradigm the state is presented either as a referee or one participant among many who have helped to shape the rules; the rules are just another manifestation of the bargaining process.

In contrast, corporatism with its adherence to state domination cannot regard the bargaining process from the same standpoint. Corporatists are not just proposing a maldistribution of power; they are questioning the fundamental basis of state–group bargaining. They regard state–group bargaining as an integral part of a system of state domination. So, for example, Leo Panitch defines the corporatist political structure not solely in terms of 'an actual linkage between the state and functional interest groups [...] constituted by institutionalised representation in economic policy making', but, adds that this confers 'an element of state control over the groups whereby this autonomy is limited and they are employed as agencies of mobilization or administration for state policy'.[88] Likewise, Alan Cawson writing in 1978 defined corporatism as involving 'state direction of the activities of predominantly privately-owned business in partnership with the representatives of [...] interest groups',[89] while for Jessop corporatism is a state form that generates an adequate social base to secure 'effective state power' to maintain bourgeois domination.[90]

Within the corporatist literature one can distinguish two general outlooks on state domination and state–group relations. One strand places the emphasis on 'control' by the state. This is the line taken, for example, by Leo Panitch. On the other side, there is an emphasis on group–state and also group–group bargaining generating a consensus about economic policy, a consensus that does not reflect the interests of group membership but is favourable to the interests the state represents. There is, in effect, a false consensus, that as Lehmbruch suggests serves the imperatives of capitalism by allowing for the regulation of 'the conflict of social classes in the distribution of national income and in the structure of industrial relations'.[91] Indeed, Lehmbruch suggests that economic policy making can no longer rely on 'controls' but has to move towards 'consensus-building'.[92]

It is the view of the present author that both notions of 'control' and 'consensus' – certainly as they stand in the literature – are misleading. What at a basic level corporatist theory is seeking to explain is how the state authorities can make policies and implement them with a degree of effectiveness that serve the interests they represent. Or, put another way, why do private actors consent to authoritative decisions that are so markedly biased against their real interests when state dependence upon them should facilitate a more effective pursuit of such interests/or challenge to state authority.

If one takes wage restraint as an example of such authoritative decisions – as frequently occurs in the corporatist literature – the suggestion of state control lacks specificity, being a generic term for a relationship based on a range of forms of power.[93] While readily accepting that a control relation may involve a variety of forms, it is obvious that group authority bargaining over wage restraint had predominantly been concerned to achieve agreement so that there would be general consent to such regulation. It is very unlikely that such bargaining is part of a process of coercion, though the threat of coercion may well be a resource used in the bargain by the state authorities and the use of coercion may act to reinforce other means of gaining compliance. On the other hand, if the authorities were going to rely on primarily coercive means to control wage increases, bargaining agreements would seem rather irrelevant. Bargaining and consultation imply attempts to secure consent.

For similar reasons, the notion of domination by the state resulting from a false consensus being bargained is not analytically useful. To quote Dunsire: 'agreement without persuasion may be arrived at by negotiation and *bargaining*, where objectives are traded rather than surrendered. Continuing conflict is acknowledged, but immediate problems are removed without destroying the group'.[94] Consensus, in contrast, suggests agreement without conflict; shared values and objectives that do not need to be traded. This is not to argue that a 'false consensus' is not important; indeed it may be fundamental given that conflict is not necessary to power. As Lukes observes: 'the most effective and insidious use of power is to prevent such conflict from arising in the first place'.[95] There may be a consensus, but it is an imposed consensus, not a genuine one.[96] But to reiterate the point, corporatist structures, with their suggested attendant features of bargaining and exchange, cannot be directly linked to generating a false consensus. This is not to deny that a false consensus will be important in sustaining corporatism, as it sustains other political structures of a particular regime, by excluding *potential issues* or *real interests* from the political process: these issues and interests would be an effective threat to the system of domination *per se* – of which corporatism is only a part. Corporatism should be regarded as a response to increasingly effective particularistic demands which threaten the existing order from within; if the existing order is challenged *in toto* then such threatening particularistic demands are of no great import. Nonetheless, it is worth recognising, as Jessop points out, that the engendering of a consensus and the operation of corporatism can to some degree stand in contradiction to each other.[97]

Summary

This chapter has sought to argue that corporatism in contemporary political analysis should be regarded as a set of political structures designed to maintain a position of state domination. Thus it stands conceptually distinct from pluralism, though this has not been a consistent

position in current writings. That said, however, one has to fully acknowledge that corporatism, like modern pluralism, focuses upon the phenomenon of the close, symbiotic relationship between the state authorities and
economic interest groups that developed under the managed capitalist
economy. Recourse to such forms of intervention as incomes and prices
policies, industrial development policies, manpower training and the
provision of certain welfare services led to increasing state dependence
upon private actors for the successful implementation of these policies.
The potential power this afforded economic actors had to be accommo-
dated by the state, leading to state–group partnerships where private
actors, usually through their interest associations, participated in authoritative decision making through negotiations and so on. To the pluralists
such partnerships, if not evidence of increased democratisation, were at
least further evidence that the 'elite–mass' or 'dominant–subordinate'
dichotomies were not valid characterisations. Conversely, for radical and
Marxist writers, who adhered to such dichotomies, the apparently
increased dependence of the state and the new status of functional and
subordinate interests presented a puzzle. It is to resolving that puzzle
theoretically that the bulk of corporatist writings has been directed. In
reality the puzzle has been two-sided: how does the state maintain its
dominance through such structures? And what are the implications of this
for social change?

Given that pluralists and the corporatists focus upon the same phenomena – with the exception of those corporatists who make institutional
structures salient – there is limited utility to be drawn from descriptive,
static models of corporatism. Instead, corporatism must be a dynamic and
theoretic model to offer analysis, something other than a name. And in
effect this necessitates developing within corporatists' constructs theories
of power and of the state. If this can be realised – and much advance has
already been accomplished – then the criticisms from pluralists of corporatist theory will no longer be able to rest upon the already creaking platform
of pluralist premises, methods and macro-theoretical perspectives and
their assumed validity. The following chapter will elaborate upon this
problématique of attendent theories of power and the state. Further, it will
also be necessary to extend the boundary of corporatist theory to incorporate the dimension of the role interest organisations perform as agencies
for implementing the policies of the state authorities.

10

Towards the development of a framework of contract-corporatist theory

In the previous chapter it was proposed that corporatist theory should be developed around the phenomenon of state-group bargaining incorporating attendant theories of power and of the state. Several writers, however, have already set down a number of theoretical approaches to corporatism based upon bargaining, and so it is necessary to consider this segment of the literature before launching off ourselves.

Corporatism and bargaining: existing approaches

To date corporatist theory in providing explanations of state-group bargaining has been limited; too extensively do conclusions rely upon in-built assumptions about power rather than on testable propositions. This feature is most evident in the work of Gerhard Lehmbruch. He sees corporatism as 'an institutional pattern of policy-formation in which large interest organisations cooperate with each other and with public authorities not only in the articulation (or even "intermediation") of interests, but – in its developed forms – in the "authoritative allocations of values" and in the implementation of policies'. This phenomenon, however, entails not simply more consultation and cooperation between government and organised interest groups, but is distinguished above all by 'a high degree of collaboration among these groups themselves in shaping economic policy'.[1] Such bargaining, which can take a variety of forms[2] serves the imperatives of capitalism 'by regulating the conflict of social classes in the distribution of national incomes and the structure of industrial relations', thereby building a consensus about regulating the economy in such areas as prices and incomes.[3] Lehmbruch's approach is, however, full of pitfalls. For one thing, the terminology employed remains under-elaborated. Cooperation is utilised in a loose manner that ignores its various forms and levels. Further, it is suggested that 'the distinguishing trait of liberal corporatism is a high degree of collaboration' among groups 'in shaping economic policy',[4] but there are no propositions as to why bargaining produces collaboration and how it produces collaboration that serves a particular interest. At best there are some highly generalised hypotheses, but nothing testable and nothing to support the conclusions expressed are provided.[5]

The central flaw in Lehmbruch's discussion is that he analytically fuses a particular political process (bargaining amongst state and groups) with a particular power relationship or structure (the needs of capital) without elaborating the linkages. One writer who has suggested such linkages, at least in respect of the subordination of trade unions, is Leo Panitch. He argues that the 'bias of the system is less attributable to direct pressure from business than to the logic entailed in state planning in a capitalist economy'. Planning, and presumably economic policy making in general, sets down a framework, particularly acceptance of the existing authority structure, that limits the extent to which trade unionists can positively participate, it being on terms, set by planning officials and industrial managers, prejudicial to their interest.[6] For Panitch trade unions have lost the terms, or cannot win the terms, of the argument.[7] Through what processes trade union leaders come to be seemingly entrenched in the logic of capitalism view is not, unfortunately, fully elaborated. Nor for that matter is it explained how certain sections of capital likewise have their interests subordinated to the general interests of capital. Panitch's argument which has a certain appeal, though it lacks a satisfactory capacity to explain, is to propose that corporatist arrangements are inevitably unstable, but that they are encouraged by recourse, actual or threatened, to coercive measures by the state.[8] The argument, however, centres essentially upon the reason why corporatist developments display a cyclical character. There is no move to explain how the logic is imposed on state-group relations. Some invaluable insights as to why the logic is accepted are supplied by Claus Offe and Helmut Wiesenthal who set down a range of factors contributing to differences in power that labour and capital can organise *and* in the degree of distortion of true interests.[9] In this admittedly complex schema any conflict between the true interests of labour and capital is inherently unequal. The ideas provided, valuable though they are, remain somewhat too abstract to incorporate into corporatist theory, certainly as it is envisaged here. But as we shall see in due course it does inform corporatist theorising.

In particular, neither Panitch or Offe and Wiesenthal furnish specific theoretical propositions about corporatist bargaining. Rather they supply a critique of pluralist theory and propositions concerning the fundamental inequality of power between capital and labour. While this does provide insights, especially into the process of corporatisation, it leaves us with corporatist theory 'as liberal-pluralist critique'. This is unsatisfactory for the reason that it explicitly ignores the dynamics of corporatist bargaining and thus makes it highly problematic to link this dimension of corporatism to its other dimensions or to wider political configurations. In effect, it denies the existence of a form of corporatist bargaining, a view that we shall see is not sustainable.

A writer who has provided a theoretical discussion of corporatist bargaining is Colin Couch. He presents corporatism as one of a number of strategies of domination. His variant of neo-corporatism – 'voluntaristic corporatism' – emphasises the virtual absence of coercive power by the state, and hence concentrates on other forms of power.[10] Under voluntaristic corporatism 'the active but, by and large, non-coercive state depends for its subordination of workers and others in bargaining and accommodation with other organised interest'.[11] Crouch does, however, fully recognise that bargaining and accommodation are characteristics also of the liberal model and so it has to be asked at what point does the bargaining of 'independent and hence pluralist power centres cease and become an enforced unity imposed on subordinates through a combination of sanctions and deals made over their heads between their organisations and dominant interest'. To overcome these analytical problems Crouch argues: 'Ultimately, the question is a matter of degree, and theory resolves problems of degree by stipulating extreme cases between which existing reality may be considered to be located as in a continuum.' At one end, he deposits voluntary corporatism, where 'the representatives of subordinates agree to maintain the discipline of their members for no material concessions at all, other than those that might be attained for the "general interest"'. This may be the result of the subordinate organisations' leaders having no pressure exerted on them by the membership or a strong degree of ideological unity leading to the subordinates' interests being identified with the system as a whole. At the other extreme is the liberal collectivist concept, where subordinate organisations offer no guarantee of discipline in exchange for specific concessions to the membership, and demands may be renewed at any moment. Furthermore, in practice, it will be very rarely that a purely corporatist arrangement exists or a purely liberal arrangement persists, indeed, there could be formulated an alliance between them.[12]

Crouch has labelled this mixed system of corporatist arrangements plus elements of genuine bargaining, not surprisingly, as bargained corporatism. Bargained corporatism:

involves acceptance of several strategies which compared with liberal collectivism, constitutes a set-back for workers' interests. But also it holds out the chance of advances. Unions are tempted – and frightened – by corporatist developments to sacrifice some of their entrenched but narrow and unambitious achievements in exchange for the possibility of greater political influence and more and broader power for their members in the workplace, but at the same time to accept more restraint, a more obvious role for the unions in restraining their members, more state interference and a fuller acceptance of the industrial order and its priorities.[13]

Crouch offers a basic 'theory' that can accommodate fairly readily a variety of state-organised interest relationships and allows different types of authority to be exercised. There is, however, a serious weakness because of voluntary corporatism's incorporation of a general interest. This 'general interest' is what the subordinated organisations or their leaders support and hence accept as the *raison d'être* for discipline. Quite simply, the general interest is going to be empirically impossible to identify and so distinguish from a specific interest of associations' members. The 'general interest' cannot exist in a vacuum nor can it be 'scientifically defined', it has to be enunciated by some actor(s). Once this is accepted, say that it is defined by the state authorities, then the problem arises as to what influence has been brought to bear on the authorities; in other words the 'general interest' may in part reflect the interests of subordinates beyond any 'concessions' they gain out of the other parts of the 'general interest'.

On top of the above difficulty, the basis upon which the general interest is accepted by the leaders of subordinate organisations according to Crouch is assimilation of interests. Here again there is a lack of concreteness. Groups may well support the existing system, not because it is their ideal, but because they lack the power at present to change the system to a more desirable form. A break with or an attempt to disrupt the existing system may lead to a loss of gains made in the existing system and/or a change to a less desirable one. It has to be possible for the theory to distinguish between assimilation of interest and the boundaries existing power structures place on the pursuit of strategies of influence. In some respect, it might be regarded that the concept of 'bargained corporatism' accommodates this problem by presenting corporatism as something that is not continuous, but which is bargained for. However, this does not get us away from our original difficulty of identifying corporatism whatever conditions it pertains under. In any case, 'bargained corporatism' entails interest organisations making a choice for gaining greater political influence at the expense of the members' interests, but political influence is not usually an end in itself and without any clarification as to what greater political influence will be employed for, it is difficult to evaluate what it all adds up to. If political influence is used to further members' long-term interests (or perhaps change the system?) then does corporatism still exist? If it does, then corporatism entails no more than showing restraint in the economy for gains in the polity, which raises questions about whether it is accurate to talk of 'subordinate' organisations. Even if organisations failed to gain anything through greater political influence, to what extent could this be regarded as a failed strategy rather than corporatism.

More recently Crouch has sought to address these difficulties through employment of a continuum with an exclusive discipline function for interest organisations at one end and an inclusive representative function at the other.[14] Bargained corporatism occurs when an interest organisation agrees to self-restraint and to discipline members in exchange for exemption from statutory regulation; under pluralist bargaining the organisation might support restraint by members but it would not police it.[15] But Crouch's answer to the problem is to redefine the concept to a marked degree. Gone is any allusion to domination: 'It cannot be assumed that liberal corporatist bargains achieve a worse deal for the members than pluralist lobbying; governments are often happy to delegate regulation to private, voluntary bodies and therefore willing to compromise their aims in order to achieve it.'[16] The concept of corporatism is quite explicitly played down in terms of the original. Its wider political significance,[17] and hence its distinguishing traits from established models of pluralism is unclear.

In addition, Crouch has interestingly sought to develop the continuum in terms of bargaining form in addition to the representative role. This presents corporatist bargaining in terms of a positive-sum game which certainly begins to resolve the difficulty mentioned above of subordinate interests accepting a common or general interest; quite simply there are gains to be had (positive-sum), though there needs to develop a series of positive-sum games 'on stream' so that pay-offs are regularly received, thereby reducing risks of major losses.[18] Again though the cost is the exclusion of domination from the corporatist equation, while the pluralism-corporatism division has to rest on a caricature of the former, viz pluralism does not entail mature positive-sum games. There is no doubt, nonetheless, that such an approach does offer a basis for explaining why subordinate groupings enter into corporatist arrangements and stay within them. But we have no criteria by which to assess the overall long-term benefits they derive from this strategy relative to other options available.

Alan Cawson has, like Crouch, sought to place bargaining at the centre of corporatism. But there remain in this approach difficulties concerning the role of the state. Under corporatist bargaining neither does the state direct functional interests nor is it directed by them. Instead, 'power is shared between the state and groups. Interdependence is the key to the corporatist relationship.'[19] This does not of itself appear incompatible with pluralism, but Cawson adds the distinguishing trait from pluralism by noting that under corporatism privileged access is afforded to a limited number of groups in return for their cooperative behaviour. So, under corporatism, 'the competitive role of interest groups – which is held to safeguard the democratic nature of pluralism – will be replaced by an orderly, co-operative and stable relationship'.[20] Yet, the dividing-line between corporatism and pluralism remains too blurred: 'In a corporatist model of policy-making, representation of demands and implementation (of policies) are fused within a mutually dependent bargaining relationship in which favourable policy outcomes are traded for co-operation and expertise.'[21]

Cawson's main focus, in effect, centres upon contrasting the competitive, pluralist sector with the cooperative, corporatist one, and that under the latter interests 'are structurally privileged in the formation of state policy'.[22] 'Structural privilege, no less than overt pressure, is an exercise of power, but it is not capable of being analysed within a framework of concepts derived from the competitive market models [...] corporate-sector groups represent the collective interests of producers of goods or providers of services. They have developed (or have been granted) an effective monopoly, whether legally recognised or not, of representation. Their power rests on their contribution to economic production and social provision, and their co-operation in the form of stable exchange relationships in a precondition of effective state intervention.'[23] There is no doubt that Alan Cawson has touched upon an important aspect of group-state relations, namely the basis of group power and the democratic implications of this.[24] However, this aspect of significant differences in political power resulting from the holding of different positions in the economy has been discussed before, notably by a number of pluralist writers (even if they have not followed through their analysis).

More importantly for our purposes, corporatism remains discussed by Cawson at a high level of generality. There is no elaboration upon the nature of the bargaining process and hence upon corporatist politics, except that it 'does not imply a dominant central state' and depends upon 'a degree of consensus' about existing social and political arrangements.[25] The implication is that privileged access ends pluralist competition, but there is no evidence to suggest that the relationship between the state and the privileged group is not pluralist itself (or at least not distinct from contemporary pluralist analysis). So, Cawson presents corporatism as undemocratic, but not as a form of state domination, though it is added that 'the state also has a crucial function to perform with respect to society: that of *legitimation*, or the maintenance of the social order'.[26] The problem with such a treatment of the state is that it cannot readily be constructed into a theory, i.e. tested. In any case Cawson remains ambiguous in his characterisation of the state because, while he wisely avoids seeing the state as all-dominant, he does present the state under the corporatist sector as being an instrument for pursuing the long-run interests of the dominant class.[27]

The above discussion of a number of approaches to corporatism and bargaining reveal a diversity of views. Generally one can detect a difficulty in reconciling state domination with bargaining: those writers who confront the dynamics of the bargaining process tend to move away from domination, while those who stick firmly to domination tend to by-pass bargaining dynamics. Thus analysis of corporatism either draws on in-built assumptions about the distribution of political power within the polity and deduces the nature of corporate bargaining from this or presents itself as a critique of pluralist approaches to bargaining by outlining omissions in that approach. A partial exception to these was provided by Offe and Wiesenthal who clearly extrapolate the logic of labour's subordinate position. But, if one postulates that the state safeguards the long-term interests of capital they do not provide a further necessary dimension, viz how the state regulates the behaviour of individual enterprises to ensure compatibility with capital's long-term interest. This is not to criticise the authors cited in this section; they have by no means been exclusively concerned to explicitly reconcile the issues posed by our own evolving framework. The review of existing approaches to corporatism and bargaining sought to highlight that theoretical questions surrounding domination and bargaining remain problematic. Certainly the writers all adhered to the view that bargaining – like other political processes – should not be viewed through a pluralist-theoretic perspective to power. What is needed is an alternative perspective. This in brief requires further recognition of the duality of class based political behaviour and conflict. As Offe and Wiesenthal point out there is political behaviour within political forms – 'organizational and procedural "rules of the game"' – but these rules themselves are not neutral, though they may be presented as such, and hence their determination represents a further level of political activity.[28] And in line with what will be elaborated in the next section, the second level of activity – that concerning political form, structures – is the more fundamental because it sets the parameters of the former level of activity. Indeed, we will be arguing shortly that not simply does it set the parameters so much as it can 'distort' the play of power within it. Corporatism, therefore, can be seen as a political form, a set of structures which place constraints upon the political activity conducted through them in a manner beneficial to those who determine these structures. The structures are a source of power.[29]

Before proceeding to elaborate upon this dual approach to power, one point merits further emphasis. Corporatist political structures are not obviously universal, but relate to a specific context. They are widely recognised as a response to the changing context of the role of state in the economy. In the present work this has been presented as the increased dependency of the state upon economic actors, capital and labour, resulting from particular types of economic intervention pursued in managing modern capitalist economies. A logical question that follows from this is: why was the potential power that fell to labour not used to have a hand in determining political structures? One answer may be that for ideological reasons the potential was not recognised. But whatever the accuracy of this piece of speculation, there is a more universal point implicit therein. Power is not a universal currency to be exchanged for the commodities of one's choice. So power to apply constraints upon the effectiveness of government intervention does not translate automatically into power to determine political form. Rather there would appear to be limits to the potential for translation because labour's power is of a 'transitory character'. For example, the trade union movement may press for and gain wage-rises in excess of productivity. The gain, however, is not likely to be for all time. Capital may simply begin to increase prices and thereby reduce real wages. If capital cannot recoup its losses through increased prices, at least fully so, then the ensuing profitability crisis hits not only capital but also labour as closures, transfer of capital abroad and the introduction of labour-saving investment follow. Of course the dynamics of the process may be more complex; for one thing the state may spend money to underwrite the profitability crisis but unless this can be drawn exclusively from non-producers then it will still impinge upon capital and/or labour. Thus labour being materially dependent upon the profit system results in their power being transitory and, therefore, not of the order to markedly shape political form. The above should not be regarded as a theoretical proposition, simply just an *ex ante* deduction that can be made in the face of the persistence of particular political forms. But while dominant interests know that the profit-system will in due course bring labour to heel so to speak, and hence that concessions to change political forms need not be granted, labour's transitory power poses a threat to the accumulation process, particularly if labour does not concede its gains without a protracted struggle with action against redundancies. It is the threat to the accumulation process that leads to corporatist structures developing; crises are something to be avoided because they can become cumulative, threatening national capital through import penetration. Of course, labour need not alone be the source of a crisis. Sectors of capital may choose to behave in a manner incompatible with the overall 'accumulation strategy', and so they too will have to be coordinated *via* corporatist structures.

The brief discussion above has sought to pursue a line of argument which suggests that, while labour gains enhanced potential political power under increasing state interventionist strategies, the prospects for utilising this potential to significantly shape political forms in its own interests is limited. That is not to argue that corporatist structures are inevitable, but it does in part suggest why corporatist structures are a 'dominant' form, not a 'compromise' form, despite their initial *raison d'être*. This leaves certain loose ends as to why labour, and indeed certain sectors of capital, do not simply refuse to have anything to do with these prejudicial structures or at least withdraw once their true nature is established. Once we have looked further at the nature of power and corporatist structures, this issue can be more competently confronted.

Towards the development of a theory of contract corporatism

Power and corporatist theory

So far we have argued that corporatist theory needs to treat power on two levels, but also be clearly able to link these two. It is this linkage, that is how power as a political form impinges upon the exercise of power within that particular form, which it was argued was not adequately elaborated in the approaches to bargaining and corporatism discussed in the previous section. Crudely, what is required is a theory that explains why corporatist structures are not neutral but distort the apparent balance of power in such a way that the state prevails over organised interests, and thus over socio-economic interests. Moreover, it is necessary to have a theory of power as a process, not as a relationship, because it pertains to bargaining. It must be emphasised that it is not being proposed that corporatism is a theory of power *per se*, but that a theory of power provides a theoretical framework for corporatism. Such a framework is provided, perhaps unwittingly, by the French sociologist Michel Crozier's approach to power as a process. He argues that:

To understand the basic elements and dynamics of power negotiations, one must focus on the overall organisation serving as their framework. Power then appears no longer merely as a relationship, but as a process inseparable from the organisational process. The terms of exchange result neither from chance nor from some abstract and theoretical balance of power. They are the result of a game whose constraints create compulsory hurdles and opportunities for manipulation for the players, and therefore determine their strategy.

These constraints are:

[...] the formal and informal objectives laid down by the organisation and accepted by the participants, as well as the rules imposed on them or established by them.[30]

These objectives and rules work indirectly by limiting the participant's freedom of action through creating sectors of uncertainty, and control over this uncertainty as it affects the pursuit of organisational goals and other participants' behaviour is where his power ultimately lies. So: 'Each participant in an organisation, in an organised system or even in a society as a whole, wields power over the system he belongs to and over the members of this system, insofar as he occupies a strategically favourable position as regards the problems on which the success of the system depends.' However, and significantly for our consideration, 'his power is limited by his rules of the game, which restrict the use he can make of his advantages'.[31] Moreover, in effect the rules of the game tend 'to demarcate artificial sources of uncertainty, enabling those who control them to negotiate on better terms with players whose favourable strategic situation otherwise puts them in a position of superiority'.[32] So, the state authorities may dominate the bargaining process in effect because they control the key areas of uncertainty and thus the rules are set to their advantage.

The identification of these rules will in effect be the basis of corporatist theories on bargaining so long as they can be welded into testable and explanatory propositions. The rules set 'a framework of a structure of domination'.[33] I would argue that it is important to recognise that these rules may operate at different conceptual levels. There will be 'deep rules' which would underlie any politico-economic structure in capitalist society. Above those, however, may be the rules which relate to the specific context within which corporatist structures exist. Finally, we might conceptualise rules which pertain to particular types of corporatist structures. This last level can lead us to postulate that there can exist a wide range of corporatist structures, a point the literature *en masse* already is advocating. There is, however, a clear logic to this viewpoint because corporatist structures do not exist within one fixed context but a variety, and this will certainly be relevant to temporal and international comparisons of corporatism.

Sorting out the conceptual and theoretical treatments of power will remain problematic.[34] For one thing it requires detailed analysis of both subjective interests and objective interests. However, whatever the difficulties, and indeed whatever the preferences of individual analysts, at least we will be no longer simply looking at the surface level of exchanges with an appearance of compromise, give and take, and a reasonably wide distribution of power.[35] What is required is an examination of wider and more enduring patterns. For as Benson rightly points out, analysing interactions between organisations in close-up reveals 'the entire society simply in terms of transactions and exchanges, of actors and games. By taking a broad view over a longer term, we can see that the games form patterns; that the exchanges operate with institutionally governed resources; that the games are connected, with some taking priorities over others, that there are some limits or boundaries within which the games are played'.[36]

What is central to Crozier's proposals is that, by both talking about rules and arguing that these rules operate to overturn the 'theoretical balance of power' by limiting the range of effective strategies that subordinate interests can pursue, everything is not reduced to ideological assimilation, important though this is. Instead, there is recognition that corporatist structures do not just limit the arena of conflict but also influence the form taken in the resolution of that conflict. This is a necessary area of theoretical development because as we have already argued corporatism arises in response to the requirements of a managed economy and the increased dependence of the state, not to a breakdown in ideological assimilation. In this respect corporatism can be seen as a set of structures which exist not to ensure that the interests of subordinate groupings are wedded to production for profit, to the accumulation process *per se*, but that there is consent to what Jessop terms a particular 'accumulation strategy'[37] (or more realisticaly consent to the form and substance of interventions conducted under a strategy as they impinge directly upon particular actors).

The above provides what can be regarded as a general construction of one important element of corporatist theory, though until there have been established rules that pertain to particular empirical situations it does not of itself provide anything testable. Of course, these rules have to varying degrees been presented in the literature already, but as was postulated there needs to be clarification as to what level they operate at: whether all political structures of domination, all corporatist structures or particular types of corporatist structures.

Following on from the above we need to confront the issue of voluntarism. Most writers on neo-corporatism have emphasised that entering into corporatist arrangements by organised interests is, while not obviously free of constraints and pressures, a voluntary action. Thus, if coercion is absent the problem arises as to why interests do not withdraw given the adverse effects bargaining has upon their interests. Otherwise corporatist structures would not be sustainable for very long; the rules have to remain acceptable. One obvious explanation of acceptance lies in the fact that the rules significantly determine the outcome, but that this only manifests itself at a particular level of analysis. At another level of analysis, however, the picture will be a different one – that of getting the best possible deal under the circumstances. The participants are, in other words, stuck at the operational level of viewing the system.[38] In this sense the rules are accepted because they are regarded as legitimate, that is they are not subject to questioning which is particularly likely where subordinate interests negotiated them in the first place as Crozier suggests. Nevertheless, non-acceptance of the rules remains a possibility, and will take the form of one of two courses of action. One, there could be an attempt to change the rules of the game which would require the realisation of power to negotiate the rules favourably. Such power could be realised from a variety of sources, but the net result would be to weaken corporatism. Two, the organisation could withdraw from the game, that is cease to bargain as an integrated participant and to pursue its interests through other means. Clearly such a withdrawal would incur immediate costs for both the group and the state authorities. The crucial question is whether the interest organisation can find an alternative means of regaining or compensating for the lost concessions so it is at least no worse off. If it cannot, then there is no *prima facie* rationality to its actions. The overall effect of withdrawal will also, of course, depend upon the impact it has upon the authorities. Should the state be unable to pursue an alternative strategy which allows it to overcome the absence of cooperation so that it is no worse off, then it may make further concessions or possibly renegotiate the rules of the game. What is central to the above is the range of alternative strategies, and their effectiveness, open to both state and groups outside the bargain. Corporatist theory should, therefore, seek to explain what structures limit the range and effectiveness of strategies open to groups and/or extend the range and effectiveness of those open to the state.

There is no denying that the issues around which organised interests assess the costs and benefits of withdrawal will be multifarious.[39] A further consideration in this line of thought is that of who within the organisation actually make such assessments, particularly if it is the case, as is suggested in the literature, that the leaderships are enjoying increased autonomy from the constraints imposed upon their actions by the membership.[40] There is a sound basis to believe that logically there is more likely to emerge an increasing divergence between leaders, who are involved in complex negotiations, and members, who are not so involved, as to strategic perceptions than would be the case under straightforward lobbying.[41] This is not to necessarily argue that leaders will adhere to higher threshold costs of withdrawal, but it does raise the question of whose perceptions count in such decisions. The whole issue of power and control within interest associations is one that the development of corporatism in ostensible liberal democracies, where voluntarism rather than coercion must remain a prominent operating principle for ideological reasons,[42] inevitably has to address (see below, p. 177–81). For the moment suffice it to say that the leaderships' perception of the benefits of participation may be more benign than that of the memberships.[43]

Perhaps a far more fruitful, if related, line of inquiry is that of the state raising the cost of withdrawal by making associations more dependent upon it for a wide variety of resources.[44] In this sense the state overcomes to some degree its own dependence upon interest associations (ignoring for the moment the question of member-power) by making the associations dependent upon itself. It is important to note that many of these resources, for example, representational exclusivity and control over aspects of public policy administration, while of value to the associations, do not impinge fundamentally upon the accumulation process, i.e. they are not concessions about basic forms of intervention. Moreover, it will also be valuable to analyse the possible constraints that are placed upon associational activity outside corporatist arrangements. In short, the potential for finding an effective role, even if the deprivation of certain resources is not excessive, outside the corporatist arena could be becoming narrower. Streeck in this regard makes a very telling point about German business associations. He found that associations of small business 'attributed their small membership and the ruinous competition among their organisations to their lack of access to the recognition by the state, and not *vice versa*'.[45] If associations shun access, to follow on therefore from this admittedly limited example, they may be committing themselves to serious organisational difficulties because they are no longer providing anything in political terms that the members cannot provide by themselves, viz non-compliance with certain types of intervention. (This does not dispose of the problem of member 'revolts' which will be addressed shortly.) Significantly, analysis of the limited scope for effective association action outside corporatism not only explains why withdrawal is less desirable, it would similarly explain the limited impact of new or splinter associations.

The above discussion suggests that corporatist theory cannot be solely concerned with the life of associations inside corporatist institutional arrangements, but must consider life on the other side of the divide because withdrawal or emerging 'oppositions' will affect the outcome and stability of corporatist arrangements. This in itself represents a major object of concern for corporatist theorising. We must now, however, turn to an even more central component in the corporatist model and certainly a far more enigmatical one – the state.

The state and corporatist theory

Having outlined how power as a process can be incorporated into corporatist theory centred around the state-groups bargaining process as a framework to explain state domination, we must now turn to theoretical consideration of the state itself. This is doubly problematic because of conceptual difficulties surrounding the state and the contentiousness presently enveloping theoretical treatment of the state. Certainly there is little benefit to be derived from engaging in yet another bibliographic essay so common at this point in discussions. Nor, on the other hand, can one treat the state at such an abstract level so as to leave empirical testing of the theory virtually impossible. Thus far our treatment of the state has been implicitly to regard it as another group; an unitary organisation with fairly readily identifiable interests.

However, before proceeding to move away from this unsatisfactory position it is necessary to ask what functions of the state are pertinent to corporatist structures. Following on from what was discussed earlier about the state forming partnerships with private actors, mediated through interest groups to ensure that the necessary consent was forthcoming to facilitate the successful implementation of public policies (or more accurately the minimising of political constraints[46] upon implementation), it is obvious, and well accepted in corporatist and pluralist literature, that these partnerships are with *producer* groups. Hence corporatist structures relate directly to the *production function* of the state. This hypothesis drawn from empirical observation, nonetheless, reflects the argument of Claus Offe that different state functions are characterised by different sets of decision rules.[47] Offe's categorisations, while useful and indicative, are somewhat rigid (especially the utilisation of 'bureaucratic decision rules'), and hence open to criticism when operationalised. In addition, problems arise because the categories are largely divorced from notions of power. A more satisfactory approach has recently come from Alan Cawson, who suggests that the mode of representation is dependent upon the type (producer, allocator, etc.) and hence target (function and individual) of intervention. Where the targets of intervention are 'interests constituted on the basis of their socio-economic function', as occurs in the sphere of economic management and social policy, 'the intervention has to be purposive-rational, that is, justified in terms of effective results rather than legitimate procedures'.[48] Therefore, it follows that 'for the functional group the membership *takes its interests* from the function, and the power of the functional group in part derives from what are the objectives of state policy. Interventionist policies require the cooperation, if not collaboration, of functional groups, and this fact alone helps to explain some of their power.'[49] Furthermore, this leads to the conclusion that 'for a whole range of state activities concerned with consumption, and with moral and ideological issues, the corporatist mode of representation is inappropriate'.[50]

While not discussing corporatism within the exact same terms as Alan Cawson there is, nevertheless, a sound case for concurring that corporatism relates primarily to the state's production function, though it seems wise to acknowledge that it may indirectly impinge upon its distribution and legitimation functions. This still leaves unresolved, for all that, to what overall purpose does the state perform a production function, that is, what is the overall nature of the state. As they presently stand, Marxist state theories suffer predominantly from two weaknesses: one, they operate at such an abstract level that they cannot explain concrete behaviour,[51] and hence resolve all question at the level of general theory; two, an excessively rigid approach to the identification of class interests. Furthermore, it is now widely accepted, following on from the French structuralists, that the state enjoys relative autonomy, pursuing the general interests of capital over and above its various fractions. The result of this is to treat theoretically the state as representing interests that lie beyond the readily identifiable behaviour of any particular articulated sectional interest.

At the end of the day, the potential for linking current macro-theories of the state to corporatist theory looks severely constrained because of the inherent difficulties of linking abstract and general theory to concrete and specific decisions authoritatively made. It, therefore, seems highly desirable to develop a theory of the state more specifically tailored for corporatist theory, that is one embedded in the state's production function. Thus, in effect, what one would be seeking to construct is a series of hypotheses centred around the following key issues: given the state encompasses certain dominant interests, how will the domination of these interests be realised in the range of authoritative decisions within society (including issues of non-decision making).

Clearly before proceeding to develop such hypotheses it will be necessary to identify in theoretical terms the dominant interest. This, in itself, is not without difficulties, but need not detain us here as it is not central to our development of a framework within which to construct theories of corporatism. The development of hypotheses concerning how specific authoritative decisions reflect the continued dominance of certain interests, however, remains beset by the problem of 'the non-exclusivity of interests'. Unless one adopts the absurd position of the capital logic school and dismisses any pursuit of material interests by the working class as 'commodity fetishism',[52] it has to be accepted that authoritative decisions such as in the fields of education, training, regional policy, youth unemployment and so on do confer benefits on subordinate interests. Moreover, it has to be logically accepted that the degree of benefits gained by subordinates can and does vary relatively. A number of recent Marxist theorists have argued that such gains for the working class are in capital's long term interests (i.e. worth conceding) because they reproduce labour power and improve the quality, reduce in other ways the cost of production and help to legitimise the existing social order,[53] but such arguments rest on a teleology and, therefore, cannot be empirically falsified and as such provide no basis for developing corporatist theory.[54]

So, it is necessary to develop more sophisticated theories in terms of operationalisation and testability. A possible route to constructing an operational theory of the state *en attendent* to corporatist theory is to expand and elaborate upon the state's production function which it previously has been argued is the function directly related to the emergence of corporatism and embed it firmly in decisional analysis. The performance of its production function is an imperative task for the state to carry out in advanced capitalist economies. However, performance of this function cannot be regarded as an analytic end in itself. It is how the various tasks or sub-functions within the production function are performed to create and recreate the necessary preconditions (such as particular wage levels, range and level of skills, improvement in productivity and protection from foreign competition) to ensure the conditions for accumulation that are important. What analysis should seek to achieve is some clearer identification and understanding of these preconditions, such that they can be qualitatively and/or quantitatively described for particular empirical circumstances. Thus we need to transfer attention from discussions of largely constant sub-functions to determining variable 'standards' that state authorities seek to achieve in a particular area of activity. These standards can be regarded as a kind of target, towards which the achievement of unfettered decisions taken by the state authorities will be directed; the standards when set against the conditions it is presumed will pertain if there is no change in the form of intervention in the relevant area indicates a gap, and such a ' "policy gap" may be seen as the framework within which policy problems come to be defined or formulated. This perceived policy gap indicates the extent of the observable policy problem' for the state authorities.[55]

Therefore, what in a very basic form is being suggested is that a series of standards can be identified for the range of sub-functions, which in any particular circumstance the state must achieve, *inter alia*, to ensure continued capital accumulation. However, simply identifying these standards will not of themselves provide an apposite explanation of the state authorities' behaviour. In the first place, the achievement of a particular standard must not undermine the achievement of any other standard: for example, if price controls were highly constrictive then they would deter investment and hence impair the attainment of standards relating to that particular sub-function. There has, therefore, to be recognition in the analysis of the mutual interdependence of the sub-functions, not only in their determination but also their execution. Secondly, the means by which the standards are pursued cannot conflict with other goals the state authorities seek to attain outside the production function or other values they seek to apply: to cite a British illustration, industrial policy has always encompassed instruments that at the end of the day seek to protect the autonomy of private capital at the expense of the effectiveness of intervention, which in part reflects certain values embedded in the state machinery.[56]

Thirdly, and finally, the standards the state wishes to attain and the means it seeks to utilise in pursuing these will inevitably, to varying degrees, conflict with the interests of producer groups and those they represent within society. Given that the state is dependent upon producers for the success of its intervention, to intervene effectively, the state authorities have to reach an accommodation with influential groupings. But while reaching an accommodation may well be achievable, reaching a series of 'accommodations' that is compatible with the effective performance of its production functions will be problematic for the state. Corporatist structures, in line with our earlier arguments, can be said to exist to ensure that there is such a compatibility. In consequence, corporatist structures will not of themselves determine every aspect of public policy; nor, therefore, will corporatism explain the finer detail of policy. Instead, to explain particular decisions within a policy sector[57] may necessitate a wider analysis encompassing the relative power resources amongst producer groupings and the currency of certain ideas.[58] Thus, for example, corporatist structures may lead to an accommodation which checks the average increase in wages to x%, but whether this is achieved through a 'flat-rate' or 'percentage' based policy will probably reflect more the balance of influences within the trade-union movement, views about 'what went wrong last time', and certain 'technical' and administrative considerations. The analysis seeks to use the standards as objective criteria against which to assess political behaviour. But it must be recognised that the achievement of these standards can be realised through a variety of measures; again we are focussing upon what lies below the surface. The importance of these standards analytically will lie in the fact that they prevail and that they conflict with the subjective and objective interests of what are hypothesised to be non-dominant groupings. Where such conditions prevailed there would be a theoretically validated actuality of state domination. From this basis the mobilisation of state power through corporatist structures can then be explained because we have a set of criteria by which to judge realisation of that power in a dominant manner.

Utilising the aforementioned standards as a means of analysing state behaviour remains, nonetheless, ambiguous. In the first place, identification of the standards in particular empirical situations will remain problematic. It is, however, true that such an approach to analysis is beginning to permeate the literature, as a recent essay by Benson vividly illustrates.[59] In any case, much of the analysis of specific areas of state intervention, such as incomes policy and industrial policy, has been conducted against a backcloth of some imperative criteria by which state behaviour is conditioned.[60] The problem is that such a backcloth can tend to lack precision and, therefore, the distinction with liberal analysis remains uncertain, except as regards the conclusions drawn. The difficulty lies in the evident point that in liberal terms a healthy economy is fundamentally approximate to a healthy accumulation process because for, say, a government to get itself re-elected it has to ensure the well-being of a *capitalist* economy. What alternative analysis should seek to do is focus upon how the state in securing the necessary political preconditions for accumulation favours the particular interests of a few drawn from a particular class as against the interests of the many. It is this conflict of objective interests that the employment of standards seeks to expose.

A valuable concept to employ in respect of the utilisation of the standards is that of an 'accumulation strategy'. Indeed, identifying an accumulation strategy can be regarded as a virtual prerequisite for identifying variable standards because it places them in an overall framework by relating a healthy accumulation process to a *set of necessary preconditions* which are not given but depend upon the balance of economic and political forces.[61] Thus another level of analysis is introduced into the corporatist equation. Recourse to 'accumulation strategies' will furthermore help to counterbalance a second difficulty that occurs with the employment of standards as alluded to earlier, namely the interdependence of standards which opens up the possibility that the state authorities will trade between them – making concessions on some and extracting more on others while still ensuring no threat to creating the favourable preconditions. Therefore, a standard will have to be utilised with reference to the other standards insofar as they are tradeable. Fortuitously these are not just theoretical considerations, but represent a calculation that the state authorities will have to make in practice, when bargaining with various interests.

A third problematical aspect of employing the standards is that the premiss of the analysis prescribes to the state the overall role of creating, maintaining or restoring the conditions required for capital accumulation in particular circumstances. Obviously, 'guaranteeing and safeguarding a "healthy" accumulation process'[62] is not a condition that either does or does not occur. This is compounded by the point that analysts widely accept that the state tolerates short-term threats to accumulation but ultimately operates in the long-term interests of capital and accumulation. Given that the 'necessary', 'healthy' or 'adequate' conditions for accumulation remain such an imprecise object of analysis, subject to short-term fluctuations furthermore, it is evident that any standards derived from them will themselves be imprecise – whatever problems result from their interdependency. However, this conclusion ignores a pertinent point made by Offe and Ronge that the state is committed structurally to optimisation. As they argue: 'it would be mistaken to argue that state policies of education and training are designed to provide the necessary manpower for certain industries, since no one, least of all the state bureaucracy, has any reliable information as to what industry will need, what type of skills, at what time, or in what numbers. Such policies are instead designed to provide a *maximum of exchange opportunities* to both labour and capital [...]' They add in relation to interventionist policies that: 'These policies are designed to open new markets, to shield the domestic economy against the intrusion of foreign competitors – briefly to create and maintain the commodity form of value [...]'[63] While such a thesis remains somewhat tentative it does suggest that such standards will tend to take a fairly stable, maximalist form in any particular empirical context. Obviously actually achieving in practice long-term maximisation will prove elusive, but nevertheless the standards will supply a set of criteria against which to draw valid assessments and is not of itself open to tautological reasoning if it takes into account the conflict between the standards and the interests within society. Clearly as it stands, and is likely to remain, such an approach to an analysis will not have the precision that one always desires, but given the complexity of social reality it seeks to explain this is unavoidable.

Not surprisingly, the state has presented serious difficulties in theoretical construction. What hopefully has been achieved is a basis upon which to approach a theoretical treatment of the state within the production function that can be employed to assess decisions made through corporatist structures. Only by understanding the nature of the decisions can we move on to explain and hence understand the significance of corporatist structures. And while one cannot ignore the utility of disaggregated, case-study analysis, a consequence of this approach, because of the interdependency of the standards, is to focus upon 'structures' in the plural. Finally, before leaving the issue of the state it is important to acknowledge that, as far as possible, there has been no attempt to address the debate surrounding macro-theories of the state[64] – instrumentalism, structuralism, form determination and the relational – it being a veritable quagmire in its own right. The approach adopted here would probably be amenable to all of them in some form, if to varying degrees of satisfaction.

Corporatism, groups and implementation

The need to develop corporatist theory so that it can effectively explain why group–state authority bargaining results in decisions compatible with the primary interests of the state, despite its dependence upon the producers the groups represent, has now been put foward and elaborated. Nevertheless, corporatism must logically encompass another dimension. It is necessary to consider groups as organisations with their own power structures. The leaders and representatives who negotiate with the state authorities cannot, as a general rule, command their members to comply with deals bargained on their behalf. Yet if the organisations' negotiators cannot act as an effective intermediary between the state and economic and social actors, then consent to public policies remains just as problematic for the state authorities; it is ultimately the consent of producers, not producer-group leaders, that matters. Related to this perspective of membership compliance is the view taken by many writers that corporatism encompasses a function for interest organisations as structures for implementing public policy – the bargains reached.[65] This integration into the corporatist model of the notion of interest organisations performing a quasi-public role as structures for implementing public policy, without doubt, has a precedent in corporatist ideology. The consequence of incorporating such a component into the model is the need to address theoretically the twin issues of organisational compliance and coverage. It has to be recognised, however, that the integration of interest organisations on a wider scale represents a sophisticated and developed form of corporatism, and that corporatist bargains may be implemented or administered by other agencies or indeed through government departments. As Cawson and Saunders correctly point out the form of legislation under corporatism is 'enabling'[66] and the function of administration can fall to various types of organisations, though not to excessively bureaucratic ones. Whatever the agencies involved, however, gaining consent will be a central problem for the authorities and interest-group leaders. One obvious reason why consent may be forthcoming is that the members regard the bargained decisions as legitimate, being the fruits of hard fought negotiations. As the best possible outcome at the present it has to be lived with, softened possibly by the hope of a brighter future. Nevertheless, it is possible that the bargain, or more likely the subject matter of the bargain (e.g. workers and wage restraint), may be or come to be challenged. One theoretical line followed in this respect has been taken up by Leo Panitch.

His argument is to suggest that rank-and-file dissent will inevitably emerge and corporatist arrangements will tend to break down. However, the propensity for breakdown will vary according to the relationship between group leaders and the membership. Significantly, the breakdown of arrangements 'has led in most cases to a state response of a coercive kind',[67] but this in turn is not sustainable indefinitely because to ensure such an approach is effective requires a level of coercion incompatible with liberal democracy. So the cycle, the search for corporatist arrangements begins anew.[68] Such a cycle may summarise events in several countries over the 1960s and 1970s, but it does not adequately emphasise the imperative nature for the state of ensuring that corporatist arrangements are sustainable. Further, the cycle may be a process of increasing sophistication and may hide other developments leading to enhanced consent.

These trends towards further developments in ensuring rank-and-file compliance have drawn out some of the most significant contributions from corporatist theorising. The most notable of these have sought to counter crude generalisations about increasingly bureaucratic and oligarchic tendencies among interest organisations, recognising the need for a good deal more theoretical subtlety. This reflects a number of phenomena that theory needs the capacity to deal with:

(1) There is the issue of coverage, that is the matter of non-members and the possibility of 'Exit',[69] given that the employment of the 'Voice' is of limited effectiveness in such 'oligarchic' organisations. In short, how is 'voting with the feet' to be prevented and the constituent actors kept under the jurisdiction of the 'bureaucratic' or 'oligarchic' structure.

(2) (Related to the first point) is the issue that, whatever changes they may be undergoing, interest organisations hold on to, and seem likely in logic to hold on to, some significant representative function. The question is, therefore, not one of how the representative function is quashed, but how it is distorted. Simply seeing the membership as the bottom rung of a bureaucratic structure is not a particularly illuminating perspective. (Nor, indeed, does it reflect that modern organisational analysis is increasingly studying organisations in terms of power bargaining rather than those of authority.)[70] The functions that the members perform, which the state wishes to control, are productive functions performed outside representative organisations; for example, the authority of the workplace is the authority of the capitalist firm, not the trade union or employer organisation.

(3) To ensure that the state's performance of the production function is effective is going to require more than absence of rank-and-file

opposition. Passivity is not enough, because so many interventions will require a degree of active collaboration and some form of support or identification with the objectives. People, of course, can be brought to support certain objectives when influence is brought to bear, e.g. manipulation, inducement, persuasion and encouragement without recourse to coercion or force.

Much recent corporatist analysis has indeed been concerned to study the impact upon interest associations and economic actors of the increasing fusion of the 'public' and 'private' domains at the 'micro-level',[71] particularly in respect of devolved implementation of public policies. And from what was said in the previous sub-section, as well as this one, such considerations must play a central part in the overall corporatist model. However, fusion of private actors and public functions within the context of interest associations cannot *prima facie* be regarded as exclusively corporatist because such development can readily fit into pluralist notions of power dispersal. So, just as at the 'policy-making level', also at the 'policy implementation/delivery levels' the primary concern is with the power relationships, not the institutional relationships. What is required is a way of explaining how the leadership of interest organisations, probably in conjunction with the state, can ensure consent to the decisions bargained, while taking into account the fact that the legitimacy of their leadership, and of the state, is not unlimited. Like the relation between state and association, the relation between association and member is not for ideological and practical reasons very likely to be a coercive one. Rather it must rely, at least in the main, on other forms of power. Moreover, these forms of power may well not only explain the compliance side, they could also provide explanations about the other crucial aspect, jurisdiction or coverage. In effect, what is being sought are propositions concerning the means utilised to increase the dependence of economic actors upon producer associations and/or the state such that the balance of power, originally posited as the genesis of corporatist structures, will be overturned. Claus Offe has provided a valuable approach centred around political status to illustrate how interest associations can become more dependent upon the state and concomitantly less dependent upon their members. Apart from providing a framework within which to analyse that particular processual phenomenon, this conceptual remit could be transferred down a level to encompass relations between associations and members.

Offe suggests that the attribution of public status to interest organisations means that the group 'ceases to be exclusively determined in its actions and accomplishments by the interests, ideologies, need-perceptions and so forth of its members [...] '[72] The four 'dimensions' of public status identified by Offe are for him indicative of the extent of corporatism. Offe's four 'dimensions' of corporatism relate to: (a) the extent to which the resources of an interest organisation are supplied by the state – resource status; (b) the extent to which the resources of an interest organisation is defined by political decision – representation status; (c) the extent to which internal relations between rank-and-file members of executive members of the organisation are regulated – organisation status; (d) the extent to which interest organisations are licensed, recognised, and invited to assume, together with a specified set of other participants, a role in legislation, the judicial system, policy planning, and implementation, or even granted the right of self-regulation – procedural status.[73] The more extensive these dimensions are, the greater the degree of corporatisation. But it is added that these attributions may assume a positive or negative character, e.g. resources taken away or its representational status reduced. The significance of such attribution of status is that 'Positive political status allows an organisation to enjoy partial immunity from its members as well as from other organisations.'[74]

There is little doubt that Offe's proposals are clearly moving in the direction of traditional notions of licenced corporatism where producer organisations become quasi-public agencies of the state. But there is also a distinct emphasis on the positive benefits the state can confer upon associations necessary for the neo-corporatist model where voluntarism is seen as an essential element. So if one moves away from the Germanic legalism of Offe's notions[75] there is much to be gleaned from the idea of making associations (or producers) partially dependent upon the state (or state and associations) for their capacity to perform certain types and ranges of functions: if they are so dependent then this gives the state (or association) a degree of influence over *how* these functions are performed.

Thus it is being suggested that the state, possibly *via* interest associations, can overcome its initial dependence upon economic actors by introducing devices to make the actors in turn dependent upon the state itself. For example, resources and other benefits could be directed towards the supportive, the range of representation biased towards the conformist and self-regulation placed with the trusty. Obviously such a process may be gradual, but such developments need not be associated with a cynical abuse of power. Instead, such a use of power may have a structural logic to it; the firm that 'does its bit' on training may be the most rational target for subsidies to support increased capital investment because it has the skilled workforce.

Nonetheless, one should be a bit wary of labelling all attributions of public status or similar attributions of quasi-public functions as corporatist. Such attribution should clearly be linked to other corporatist structures and functions. The state may sanction public status to interest organisations or it may have to bow to powerful groups demanding the right to regulate themselves in their own interests, thereby freeing themselves from the constraints generated from the primary interests of the state. In short, public status, notably rights of self-regulation, may reflect power structures other than those compatible with corporatism; such attributions should be explainable in terms of facilitating the performance of state intervention in production while upholding the fundamental interests the state encompasses.

Finally in this sub-section it is necessary to address the issue of whether it is essential that implementation of policies be conducted through interest associations, or whether corporatism can be said to exist when more familiar agencies are involved in administering policies. In theory at least it can be regarded as perfectly feasible for 'corporatist bargains' to be applied by more familiar state agencies. The crucial issue is that the bargains are applied intact, not so much how they are applied. That apart, it is logical to argue that an ideal or highly developed form of corporatism would entail interest associations assuming a quasi-public role in the implementation of corporatist decisions. For one thing, such a state of affairs would more closely approximate with our General Model of Corporatism. Further there are practical advantages for the state in granting such a function to producer organisations: their participation should enhance the legitimacy of state intervention; they provide the state with expertise in the productive process to draw on; and they provide a potentially more responsive and efficient structure for administering intervention. Of course, there is another side – the failure of compliance and the inadequacy of coverage threatening state domination. In such cases, because of either insufficient development or the breakdown of such structures, the state will have to rely on its own agencies; the administration of corporatist bargains will fall to more familiar organisations drawing on more traditional sources of authority. To reiterate the point, though, such a breakdown is no way tantamount to the inappropriateness of the corporatist model. In any case, it has to be recognised that in the case of large private companies they may well deal directly with the state, leaving a peripheral role to the appropriate representative association.

Overall, given that the development of neo-corporatism is not part of a grand strategy, but a series of more pragmatic, *ad hoc* strategic responses to specific contingent conditions, subject to reversal moveover,[76] a coherent overall institutional pattern will probably prove difficult to detect, though one may emerge with the passage of time. In the interim, a process that is probably of significance is the increasing appearance of hybrid arrangements, between pure 'state' or 'association' implementation structures, with many public interventionist agencies recruiting representatives from associations on to their managing boards. This might well be regarded as one step along the path to a more developed form of corporatism.

Conclusion

Theories are only more or less useful. The utility of corporatist theory must remain an open question for some time. But the potential is there. In 1983, Wyn Grant surveying the state of play felt that corporatism was in danger of being beaten up by 'the intellectual skinheads of political science' (sic), with the result that 'the corporatist project could be abandoned before corporatist theory has been fully developed or before it has been rigorously empirically tested': he further added that the 'corporatist model [may] only be fit to be tested to destruction'.[77] Grant himself may have been a shade apologetic. Corporatist theory need not be regarded as an interesting end in itself. Hopefully the present discussion has illuminated the potential of corporatism to free political analysis from the unacceptable premises and simplicities of contemporary pluralism, while not falling into the excessive abstraction and teleologies of Marxist functionalism. In short, corporatism is just as much a response to failings elsewhere as a creature of self-generation.

But corporatism cannot be regarded as meritorious on these grounds alone. It needs to be distinctive, testable and coherent. It was to move in such a direction that the discussion in this part of the book was directed. To that end there was developed a general model or organising framework of neo-corporatism. This we can term *contract corporatism* to emphasise both the centrality of bargaining and the voluntary nature of such structures. The model of contract corporatism is as on pages 184 and 185.

The model of contract corporatism represents an attempt to pull together under the rubric of the General Model of Corporatism the various components that the neo-corporatist literature has identified and to set them out in a logical manner. In addition, the theoretical issues raised by these components, given that corporatism cannot remain a static descriptive model, were aired. It is important to recognise that the fruits of the exercise undertaken in this and the previous chapter have drawn at various points extensively upon the ideas of many neo-corporatist writers. Although their contributions were possibly not acknowledged as extensively as might have been wished, and that they came in for criticism, this should not detract from the fact that in various ways their theoretical work was a prerequisite of the first order in developing the model. And this reflects the overall objective of the exercise: to try to mould reasonably disparate approaches into a general, but coherent, framework. This is not in any sense to suggest we are still at square one, because much of the theoretical work already undertaken is readily encompassed within the framework. Much of the detail has already been sketched in. What is, however, crucial is that the theoretical developments are linked satisfactorily – at least collectively, if not by individual writers – to other related political and economic configurations that are themselves the object of theoretically informed understanding. It is these linkages, I would suggest more than anything else, that the neo-corporatist writers have failed to adequately elaborate.

Table 10.1 *Model of contract corporatism*

	Components		Theoretical requirements
(1)	State domination under advanced capitalism	→	Development of macro-theories concerning nature of state under capitalism.
(2)	Need for state to effectively perform production function to ensure adequate accumulation process, but performance of production function increases dependency upon socio-economic actors and threatens successful performance of function.	→	Development of general theories of nature of production function under advanced capitalism, especially problematic nature.
(3)	State attempts to establish structures to overturn the dependency 'imbalance' of dependency and establishes corporatist structures where socio-economic actors, usually mediated through representative associations, bargain over authoritative interventions.	→	Identification of various preconditions or 'standards' state must set under a general accumulation strategy to ensure accumulation process. Further identification of how applying these standards conflicts with subjective and objective interests of subordinate groupings.
(4)	Embedded in corporatist political structures are rules which both limit the range of bargaining and distort the process of bargaining in favour of the dominant state. These rules can analytically be viewed as operating at three levels: Those which, (a) apply to all political forms under capitalism (b) apply to all corporatist structures (c) apply only to specific types of corporatist structures.	→	Development of propositions which explain how rules ensure standards are applied (acknowledging interdependency of standards) in conflict to interests of subordinates and development of more specific propositions in respect of particular types of corporatist structures for comparison over time and across states.

(5) Due to possible limits of ideological domination, conflict of interests can threaten operation and existence of corporatist structures if leadership of associations withdraw.

→ Development of propositions which explain the limitations upon the strategy of withdrawal from corporatist structures by associational leaderships, including explanations of how state raises cost of withdrawal by increasing dependence upon itself.

(6) Due to possible limits of ideological domination, socio-economic actors may threaten corporatist interventions, despite associational leaders compliance, through withdrawal, revolt or non-compliance.

→ Development of propositions which explain how state increases dependency of socio-economic actors, possibly *via* representative associations, upon itself to ensure compliance to interventions pursued by it.

(7) In most developed form interest associations will assume role of structures for implementing policies under production function.

→ Development of propositions which explain how interest associations increase dependency of members upon organisation to ensure compliance to decision agreed by leadership

and

development of propositions to explain how associations ensure the membership coverage is adequate to act as an effective implementing structure.

Part V

Retrospect and prospect

11

Conclusion: retrospect and prospect

The aim of this book has been to clarify the concept of corporatism and to extrapolate three types of the concept which can be set out in reasonably precise and coherent models. Writing a decade after the appearance of Philippe Schmitter's trail-setting essay 'Still the Century of Corporatism?', it is clear that the concept is of fundamental importance to the analysis of advanced capitalist democracies. Despite the fact that not everybody has welcomed corporatism's arrival with dancing in the streets, no one can now dismiss corporatism as a short-term visitor. It has taken up permanent residence. Probably a major reason for the preponderance of corporatist-based literature has been that the concept has triggered off widespread interest in a range of issues relating to the role of the state and interest associations in advanced capitalist societies which conventional analysis either underplayed or simply ignored. Therein lies, to return afresh to the theme raised in the introductory chapter, the fundamental *problématique* of corporatism: the concept has released a flood of objects of study, seeping through at different levels into different domains. The concent of corporatism as it at present stands, far from possessing a firm theoretical base, evokes the image of a tangle of seemingly endless threads. My aim in this study has been to cut through these threads, and to delimit the boundaries of the subject – or at least to distinguish between central and peripheral issues.

Without doubt this delimitation of corporatism has entailed more than just tidying up a few loose ends. Many leading analysts involved in studying corporatism today do not work with a conceptual remit of a dominant state. Indeed, it is fair to say that a number of contemporary writers have moved away from the dominant state position. Philippe Schmitter is one writer who now posits corporatism outside such a perspective; rather neo-corporatism entails 'class compromise' though not necessarily a balance of class forces.[1] The emergence of neo-corporatist arrangements is not explained by the 'macro-functional imperatives of

189

capitalist reproduction', while 'the micro-behavioural preferences of civil servants' does not explain its significance. Instead the answer lies at 'the meso-level', i.e. in the relationship between the interests of class/sectional organisations and the interests of the state as an institution.[2] Corporatism is seen, therefore, not as a grand political design but as a 'policy instrument', an arrangement of 'mutual convenience between representatives of interest associations and representatives of state authority'. Of benefit to interest associations is the backing of state authority to prevent 'free-riding' and 'free-booting' by rendering 'member contributions and compliances compulsory', thus giving greater influence over public policy 'to ensure stable or expanding rewards under the existing order'. The state benefits, conversely, from obtaining our old friends 'necessary information' and 'consent'.[3]

Central to the working of corporatist arrangements is the notion of 'Private Interest Government', that is the arrangement whereby the state delegates public regulatory authority, to interest associations. Such arrangements base their legitimacy on the claim that self-regulation is conducted in the public interest. The associations are encouraged to espouse the public interest under threat of something worse – usually direct regulation. How serious a threat this will prove to be is another matter for Schmitter opines: 'The state must be weak enough to recognise that the cost of authoritively implementing a given policy will exceed its likely benefits [. . .]'.[4] Neither state control nor private government, but a symmetery, is now the key to neo-corporatist arrangements, with the essential factor being self-discipline by associations over compromise 'pacts' whereby benefits accrue to state, associational leaders and their members. Through an associative-corporative order short-term advantages are not pushed to their full advantage; instead trust is built up, mutual recognition of status and entitlements is pursued, and stability and certainty gained. Rather than mutual interdependence leading to mutual disruption, a mutual 'satisficing' order is achieved. Thus in an overloaded system the fact is recognised that it may be a matter of 'sink together, or swim together'.[5]

In some respects the associative-corporative model is close to contemporary pluralist ones that seek to confront so-called overloaded governmental systems, where widespread non-compliance threatens the interests of all because the system as a whole greatly 'under-achieves'. Pluralists suggest that the group process becomes more highly institutionalised as the participants acknowledge their increased interdependency and accept a framework of rules, norms of behaviour, that sacrifice pursuit of short-term interests for a more stable long-term environment.[6] There are, however, important differences, if not absolutely, at least in terms of emphasis. Firstly, the structure of associations under corporatism is regarded as more ordered and far more explicitly shaped by the state; the structures and functions of associations have far less to do with spontaneity. Secondly, the associative-corporatist model more explicitly emphasises cleavages between leaders and members of associations. Thirdly, and distinctively it is argued that interest organisations are not just passive recipients of preferences but, through interaction with their societal constituencies, help to shape them; that is the collective interest depends in part upon the way it is organised.[7] Finally, a key difference is the delegation of public authority to associations. Such delegation is granted to guarantee the compliance of the members to public regulations and to ensure these regulations are applied in a public regarding manner.[8]

These dimensions listed above, particularly the latter one, quite clearly approximate to our own conceptualisations and models of corporatism. But obviously excluded from the conceptual remit, although probably greater emphasis is placed upon the influence of the state than is the case under pluralist models, is the notion of a dominant state. Schmitter notes that neo-corporatist arrangements are imbedded in the institutional interests of relatively autonomous states.[9] Compromise, however, is the product of such arrangements. Colin Crouch, likewise, has now sought to present 'bargained corporatism' as a system where association leaders regulate the members in accord with the general principles negotiated between the association and the public authorities. The motivation for associations is again the avoidance of direct regulation, while compromise rather than domination is the key.[10]

This emphasis upon interest associations disciplining members in accordance with public goals and being afforded some form of public authority to do so has now become a central focus of neo-corporatist study. But the absence of a dominant state within such arrangements poses a question as to whether we are dealing with a form of corporatism or not. In terms of corporatist ideology and authoritarian practice of corporatism the interests imbedded within the state were seen to be predominant. Further, in developing our own theoretical framework of neo-corporatism, the model of contract corporatism, a dominant state was held to be an integral component. This embraces what has been argued to be a fundamental nostrum of corporatism, namely that the state encompasses interests that extend beyond its aggregated and disaggregated interests for institutional survival and that it establishes and maintains a particular socio-economic order over and above popular and particular interests. Evidently, non-state producer associations have themselves an integral role to play in the exercise of dominance by the state, but corporatism, 'neo' or otherwise, cannot rest exclusively on associational discipline, even if it is public regarding. The argument against the case for so including this limited phenomenon is that central to corporatism was the notion of state dominance over producers achieved through producer associations, not a *compromise* exchange because of limited organisational capacity of the state to effectively implement regulations and interest associations to effectively mobilise members to influence public policy. Instead, the term *private interest government* is preferable, reflecting *inter alia* the more limited nature of the phenomenon. It has nevertheless to be recognised that private interest government could well be a part of corporatist arrangements as argued in Chapter 10. Schmitter, however, presents private interest government as imbedded in a context of 'mutual deterrence' among the parties where, for collective self-interest with a more symmetrical distribution of rewards, mediated through mutual recognitions of status and entitlements, there is generated consent and hence social peace.[11] The implication is one of shared benefits, though this does not mean we are back to the pluralist model for the four reasons listed above.

The lengthy discussion of Schmitter's more recent theoretical deliberations illustrate vividly a wider point, and one very much at the heart of this present work, namely that corporatism be conceptually treated as a *Gestalt*. The emphasis in our discussion has been to treat corporatism as a melody, not a collection of individual notes. Therefore, when individual components of the corporatist model were held to accord with a particular empirical example it was argued that this of itself did not represent evidence of corporatism. Nor indeed is it necessarily very helpful to label such phenomena 'corporatist'. So, for example, it is argued that evidence of participation in, or acquisition of, the exercise of public authority by interest associations should not *per se* be regarded as corporatism. In this sense then, the approach to corporatism has been essentially political in emphasis, rather than legal-institutional, though it by no means excludes the legal-institutional angle from consideration.

One major consequence, noted in the first chapter, of conceptualising corporatism as a totality, emphasising the interrelatedness of the components, has been to delimit corporatism conceptually, and hence in applicability, to a much narrower arena. Some of the usages and applications so excluded were so loose as to be no great loss and carried no great weight in the field of study anyway. Other analytic approaches and studies, however, are far too important and insightful to be simply brushed aside. For example, apart from the approaches of major contemporary theorists like Philippe Schmitter and his associates, our present conceptualisations would challenge the definitional credentials of 'corporatist arrangements' set out by the Corporatism and Accountability Panel of the British Economic and Social Research Council which looks very like an approximation to contemporary pluralism.[12] In particular, many theorists of corporatism have, for normative and other reasons, conceptualised the state in a non-dominant form. (Indeed, it is not unfair to say that, with the exception of the works of Bob Jessop and Alan Cawson, corporatist conceptualisations of the state have been somewhat wanting up to this point.)

Ignoring for the moment the preferences and arguments presented herein for a dominant state, it is necessary to acknowledge the important similarities between our own framework of contract corporatism and certain other forms of neo-corporatism. Many of these forms are more than just variants of pluralism with their highlighting of privileged access enjoyed by certain associations and the regulation of the membership in line with public policy objectives by the representative organisations. Instead of a dominant state we have a coalition of the state and privileged associations negotiating authoritative decisions, with these associations acting as intermediaries by applying the decisions on the membership. And further if we posit a degree of consensus between the state and privileged associations (i.e. it is more advantageous to make capitalism work in a particular manner that guarantees certain and probably increasing benefits, than to have a self-defeating free-for-all) and that membership preferences are only partially reflected in decisions agreed and applied, then we are significantly close to our own conceptualisations of corporatism. How close in practice will depend upon a number of factors centered around the interests of the various participants and how far they are realised in authoritative allocations. In effect, what we are discussing is a relatively weak version of contract corporatism, where the state is not dominant and so has to build up a coalition of support from key associations and make genuine concessions on its own interests. Depending upon the degree of weakness the theoretical framework of contract corporatism should, either in an extrapolated manner or used in conjunction with other models, provide a valuable analytic model. However, because such constructs and related empirical cases will not entail a dominant state, they will not be in conformity with our General Model of Corporatism and as such cannot be regarded as a pure variety, but a hybrid of corporatism. This is not to diminish the potential utility of mixed or hybrid models, but it is intended to ensure that corporatism as a concept maintains its historical integrity. Obviously when models are applied to empirical conditions they are not always going to provide a perfect match by any standards, and it evident that many contemporary analysts working within the wider corporatist *milieu* do not deem the state in advanced capitalist economies to be dominant. It seems, therefore, undesirable, not to say impractical, to render neo-corporatism the exclusive property of those of a marxist or radical persuasion. My dispute here is not with attempts to adapt models for reasons of empirical finding or normative preference, but I am proposing that corporatism be discussed by continual reference to some relatively precise base. This is, after all, what happened to some degree at least with the revisions of pluralism in the 1960s and 1970s. Such an outlook is not just an act of gregariousness. It reflects a fundamental notion embedded within the concept of corporatism that appears to be of growing empirical importance in a range of industrialised polities: the employment by the state of associations of producers as a structure for gaining some degree of formalised control over individual producers. Such a state of affairs from a variety a normative perspectives was hardly surprising given the extensive intervention of the state in managed market economies and the resultant development of organised interests. But it posed a problem for political and social analysis. The paradigms and analytic frameworks that encompassed organised interests as more than just private, voluntary and representative associations, but also afforded them some public, compulsory and regulatory aspects, were seriously underdeveloped.

Of course we saw in Part II that corporatist economic and social theorists very much emphasised these latter aspects. To them trades or professions were natural communities of civil society, and as such partook of a public character. Hegel put the point simply: 'As the family was the first, so the Corporation is the second ethical root of the state, the one planted in civil society.'[13] So the Corporation was integrally related to the state providing an institution of protection for the atomistic individuals of society and a means for 'public surveillance' over economic and welfare regulations.[14] It was this idea that was central to the theorists – a means to the public authority overseeing the economic and social order that had a moral basis and hence was harmonious. While the intermediary Corporation was to have a quasi-public status and be subordinate to the authority of the state as a higher moral entity, thereby empowering the state to determine the general socio-economic order, respect for the natural authority of the intermediaries would protect their autonomy and avoid étatisme. The corporatist order rested upon a mutual respect between the state and intermediary for each other's authority to avoid the necessity of large-scale state interference to maintain its authority and to prevent 'illegitimate' incursions by the state.

When, however, corporatist ideology came to be applied in a number of authoritarian regimes in the period between the two world wars there was no such mutual respect; the state with varying degrees of commitment severely curtailed the autonomy of the licenced intermediary associations. It was unlikely – as a few theorists predicted – that the intermediaries given half a chance would have displayed the commensurate respect either. However, afforded little or no opportunity to test this hypothesis, the intermediaries and most producers saw an order imposed upon them that reflected not a higher moral purpose, but more basic private purposes of certain dominant groupings. The corporatist system was highly *étatiste*, while the state overran non-conformity with a generous recourse to sanctions which threatened liberty and livelihood. Corporatist ideology was only selectively applied, and to some degree was re-written to reflect the more imposing role the state had assumed. Nonetheless, pure corporatist ideology often found itself as a cynically employed instrument of legitimation.

Nor did the two examples we studied in detail prove to be the only cases. In Europe itself during the same era a similar system emerged in Spain, and one can detect a corporatist pattern emerging in Austria under Dollfuss,[15] and in Vichy France.[16] Further, authoritarian corporatism, if in a somewhat disjointed manner, manifested itself in a number of Latin American countries after 1945. That corporatism should take an overtly authoritarian form, or at least be adapted by authoritarian rulers, is not surprising in the light of what was revealed in our examination of corporatist thought. In the body of thought there was a continual emphasis upon a social order welded together by a deeply embedded and widespread morality encompassing state and civil society, rendering state and society at one, bonded in a single non-hedonistic purpose. As Gaeton Pirou and other sceptically suggested, without such a moral transformation of society the corporatist edifice would collapse either into chaos or rampant authoritarianism.

Outside Iberia, European corporatism at first sight appeared to collapse and die with the military defeat of the authoritarian axis powers which had sustained it, although some observers were not so certain that it had vanished completely without trace. But since the 1970s corporatism – admittedly reincarnated in a new form set within obstensible liberal democracies – returned with a vengeance. It is hard to find an advanced capitalist society that has failed to show such trends at least to some observers.[17] Indeed, many of these observers traced such developments well back beyond the 1970s. Since the 'rediscovery of corporatism' a vast amount of knowledge and understanding has been reaped; equally, however, an extensive amount of confusion continues to rein. Corporatism has appeared in a veritable plethora of forms and models. In addition, the emergence of corporatist analysis generated a great deal of conflict within the social science community. Corporatism challenged the assumptions and conclusions of pluralism, and raised fundamental questions about the democratic credentials of the group system. Much of the conflict was no more than a tussle among straw men. There was fortuitously, in addition, a more substantial debate. Probably the most significant topic in the contest was the state. Conventional analysis had treated the state in liberal democracies as residual, a product of democratic rule not an instrument of class rule. The state was regarded as part of the wider democratic-pluralist society, and not as an autonomous entity distorting liberal pluralism below the surface. However, even after the passage of not inconsiderable time since the resurrection of the state in political analysis, it remains a problematic concept to employ: state 'theory' has been either too abstract or riddled with self-fulfilling premises to provide a basis for solid understanding. In consequence 'the state' is mentioned a great deal more, but it seldom effectively holds the centre of analysis. This is true of corporatist analysis. Having thrown the state into the spotlight, the act is taking a long time to get together. Indeed, it is difficult to see, given that the corporatist model has raised the issues of the state shaping interests, granting privileged access and overseeing producers, how the act can work without a substantial theory of the state – unless the performance is to be exclusively descriptive-institutional. Without a theory of the state the behaviour of what is seen as a crucial political actor will remain open to speculation rather than effective analysis. How, for example, a lengthy discussion of the compatibility between democratic norms and neo-corporatist practice[18] can be seriously engaged in, without certain propositions concerning the role of the state under corporatism being granted full consideration, is difficult to discern.

Thus, the development of state theory is now more than ever an imperative factor in the future of corporatist analysis, whether one is operating with pure (ie dominant state) corporatism or some hybrid form. Theoretical development concerning the role of the state, it must be stressed, has to go hand in hand with the accumulation of the relevant empirical material. Theorising cannot continue endlessly in a vacuum, just as empirical evidence does not speak for itself. Until such time as theories of the state which are satisfactorily operational have been developed our understanding of corporatism in advanced capitalist societies will remain limited.

Our discussion of corporatism has been conceptual in nature. A good deal of the existing literature on neo-corporatism, however, has contained extensive applications of the concept to empirical data. Much of the literature has readily and unambiguously identified the existence or absence of corporatist 'traits' in a wide array of contexts. Such sightings of corporatism have not, it must be added, been the random reports of individuals with some esoteric notion of what corporatism actually is. Indeed, there has been a notable degree of agreement as to the whereabouts of corporatism. There is, however, in the light of foregoing discussion doubts about such accreditations. Perhaps the most manifest sign of this propensity to identify corporatism has been the ranking of polities according to the degree of 'corporatisation'. Such a ranking puts Austria at the head of the corporatist league table; then comes the Netherlands and the Scandinavian countries. The larger industrialised polities fall in the middle and lower rankings.[19] The question, therefore, arises as to what such differences in ranking signify. But before we move into discussions of distinctive national variables, we need to address the bases of the ranking. In the case of Schmitter's and Lehmbruch's assessments, their focus is upon the degree of organisational centralisation and associational monopoly of socio-economic interests.[20] Their approach towards corporatism – an approach adhered to by other writers[21] – is to focus upon two variables that might be regarded as central to state–interest intermediation, namely, control and coverage. Corporatism is thus strongly identified with how 'organised' the group system is. In this respect it is hardly surprising that it is the smaller nations which display the corporatist traits.

There is no doubt that these polities do display markedly more formalised and institutionalised relations between state and organised interests than the larger nations. It is the stable basis of the relationship between state and interests, not the fluidity associated with American pluralism,[22] that is the central aspect of attention. Such institutionalised stability is well reflected in the case of Norway where there is a vast array of governmental committees, mostly permanent ones, of which approximately 40% afford representation to outside interests. However, as Olsen points out such committees remain largely concerned with specific, limited issues, and not with wider economic matters which organised interests are reluctant to get involved in.[23] Olsen adds that there is more extensive participation 'in structural decisions establishing general rules for future choices than in one-slot decisions'.[24] Further, it is noted that organisational coverage is high, but based upon small organisation sets, and that organisations use specialised, not general, channels for contacting government.[25] The picture presented is certainly one of stability, though stability is just as likely to be a cause of, as an effect of, the system, with the common feature being one of discreet specialised arenas for interest participation where issues are dealt with in a fairly routinised, regularised manner. These specialised arenas seem to be cut off from each other and wider political and policy considerations.[26] As Kvavik argues: 'fragmentation of both groups and the potential arenas for the formulation of policy is low [...] Fragmentation is orderly and occurs along well-defined functional lines.'[27]

Sweden presents a similar picture to Norway. Organised interests, which are strongly centralised and enjoy very high membership levels, are well represented on government commissions involved in formulating policy. They additionally, under the 'remiss' system, have the opportunity to comment on commission proposals. The more important groups also can benefit from well-established procedures of informal contacts with government.[28] Interestingly, Ruin points out that such a well-established system of incorporating organised interests led to dissatisfaction amongst those excluded, that is the grass-roots, in the 1970s when demands for participation increased. The government response was to extend participation to 'discontented' sections of the community on to policy commissions and to afford the grass-roots a role in the implementation of policy by granting them places on public agencies.[29] Such extensions of participation were clearly an attempt to pacify, but they have also produced problems in that the policy process has become pedantic and highly prone to fudge over disagreements.

The highly formalised integration of outside interest into the public policy process found in Sweden and Norway is also a common trait of the other Scandinavian countries. Denmark has a well-established system of committees, commissions, boards and so on, dating back to the 1930s, upon which private and local or semi-autonomous state interests often have representation. The bulk of such representation – some 80% in fact – is taken up by producer interests. Further, given the vast range of committees, high specialisation, as elsewhere, appears to be a feature of the committee structure. But it is worth noting that Johansen and Kristensen do not regard the Danish system as overtly centralised or monopolistic.[30] Additionally, it is worth noting that, while the Danish system is highly organised, it is not unified: there are 'great variations in the intensity and scope of the interplay between interest groups and public bureaucracy. These variations can be seen across types of interest groups, organizational resources and structures, and political issue areas.'[31] Somewhat differently, Helander's study of the Finnish committee system reveals that along with the extension and increasing permanence of committees there has been a notable degree of concentration in interest representation and within the representative organisations themselves. Unlike certain others of the Scandinavian systems, there has been the arrival of new peak labour and industry associations playing a prominent role in the Finnish polity.[32]

So we can see that while there is evidently a Scandinavian pattern of an array of committees, largely permanent and formalised in character, which afford organised interests a direct role in authoritative decision making and administering policy decisions, there are significant variations in the structure of such systems of intermediation.[33] Indeed, if we cast the net wider to include non-Scandinavian polities such as Holland – a suggested example of corporatism – it is possible to detect wide variations in modes of operation – according to departmental, and, indeed, divisional 'styles' – within the national system. The main feature of the Dutch system in fact appears to be one of extreme sectorisation such that there is no effective coordination of government activity.[34] (The Dutch machinery also differs from other examples of 'corporatism' in that Holland has an example of the archetypal corporatist national council of economic and social interests, the Social and Economic Council. The Council, which was established in 1950, consists of fifteen members each from employers, trade unions and independents nominated by the Cabinet – usually university professors – and has the right to be consulted on all social and economic legislation and policies, as well as that of offering unsolicited advice. The Council is highly influential, its unanimous recommendations generally being accepted in full by government.)[35] Yet despite variations in format, Norway, Sweden, Denmark, Finland, Holland and Austria[36] with their highly institutionalised system of integrating interest associations into authoritative decision making processes, have clearly been held up as examples of neo-corporatism.[37] We would, however, question whether such arrangements can so readily be labelled corporatist. In Part IV the argument was put forward that to discuss corporatism in institutional terms is ultimately unsatisfactory, never allowing for a clear distinction between itself and pluralism to be drawn. The question that remains from the empirical studies is simple, but fundamental: are these countries not just examples of institutionally developed forms of pluralism? As the scourge of Schmitter, Grant Jordan, validly argues there is nothing *per se* in policy sectorisation, group integration and consultation which means accepting the need to abandon the pluralist approach to analysis.[38]

The issues that need to be addressed concern influence over political decisions. From the literature just cited it is difficult at all to see what impact such institutionalisation has upon the relative influence of state and societal interests *vis à vis* less structured systems of interest representation. Indeed, the Scandinavian literature reads rather closely to pluralist analyses of Britain, except the former has more facts and figures. There is no serious consideration of how the agenda of such committees are structured, how decisions are taken, what the conflicts of interests are, what are the opportunities for mobilising resources and how participation may shape perceptions. Instead, there seems to be a gut reaction against the rather cosy, consensual atmosphere of such committees which suggests that something is not quite right. But this does not clinch any argument – the consensus may be genuine or it may be false.

In short the literature does not pick up on the questions set out in our model of Contract Corporatism, and, without a consideration of such questions, whether any of these countries are corporatist or not remains inadequately tested. In fact, whether less highly institutionalised systems might not provide better examples of corporatism remains uncertain.[39] One suggested feature of significance that pertains to these designated corporatist systems is that the consensuses they generate ensure greater politico-economic stability: 'there is a strong positive relationship between a societal corporatist mode of interest intermediation and relative governability'.[40] Ignoring the application of the term 'corporatism', this itself remains open to doubt; quite possibly effective government with high growth and so forth produces the kind of consensual attitudes that allow for stable, routinised relations between state and organised interests (or maybe for a complex process of interaction).

Quite clearly the gap between the promise and fulfilment of neo-corporatism is still marked. A large amount of work developing and refining neo-corporatist theory remains to be completed before the supply of satisfactory answers begin to equate with the significant questions the corporatist challenge has posed. What the above suggests is that in refining and applying models of corporatism one would be advised not only to act with caution concerning current claims and assessments about the existence of corporatism, but also to retain an open mind as to its likely incidence. The current literature is without doubt interesting and indicative, but it is nowhere near to conclusive. Thus wariness about Wyn Grant's skinheads should be balanced by a measure of suspicion for entrepreneurial barrow-boys selling corporatism as a panacea for contemporary political analysis.

Of course, the analytic importance of corporatism does not just depend upon further refinement of models, it is also contingent upon what happens in the actual practice of state authorities in managing the economies of Western capitalist countries. The 1980s have seen a general tendency for states to withdraw from the economy and to rely on the market, sustained by the appropriate fiscal and monetary policies, to achieve macro-economic goals. In part, this move towards liberalisation has proved illusory, governments have withdrawn in certain types of activity only to extend into others. To some observers this withdrawing by the state reflects *inter alia* growing dissatisfaction with the 'corporatism' of the 1960s and 1970s. Those of liberal leanings appear to welcome the end of behind-the-scenes deals and a move away from 'fascism with a human face', and particularly rejoice that the political status of trade union leaders has been cut down to size. But while some of the more prominent and public incidents of corporatism – for example national tripartite negotiations – may have declined, there is no reason to believe *prima facie* that the new political economy entails a down-grading of corporatist arrangements. It may well be that just as the role of the state is changing rather than declining, so are corporatist arrangements altering in incidence and form rather than diminishing. Indeed, many of the areas which are increasingly subject to state intervention such as manpower retraining, energy saving and inner-city community development projects are just as amenable to corporatism as incomes policies or national planning – the key issue remains the extent to which the state continues to be dependent upon producers for the effective implementation of economic policies. The state may presently regulate by less direct means, handing back greater responsibilities to producers, but the overall dependence will continue to pertain and hence so will the imperative need to overcome such dependence through corporatist structures – if in a different form. The important point to note is that corporatism should not be regarded in terms of the existence of certain prominent national institutions, but has to be seen in a more dynamic evolutionary manner, reflecting the changing role of the state in advanced capitalist economies. Corporatism is not fruitfully regarded as something that is transitory, pertaining to a particular era of the state in the post-war economy. From our contextual discussions it would appear to have a more permanent character.

This concluding chapter has been directed largely at a further consideration of neo-corporatism. Such a focus reflected more than anything else the fact that as a purely analytic concept, as opposed to a system of ideas or a generic model of certain actual political-economic systems, neo-corporatism presents many more loose-ends and generates major theoretical controversies which were in need of at least tidying-up. In particular, while the preceding discussion on developing a theory of neo-corporatism *via* the model of contract corporatism sought to provide a limited and clear conceptualisation that was linked to the other varieties discussed earlier, this should not be read as advocating rigidity. Rather in this chapter I have been advocating the need to balance analytical requirements of flexibility with the need to maintain a clear conceptual base. Nor is this simply an exercise to defend the purity of corporatism's family-name. In line with the arguments set out in Chapter 9 there are valid analytic grounds for this, though normative preference inevitably played its part.

In saying the above it is not suggested that we know all there is to know about corporatist ideology or authoritarian-corporatist practice. Hopefully, the models of consensual-licenced and authoritarian-licenced corporatism will in some manner enhance any such work to extend our knowledge in either direction. Certainly there appears to be a strong case for studies into the identification and elaboration of, not to mention comparisons between, different traditions within the *corpus* of corporatist economic and social theory. Moreover, there are still significant gaps in our knowledge concerning the practice of corporatism in several authoritarian regimes, while the wider forces which moulded such political-economic organisations in so many countries remain far from fully understood.

Perhaps the 'last word' should be left to Mihail Manoilesco, all the more so because it is exactly fifty years since his *Le Siècle du Corporatisme* was first published. Many of his predictions and arguments have not proved so coldly logical as he suggested. But he did highlight some prominent features of state regulation in capitalist economies: that the state would turn outwards, away from its own institutions, to semi-autonomous producer associations as the *appareil mécanisme* of regulation. In short, the Romanian political economist was not so wholly wide of the mark when he stated: 'Or, la direction générale pour notre époque, c'est l'organisation de chaque collectivité nationale par le corporatisme.'[41] Quite how close to the mark, and in what forms, and with what variations across states requires further invstigation.

Notes

Chapter 1

1 G. A. Almond, 'Corporatism, Pluralism and Professional Memory', *World Politics*, Vol. 35 (1983), pp. 250–1.
2 H. B. Milward and R. A. Francisco, 'Subsystem Politics and Corporatism in the United States' in *Policy and Politics*, Vol. 11 (1983), pp. 273–93.
3 V. Bunce, 'The Political Economy of the Brezhnev Era: The Rise and Fall of Corporatism' in *British Journal of Political Science*, Vol. 13 (1983), pp. 129–58.
4 Examples of loose and ambiguous employment of corporatism include R. Rhodes, *Control and Power in Central-Local Government* (Farnborough: Gower, 1981), pp. 3–7 and 112–14; O. Ruin, 'Participatory Democracy and Corporatism: The Case of Sweden', *Scandinavian Political Studies*, Vol. 9 (1974), pp. 171–84; A. Gould, 'The Salarical Middle Class in the Corporatist Welfare State', *Policy and Politics*, Vol. 9 (1981), pp. 401–18, and R. Klein, 'Corporate state, health service and professions', *New Universities Quarterly*, Vol. 2, (1977), pp. 161–180.
5 *Review of Politics*, Vol. 36 (1974), pp. 85–131. In Britain the earliest impetus to the take-off of interest in neo-corporatism came from sociologists Jack Winkler and Ray Pahl. However, despite being the front runners, their own framework was soon superseded in credence by those of other writers, most notable among them being Schmitter himself. For Pahl and Winkler's original work see, 'The Coming Corporatism', *New Society*, 10 October 1974.
6 For one suggested listing see H. J. Wiarda, 'Corporatist Theory and Ideology: A Latin American Development Paradigm', *Journal of Church and State*, Vol. 20 (1978), pp. 42–3.
7 See, for example, H. J. Wiarda, 'Toward a Framework for the Study of Political Change in the Iberic-Latin Tradition', *World Politics*, Vol. 25 (1973), pp. 206–35; and R. Rogowski and L. Wasserspring, *Does Political Development Exist? Corporatism in Old and New Societies* (London: Sage, 1971).
8 See H. J. Wiarda, 'The Corporatist Tradition and the Corporative System in Portugal: Structured, Evolving, Transcended, Persistent', in L. S. Graham and H. Makler (eds) *Contemporary Portugal* (London: University of Texas Press, 1979).
9 Rogowski and Wasserspring, *op. cit.*, p. 7.
10 Support for this view comes from Phillipe Schmitter, 'Still the Century of Corporatism?' in P. C. Schmitter and G. Lehmbruch (eds). *Trends Towards Corporatist Intermediation* (London: Sage, 1979), pp. 10–13.
11 Peter J. Williamson, *Corporatism in Theory and Practice and Contemporary British Politics*. (Ph.D. Thesis, University of Aberdeen, 1982), Part 4.
12 For an example of a very 'broad brush' view, see L. P. Carpenter, 'Corporatism in Britain 1930–45', *Journal of Contemporary History*, Vol. 11 (1976),

pp. 3–25. See also N. Harris, *Competition and the Corporate Society* (London: Methuen, 1972), Ch. 4. In any case many of the prescriptive writers marshalled into the corporatist camp more obviously fit into other ideological traditions.

Chapter 2

1 G. Boivin and M. Bouvier-Ajam, *Vers une Economie politique morale,* (Paris: Recueil Sirey, 1938), p. 50, quoted in M. H. Elbow, *French Corporative Theory 1789–1948* (New York: Columbia University Press, 1953), p. 135.

2 H. Maine, *Ancient Law* (London: J. Murray, 1901), p. 170.

3 A. Murat, *Le Corporatisme* (Paris: Les Publications Techniques, 1944), p. 187.

4 O. Newman, *The Challenge of Corporatism* (London: Macmillan, 1981), pp. 36–7.

5 G. Ionescu, *The Political Thought of Saint-Simon* (London: Oxford University Press, 1976), pp. 18–20.

6 This is particularly true of French writers, but I believe the argument holds for other countries. For a discussion of such linkages in respect of Charles Maurras, see M. Sutton, *Nationalism, Positivism and Catholicism* (Cambridge: Cambridge University Press, 1982). A. Black, *Guilds and Civil Society* (London: Methuen, 1984) pp. 220–1 very seriously under-estimates the influence of Catholicism on corporatist thought.

7 See H. J. Wiarda, 'Corporatist Theory and Ideology: A Latin American Development Paradigm', *Journal of Church and State*, Vol. 20 (1978), pp. 31–6.

8 G. Valois, *L'Économie nouvelle* (Paris: Nouvelle Librarie Nationale, 1919), p. 129. Valois at the time of the publication of the above work was associated with the Action Française, but he split from the 'too intellectual' Maurras for Fascist action in 1925. A discussion of Valois and his contribution to French fascism – the authors present him as the founder of French fascism – and some of his ideas are found in J. Plumyene et R. Lasierra, *Les Fascismes Français 1923–63* (Paris: Éditions du Seuil, 1966), pp. 31–44. Valois' relationship with Maurras is fully detailed in P. Bontang, *Maurras: La Destine et l'Œuvre* (Paris: Plon, 1984), Book VII, Ch. 3.

9 P. Lucius, *Une grande Industrie dans la tourmente* (Paris: Les Œuvres Françaises, 1935), p. 10, quoted in Elbow, *op. cit.,* p. 136.

10 See, for example, La Tour du Pin, *Vers un Ordre social chrétien* (Paris: Gabriel Beauchiane, 1929), p. 33, although throughout the work similar points are made. Charles Humbert René, Comte de la Tour du Pin Chambly, Marquis de la Chance (1834–1924) was a member of the French nobility who spent his early years in the French army. However, he resigned from the military in 1881 and spent most of the rest of his life concerned with the 'social question' and the development of Catholic corporatist doctrine (although he was fervently royalist and anti-republican despite Leo XIII's support of the Republic in 1892), and organised workers in Catholic associations. His influence was extensive – ranging from Leo XIII's *Rerum Novarum* to Charles Maurras and to Maréchal Pétain. His seminal work, *Vers un Ordre social chrétien* was first published in 1907.

11 See R. H. Bowen, *German Theories of the Corporative State* (New York: Russel and Russel, 1947), pp. 192–3. Wichard von Moellendorff, along with

Walther Rathenau, was the main proponent of the 'new collective economy' as a means to national reconstruction after the war of 1914–18. During and after that war, he had been a civil servant and he had some success in influencing the right-wing Social Democratic cabinet ministers under whom he served as a high-ranking civil servant during the early years of the Weimar Republic.

12 See E.A. Clark, 'Adolf Wagner: From National Economist to National Socialist', *Political Science Quarterly* Vol. 55 (1940), p. 393. Wagner was born in 1835 and was one of the major proponents of the doctrines of national economics in Germany stemming from Adam Müller and others. His nationalism was extremely intolerant and in 1935 he was posthumously honoured as one of the fathers of Nazism.

13 See J. Azpiazu, *The Corporate State* (St Louis, Mo.: B. Herder, 1951), pp. 133–4.

14 See O. Spann, *Der wahre Staat* (Leipzig: Quelle and Meyer, 1923), particularly pp. 123–39, for Spann's criticism of capitalism which he rested on the spiritual malaise emanating from individualism upon which capitalism was based. For a background to Spann's theoretical premisses of universalism, see A. Emery, 'The Totalitarian Economics of Othmar Spann', *Journal of Social Philosophy* Vol. 1 (1936), pp. 263–77.

15 See A. Diamant, *Austrian Catholics and the First Republic* (Princeton, N.J.: Princeton University Press, 1960), p. 241.

16 See H. Denis, *La Corporation* (Paris: Presses Universitaires, Françaises, 1941), p. 42 cited in P. Vignaux, 'Corporativism in Europe', *The Review of Politics* Vol. 4 (1942), p. 203.

17 See Bowen, *op. cit.*, p. 38.

18 See Vignaux, *op. cit.*, p. 196.

19 Some corporatists regarded liberalism as a system of false liberty. See a discussion of Wilhelm Emmanual, Baron von Ketteler's criticism of liberalism in W.E. Hogan, *The Development of William Emmanual von Ketteler's Interpretation of the Social Problem* (Washington: Catholic University of America 1946), pp. 76–80. Ketteler's discussion of the falseness of liberalism's liberty is very similar to other corporatists and was set out in his book *Freiheit, Autorität, und Kirche* (Liberty, Authority and the Church) published first in 1862. Ketteler was the most important of the social Catholic corporatists. He became Bishop of Mainz in 1850 at the express desire of Pius IX and influenced more than anyone else Leo XIII's *Rerum Novarum*.

20 For an examination of the basis of economic liberalism see D. J. Manning, *Liberalism* (London: Dent, 1976) pp. 19–21.

21 For example, Franz Hitze; see Bowen, *op. cit.*, p. 95. Hitze was a German Social Catholic (1851–1921) who was ordained in 1878 and spent much of his time studying scholastic theology, particularly the social philosophy of St Thomas Aquinas. His main corporatist study was published in 1880 'Kapital und Arbeit und die Reorganisation der Gesellschaft' in *Deutsche Arbeit*, 6 January 1921 (*Capital and Labour and the Reorganization of Society*).

22 See G. de Michelis *World Reorganization on Corporatist Lines* (London: Unwin Bros, 1935), pp. 29–30.

23 See Azpiazu, *op. cit.*, pp. 75–6.

24 See C. Gide and C. Rist, *A History of Economic Doctrines* (London: G. Harrap, 1948) p. 531. In his Encyclical *Immortale Dei*, Leo XIII stated 'The State is the minister of God for Good.'

25 P. Chanson, *Les Droits du travailleur et le corporatisme* (Paris: Desclée de Brouwer, 1935), p. 214. Paul Chanson was President of the Calais Maritime Employers' Syndicate and based his corporatist proposals on the two papal encyclicals *Rerum Novarum* and *Quadragesimo Anno*.

26 See F. Perroux, *Capitalisme et communauté de travail* (Paris: Recueil Sirey, 1937), p. 18. Perroux was a colleague of Pirou in the Faculty of Law (i.e. economics) in Paris. His works were based on a strange juxtaposition of rigorous abstract theory and moving appeals to the heart. He was made a member of the Economic Council under Pétain.

27 See Valois, *op. cit.*, p. 15.

28 See O. Spann, *Types of Economic Theory* (London: Allen and Unwin, 1930), p. 163. Müller (1779–1829) was the only member of the German 'Romantic School' to occupy himself exclusively with political speculation (because he lacked any artistic talent). He was a strong supporter of the monarchy.

29 See E. A. Clark, 'Adolf Wagner: From National Economist to National Socialist', *Political Science Quarterly*, Vol. 55 (1940), pp. 394–7.

30 See Taylor Cole, 'Corporative Organization of the Third Reich', *Review of Politics*, Vol. 2 (1940), p. 448. Frauendorfer headed the Nazi Party's Bureaux for Corporative Organisation in the Party and Labour Front.

31 See C. T. Muret, *French Royalist Doctrines Since the Revolution* (New York: Columbia University Press, 1933), pp. 200–16.

32 Valois, *op. cit.*, p. 15.

33 Elbow, *op. cit.*, p. 141. See also L. Baudin *Le Corporatisme* (Paris: Librarie Générale de Droit et Jurisprudence, 1942), pp. 17–21. The latter, being an 'academic' work also includes a general examination of the other theorists.

34 See Bowen, *op. cit.*, p. 185.

35 W. Rathenau, *Der neue Staat* (Berlin: S. Fischer, 1919), p. 32. Walther Rathenau (1867–1922) was the chief architect of the German Collective Economy. His career began in his father's large electrical combine AEG and during the war he played a prominent part in planning the German economy. Although he played no public part in the events attending and immediately following the Revolution of 1918, his views on Germany's political and social future achieved almost universal currency during the period between the armistice and promulgation of the new constitution.

The extensive and consequential rationalisation movement in German industry owed much to his ideas of industrial organisation. Many of his ideas were drawn, although altered (without acknowledgement) from G. D. H. Cole's works on Guild Socialism. His emotional loyalties were bound up with many of the most intensely conservative elements of the German nationalistic tradition, although his intellectual conclusions were often in conflict with these emotions. In 1922, he became foreign minister, an important post involved in reparation discussions with Britain and France, but his most important job was signing the Treaty of Rapallo with the Russians. The apparent 'defeatism' of the Treaty and the fact that he was a Jew, led to him being shot dead by a group of nationalists in June 1922. As an industrial administrator and politician/diplomat, as well as social theorist, Rathenau has attracted many biographers. The most accessible are H. Kesseler (trans W. D. Robson-Scott and L. Hyde) *Walther Rathenau* (London: C. Howe Ltd, 1929) and J. Joll 'Walther Rathenau', in his *Intellectuals in Politics* (London: Weidenfeld and Nicolson, 1960).

36 See W. Rathenau, *The New Society* (London: Williams and Norgate, 1921), pp. 12–13 and 28–9.

37 See Elbow, *op. cit.*, p. 167.

38 See M. Manoilesco, *Le Siècle du corporatisme* (Paris: Librarie Félix Alcan, 1934), p. 115. Manoilesco was in fact Romanian and was one of the few theorists to be an economist, being Professor of Political Economy in Bucharest. For a brief period he was Minister of Commerce in his native Romania, but after his political career was cut short, he wrote his major work – *The Century of Corporatism* – and published it in Paris where his work found a receptive audience in 1934.

39 See Cole, *op. cit.*, p. 449.

40 See A. Rocco, 'The Syndicates and the Crisis Within the State', (1920), in A. Lyttleton, *Italian Fascisms* (London: Cape, 1973) p. 280. Rocco was Professor of Commercial Law at the University of Turin. Latterly his politics were nationalist conservative. He held the post of Minister of Justice under Mussolini from 1925–32, which gave him extensive influence over the creation of the Italian corporative state.

41 See Elbow, *op. cit.*, p. 138.

42 Quoted in Bowen, *op. cit.*, p. 96.

43 See Azpiazu, *op. cit.*, p. 194.

44 See Valois, *op. cit.*, p. 184.

45 See Spann, *Der wahre Staat*, pp. 290–4 for suggestions to give the system a dynamic element through 'latent' competition.

46 See Elbow, *op. cit.*, pp. 148–9.

47 See Diamant, *op. cit.*, p. 196.

48 See *ibid*, p. 197. Both Messner and Dobrestberger were Austrian social Catholics who tried to introduce greater realism into Catholic corporatist thought as compared with the Romantics. Their work comes from the inter-war era.

49 See Bowen, *op. cit.*, pp. 26–31. Johann Fichte (1762–1814) was at one time the most noted disciple of Kant. In the early nineteenth century he abandoned his support for individualism in place of an organic view of the state combined with the emergent militant nationalism of the time. His influence can be traced through all subsequent generations of German theorists.

50 Spann, *Types of Economic Theory*, pp. 159–66.

51 *ibid*, p. 171.

52 Clark, *op. cit.*, p. 393.

53 La Tour, *op. cit.*, pp. 34, 63, and 327.

54 Valois, *op. cit.*, pp. 1–13 and 294–301. See also F. Baconnier *La Salut par le corporation* (Paris: Les Œuvres Françaises, 1935), passim.

55 Spann, *Types of Economic Theory*, pp. 196–201.

56 See W. Rathenau, *Die neue Wirtschaft* (Berlin: S. Fischer, 1918).

57 See M. Manoilesco, *The Theory of Protectionism and International Trade* (London: P. S. King and Sons, 1931); and *Le Siècle du corporatisme*, pp. 27–49.

58 Spann and Manoilesco were both economics professors, while Rathenau was an industrialist and government planner.

59 W. von Ketteler, *Die Arbeiterfrage und das Christenthum* (Mainz: F. Kirchheim, 1864), p. 57.

60 Azpiazu, *op. cit.*, passim.

61 See G. Lefranc, *Histoire des doctrines sociales*, Vol. 2 (Paris: Aubier-Montaigne, 1966), pp. 161–2. Both La Tour and de Mun participated in the

Union of Bribourg conferences which strongly supported private property in their report to Leo XIII in 1888; see also La Tour, *op. cit.*, p. 141.

62 See J. N. Mood (ed), *Church and Society* (New York: Arts Inc, 1953), p. 241.

63 La Tour, *op. cit.*, p. 93.

64 P. Andrau, 'Le Vrai Visage de La Tour du Pin', *Esprit*, 1 June 1934. The charge that La Tour was a socialist cannot be sustained by wider reference to his works.

65 London: Catholic Truth Society, 1960, pp. 33–34.

66 London: Catholic Truth Society, 1960, pp. 29–30. See also R. L. Camp, *The Papal Ideology of Social Reform* (Leiden: E. J. Brill, 1969), pp. 55–6 and 65–6.

67 See La Tour, *op. cit.*, p. 93; Moody, *op. cit.*, p. 403; and J. Messner, *Social Ethics* (London: B. Herder, 1964), pp. 821–6.

68 See W. Rathenau, *In Days to Come* (London: Allen and Unwin, 1921), p. 93.

69 *Ibid*, p. 114.

70 W. Rathenau, *Die neue Wirtschaft.*

71 F. Redlich, 'German Economic Planning for War and Peace', *Review of Politics* Vol. 6 (1944), p. 329.

72 See A. C. Coutinho, 'The Federalism of Karl Marlo and Konstantin Frantz', *Political Science Quarterly*, Vol. 53 (1938), p. 148.

73 Bowen, *op. cit.*, pp. 131 and 122–123.

74 Gide and Rist, *op. cit.*, p. 444.

75 See, for example, Perroux *op. cit.*, p. 21; Bacconnier, *op. cit.*, pp. 163–7; and C. De La Rocque, *The Fiery Cross* (London: Lovat Dickson, 1936), pp. 105–6. Lt Col De La Rocque was head of the Fascist organisation, the *Croix de Feu*, which became powerful after the riots of February 1934. In 1936 when the government disbanded political leagues, it became the Parti Social Français. *The Fiery Cross* is the English translation of *Service publique* (1934).

76 See P. Lucius, *Révolutions au XXe Siècle* (Paris: Payot, 1934), pp. 341–2; and Chanson, *op. cit.*, p. 243.

77 Manoilesco, *Le Siècle du corporatisme*, pp. 101–5.

78 De Michelis, *op. cit.*, pp. 25 and 208.

79 Baudin, *op. cit.*, pp. 24–5.

80 Diamant, *op. cit.*, pp. 162–3.

81 Pius XI, *op. cit.*, pp. 45–6.

82 Coutinho, *op. cit.*, p. 421; Bowen, *op. cit.*, pp. 122–3 and 131.

83 Clark, *op. cit.*, p. 444.

84 See C. B. Macpherson, 'Capitalism and the Changing Concept of Property', in E. Kamendu and R. S. Neale (eds) *Feudalism, Capitalism and Beyond* (London: St Martin, 1976), p. 106.

85 *Ibid*, p. 109.

86 F. Baader, 'Evolution and Revolutionism' (1834) quoted in Moody, *op. cit.*, p. 403.

87 Azpiazu, *op. cit.*, pp. 59 and 148–50; Messner, *op. cit.*, pp. 826–7; Leo XIII, *op. cit.*, pp. 20–1; A. de Mun *Discours* (Paris: Librarie Ch. Poussielgue, 1895), Vol. 1, p. 403; H. Pesch 'Principles of a Christian Social and Economic Theory', in Moody, *op. cit.*, p. 548; Hogan, *op. cit.*, pp. 60–64; and Ketteler, *op. cit.*, pp. 77–78 and 149–56.

88 Pesch in Moody, *op. cit.*, pp. 547–548.

89 La Tour, *op. cit.*, p. 33.

90 Rathenau, *In Days to Come*, pp. 120–8 and 147–9. See also *Die neue Wirtschaft*, passim.

91 Manoilesco, *op. cit.*, pp. 102–5.
92 Clark, *op. cit.*, pp. 395–7.
93 De Michelis, *op. cit.*, pp. 208–9.
94 A good illustration of the corporatist position on regulation is found in
   G. Pirou, *Essais sur le corporatisme* (Paris: Librairie du Recueil Sirey, 1935),
   pp. 125–34. Here Pirou not only outlines his own position but discusses the
   works of other contemporary French theorists. See also Baudin, *op. cit.*,
   pp. 32–40; Perroux, *op. cit.*, p. 18 and passim; and F. Vito, *Economia
   Politica Corporativa* (Milan: A. Giuffre, 1939).
95 See A. P. Evans, 'The Problem of Control in Medieval Industry', *Political
   Science Quarterly* Vol. 36 (1921), pp. 607–8.
96 Spann, *Der wahre Staat*, p. 261. See also Diamant, *op. cit.*, pp. 54 and 59 on
   Adam Müller and Vogelsang respectively.
97 One exception to this was Louis Baudin who discussed at some length 'des
   bénéfices normaux'. See Baudin, *op. cit.*, pp. 34ff.
98 See De Michelis, *op. cit.*, pp. 28–9; Rathenau, *In Days to Come*, pp. 93 and
   111; and Gide and Rist, *op. cit.*, p. 444 on Wagner.
99 Ketteler, *op. cit.*, pp. 53–7.
100 Azpiazu, *op. cit.*, pp. 16–17.
101 See La Tour, *op. cit.*, p. 27; Rathenau, *In Days to Come*, pp. 71–2 and 127–8;
   De Michelis, *op. cit.*, pp. 208–9; Pirou, *Essais sur le corporatisme*, p. 127;
   Manoilesco, *op. cit.*, pp. 102–5.
102 See, for example, Manoilesco, *op. cit.*, pp. 287–98; Pirou, *Essais sur le
   corporatisme*, pp. 287–98; Chanson, *op. cit.*, passim; Messner, *op. cit.*, esp.
   pp. 795–6; La Tour, *op. cit.*, pp. 71–105, and *Aphorismes de politique social*
   (Paris: Nouvelle Librairie Nationale, 1909), pp. 54–66; Rathenau, *In Days to
   Come*, passim; and Pesch in Moody, *op. cit.*, p. 547.
103 See, for example, Valois' critique of Marxism, *op. cit.*, pp. 15 and 68.
104 See Azpiazu, *op. cit.*, pp. 167–9.
105 A discussion of the theoretical premises of the just wage is found in M. P.
   Fogarty *The Just Wage* (London: Chapman, 1961), Appendix 1.
106 Ketteler, *op. cit.*, pp. 112–15. See also Hogan, *op. cit.*, pp. 117–20.
107 Ketteler, *op. cit.*, pp. 15–17 and ff.; La Tour, *op. cit.*, pp. 14 and 145–6;
   Azpiazu, *op. cit.*, pp. 173–5 and 177–83; de Mun, *op. cit.*, Vols 1 and 2
   passim; Messner, *op. cit.*, p. 802; and Moody, *op. cit.*, pp. 401–6 and 536–8
   (Franz Baader).
108 See Fogarty, *op. cit.*, esp. pp. 297–8.
109 Azpiazu, *op. cit.*, pp. 29–50. See also La Tour, *op. cit.*, p. 140.
110 See G. Pirou, *Néo-Liberalisme, néo-corporatisme, néo-socialisme* (Paris:
   Gallimard, 1939), p. 83; and Manoilesco, *op. cit.*, pp. 110–12.
111 Rathenau *In Days to Come*, passim. See also de La Rocque, *op. cit.*, p. 187;
   and Bowen, *op. cit.*, pp. 56–7 (Marlo).
112 Manoilesco, *op. cit.*, pp. 277 and 279–80.
113 Messner, *op. cit.*, pp. 799–802.
114 Azpiazu, *op. cit.*, pp. 177–83.
115 Pius XI, *op. cit.*, p. 33.
116 La Tour, *op. cit.*, pp. 12–13.
117 Hogan, *op. cit.*, pp. 162–3.
118 Pius XI, *op. cit.*, pp. 32–3, for example.
119 For a general summary see Vito, *op. cit.*, Ch. 3.

120 E. Durkheim, *De la Division du travail social* (Paris: Félix Alcan, 1926), p. xxxi.

121 La Tour, *op. cit.*, p. 27.

122 De Mun, *op. cit.*, Vol. 4, pp. 21–37; and F. B. Martin *Count Albert De Mun* (Chapel Hill: University of North Carolina Press, 1978), pp. 53–4 and 113–14.

123 Martin, *op. cit.* De Mun's career is similar to that of La Tour, a Catholic with an aristocratic and military background. However, he was more of an orator and organiser than a writer. He was elected to the Chamber of Deputies in 1881 and was a constant campaigner for social reform. Martin provides an excellent biography.

124 De La Rocque, *op. cit.*, pp. 188–9; Pirou, *Néo-Liberalisme, néo-corporatisme, néo-socialisme*, p. 83; Chanson, *op. cit.*, pp. 182–8; J. Brethe de la Gressay *Le Syndicalisme: l'organisation professionnel de l'État* (Paris: Recueil Sirey, 1930), pp. 259–61; and Firmin Bacconnier's article in *Action Française*, 1 April 1934. Some other benefits were sometimes mentioned, such as housing.

125 F. Nitti, *Catholic Socialism* (London: Swann Sonnescheim and Co, 1895), pp. 153–4 (Hitze); and Manoilesco, *op. cit.*, pp. 275–6. Azpiazu, *op. cit.*, pp. 99, 203 and 209–10; F. Baader 'On the Present Faulty Relationship between the Propertyless, or Proletarians, and the Propertied Class of Society' (1835), in Moody, *op. cit.*; Bowen, *op. cit.*, pp. 133–4 (Schäffle); Rathenau, *In Days to Come*, p. 111.

126 Ketteler, *op. cit.*, Chs. 2 and 7.

127 W. Rathenau, *The New Society*, p. 7.

128 *ibid*, p. 58.

129 Manoilesco, *op. cit.*, pp. 109–10. See also Pirou *Néo-Liberalisme, néo-corporatisme, néo-socialisme*, p. 178.

130 Azpiazu, *op. cit.*, p. 46. See also Messner, *op. cit.*, pp. 331–4.

131 Spann, *Der wahre Staat*, p. 125; and La Tour, *Aphorismes de politique social*, p. 43.

132 See Emery, *op. cit.*, pp. 265–8. See also Coutinho, *op. cit.*, on Marlo and Frantz.

133 Spann, *Der wahre Staat*, pp. 290–4.

134 La Tour, *op. cit.*, p. 24.

135 De Mun, *op. cit.*, Vol. 1, p. 403.

136 Elbow, *op. cit.*, p. 146.

137 See, for example, Bacconnier in *Action Française*, *op. cit.*

138 Messner, *op. cit.*, p. 840.

139 Redlich, *op. cit.*, p. 336.

140 On employment rights see also Rathenau, *The New Society*, pp. 107–14 and *In Days to Come*, p. 127; J. Fichte, *The Science of Rights* (London: Routledge and Kegan Paul, 1970), p. 215; Azpiazu, *op. cit.*, pp. 99 and 125; Manoilesco, *op. cit.*, pp. 110 and 297–8; and Nitti, *op. cit.*, p. 150 (Hitze).

141 Brethe de la Gressaye, *op. cit.*, p. 261.

142 Messner, *op. cit.*, p. 835.

143 Manoilesco, *op. cit.*, pp. 278–9.

Chapter 3

1 A.-H. Chroust, 'The Corporate Idea and the Body Politic in the Middle Ages', *The Review of Politics*, Vol. 9 (1947), pp. 423–30.

2 R. La Tour du Pin, *Vers un Ordre sociale chrétien*, p. 117.

3 *ibid*, p. 499. La Tour, in fact, saw the corporation comprising all elements which constituted the profession, including employers, clerks and workers in large industry; masters, workers and apprentices in trades; and proprietors, tenants and cultivators in agriculture. In large industry capital was to be represented as well as management.

4 De Mun, *Discours* (Paris, 1895), Vol. 1, p. 403.

5 See Hogan, *The Development of William Emmanuel von Ketteler's Interpretation of The Social Problem* (Washington, 1946), pp. 227–9.

6 P. Lucius, *Rénovation du capitalisme* (Paris: Payot, 1933), p. 303. Lucius was an interbellum French corporatist who was an employer in the leather industry. His writings reflected very much the traditions of corporatist thought.

7 See G. L. Mosse, *Germans and Jews* (London: Orbach and Chambers, 1971), p. 130.

8 This sentence deliberately paraphrases M. Manoilesco, *Le Siècle du corporatisme*, pp. 106–7.

9 This is not to say that some writers did not identify processes which encouraged corporatist developments. International competition was common; see F. Bacconnier, *Le Salut par la corporation*, pp. 114–31.

10 See La Tour, *op. cit.*, pp. 23–4. A *corps d'état* is defined by La Tour as 'the ensemble of all the workshops where the same profession is practised', p. 409.

11 See M. Elbow, *French Corporative Theory 1789–1948*, (New York, 1953), p. 159.

12 See W. Rathenau, *Die neue Wirtschaft*, p. 56.

13 See E. Barker in his translation of Gierke's *Natural Law and the Theory of Society: 1500–1800* (Cambridge: Cambridge University Press, 1934), pp. ix–x.

14 O. von Gierke, *Political Theories of the Middle Age* (Cambridge: Cambridge University Press, 1900), p. 95.

15 *ibid*, pp. 99–100.

16 Those who influenced corporatist theorists are not of primary concern here, but it has been worth examining Gierke in some detail because his writings, which are readily accessible, thanks to Maitland, offer a good insight into the corporatist position which drew its ideas from the medieval thought Gierke examined. For further discussion on Gierke, see Black, *Guilds and Civil Society* (London, 1984), pp. 210–17.

17 See Kessler, *Walther Rathenau* (London, 1929), p. 218.

18 See Rathenau, *Die neue Wirtschaft*, pp. 27–8 and 75.

19 G. Hegel, *Philosophy of Right* (Oxford: Oxford University Press, 1942), p. 255.

20 For a discussion of Hegel's view see S. Avineri, *Hegel's Theory of the Modern State* (Cambridge: Cambridge University Press, 1972), pp. 164–7; and Black, *op. cit.*, Ch. 17.

21 See Bowen, *German Theories of the Cooperative State* (New York, 1947), p. 57. Karl Marlo was the literary name of Karl Winkelbeck (1810–1865). His writings reflected concern that the advance of capitalism was destroying small businesses and independent craftsmen and his proposals were clearly designed to stave off such developments.

22 *ibid*, pp. 61–2. Von Gerlach (1795–1877) was descended from one of the

oldest Prussian noble families and was a principal founder of the Conservative Party in Prussia.

23 Clark, 'Adolph Wagner', *Political Science Quarterly*, Vol. 55 (1940), p. 397.

24 See La Tour, *op. cit.* p. 183.

25 See G. Pirou, 'Léon Duguit et L'Économie Politique', *Revue D'Économie politique* Vol. 47 (1933).

26 See R. Soltau, *French Political Thought in the Nineteenth Century* (London: E. Benn Ltd., 1931), pp. 475–476. Duguit's syndicates were not integrated organisations like the corporation but were combinations like trade unions and trade associations.

27 Valois, *L'Économie nouvelle* (Paris, 1919), p. 15.

28 See De La Rocque, *The Fiery Cross* (London, 1936), p. 117.

29 Lucius *Rénovation du capitalisme*, p. 300 (my emphasis).

30 See Baudin, *Le Corporatisme* (Paris, 1942), p. 12.

31 R. Schmitz, *Der Weg zur berufsständischen Ordnung in Österreich*, p. 29–30, quoted in Diamant, *Austrian Catholics* (Princeton, 1960), p. 244. The work quoted was published in 1934. See also Messner, *Social Ethics* (London, 1964), p. 442. Messner, who wrote in the 1920s and 1930s, was not a member of the Austrian Romantic School but a 'realist'. He, therefore, continued to expound his ideas of 'democratic corporatism' after the fall of Dolfuss's Austrian corporative Republic. The work cited was first published in 1949.

32 See P. Dodge *Beyond Marxism: The Faith and Works of Hendrik de Man* (The Hague; Martinus Nijhoff, 1966), p. 160. De Man was a member of, and indeed became President of, the *Parti Ouvrier Belge*. He also held ministerial posts and was a senator in Belgium between the wars. Much of his writing concerned economic planning. His corporatist proposals reflected his desire to achieve socialist/social democratic goals without resource to extensive state involvement. In effect, his ideas lay somewhere between corporatism and guild socialism, but it is, nevertheless, worth pointing out the wide appeal even to those whose objectives were not corporatist – the appeal of corporatism's anti-étatisme.

33 Many of the references already cited indicate this view of the state. Chanson, *Les Droits du Travaillent* (Paris, 1935), p. 214, concisely reflects the view of all of them.

34 See, for example, Manoilesco, *Le Siècle du corporatisme* (Paris, 1934), p. 79.

35 On this point see Baudin *op. cit.*, pp. 13–14. Baudin points out that the theorists 'underlined the necessity of an appropriate education'.

36 G. Pirou, *Le Corporatisme* (Paris: Librarie du Receuil Sirey, 1935), pp. 40–61.

37 *ibid*, pp. 62–7.

38 P. C. Schmitter 'Still the Century of Corporatism?', Schmitter and Lehmbruch (eds).

39 Manoilesco, *op. cit.*, pp. 156–60.

40 *ibid*, pp. 163–4.

41 *ibid*, pp. 160–2.

42 Azpiazu, *op. cit.*, p. 91.

43 De Mun, *op. cit.*, Vol. 1, p. 403.

44 Manoilesco, *op. cit.*, pp. 176–7.

45 Baudin, *op. cit.*, p. 12.

46 La Tour, *op. cit.*, p. 23.

47 Azpiazu, *op. cit.*, p. 91.
48 *ibid*, p. 96; La Tour, *op. cit.*, p. 31; and Rathenau *Der neue Staat*, p. 35.
49 Bowen, *op. cit.*, p. 85. Ketteler was primarily concerned with the 'labour question' and not with production.
50 Nitti, *Catholic Socialism* (London, 1895), p. 152.
51 See Diamant, *op. cit.*, p. 61. Von Vogelsang (1818–90) was born into the Austrian landed nobility. Although born into a Protestant family, his acquaintance with Ketteler in Germany brought out his pro-Catholic inclinations. He combined in his ideas romanticist conceptions of medieval guilds and monarchism, drawn from Müller, with concern for the social question, taken from Ketteler, into an ideal social system called 'social monarchy'. His most influential works, which were journalistic in form, date from 1875 to 1890. He was one of the most influential of Austrian social-Catholic corporatists.
52 Nitti, *op. cit.*, p. 276.
53 Rathenau, *Die neue Wirtschaft* p. 56f.
54 Chanson, *op. cit.*, p. 228.
55 Pirou *Le Corporatisme*, pp. 32–4.
56 La Tour, *op. cit.*, pp. 23–4.
57 Azpiazu, *op. cit.*, pp. 250–1 and passim.
58 Quite what Manoilesco is driving at is not quite clear, see *Le Siècle*, p. 176.
59 Of course it is not necessary that every single economic function became encompassed in such monopolies, nor that all engaged in a function, particularly at the periphery, would be brought into the system. For example, some writers felt small businesses need not be included.
60 Bacconier, *Le Salut par la corporation*, p. 163.
61 La Tour, *op. cit.*, p. 29. for example.
62 *ibid*, pp. 140–5.
63 Durkheim, *De la Division du travail social* (Paris, 1926), p. vi.
64 Valois, *op. cit.*, pp. 282–3. Valois in fact outlined a hypothetical corporation based upon the profession he knew best, book production (pp. 284–5).
65 Bacconier, *Le Salut par la corporation*, p. 139.
66 De la Rocque, *op. cit.*, pp. 119–22.
67 Elbow, *French Corporative Theory* (New York, 1953), pp. 150–1.
68 Rocco, 'The Syndicates and the Crisis Within the State', in Lyttleton (ed.) *Italian Fascisms* (London, 1973), p. 280.
69 Cole, 'Corporative Organisation of the Third Reich', *Review of Politics*, Vol. 2 (1940), p. 448.
70 Clark, *op. cit.*, p. 397.
71 Manoilesco, *op. cit.*, pp. 249–54. See also Messner, *op. cit.*, pp. 443–5 for a view that placed more emphasis on building upon existing syndical associations.
72 La Tour, *op. cit.*, p. 33.
73 Rathenau, *Die neue Wirtschaft*, p. 61.
74 Baudin, *op. cit.*, pp.. 32–40.
75 Manoilesco, *op. cit.*, pp. 288–90.
76 A. P. Evans, 'The Problem of Control in Medieval Industry', *Political Science Quarterly*, Vol. 26 (1921), p.. 608.
77 For a discussion of the issues see Pirou, *Essais sur le corporatisme*, pp. 127–34. Pirou was somewhat sceptical of the practicalities of such a *modus operandi*,

coming down in favour of state planning with the corporations bringing about simply 'harmonisation'. See again Baudin, *op. cit.*, pp. 32–40.

78 Valois, *op. cit.*, p. 184.
79 Rathenau, *Die neue Wirtschaft*, passim.
80 For further details on price regulation see F. Redlich, *op. cit.*, pp. 329–30 (Von Moellendorff); Bowen, *op. cit.*, p. 117 (Pesch): and Elbow, *op. cit.*, pp. 147–9.
81 See W. Rathenau 'Die neue Wirtschaft' in *Gesammelte Schriften in funf Bänden* (Berlin: S. Fischer, 1925), pp. 231–5.
82 Rathenau, *In Days to Come*, p. 127.
83 Redlich, *op. cit.*, 328–32 for Moellendorff's proposals and his differences with Rathenau.
84 Manoilesco, *op. cit.*, pp. 291–2.
85 La Tour, *op. cit.*, pp. 145–6.
86 For further examples see Azpiazu, *op. cit.*, pp. 194–6; De Michelis, *World Reorganization on Corporativist Lines* (London, 1935), pp. 26–9; De La Rocque, *op. cit.*, pp. 116–17; Appendix in *Quarterly Journal of Economics*, Vol. 1, 1886–7, pp. 113–33 (Wagner); and Coutinho 'The Federalism of Karl Marlo and Konstantin Frantz', *op. cit.*, pp. 420–1.
87 See Pirou, *Essais sur le Corporatisme*, pp. 122–34 for a discussion of the issues and divisions among French corporatists. Manoilesco, *op. cit.*, p. 287, held that the economic functions of the corporation would be carried out by the syndicate of entrepreneurs alone. Schäffle felt that for the forseeable future the employer would have an important leadership task over labour, see Bowen, *op. cit.*, p. 131. For an example of divisions of competence see E. Duthoit, 'Par une Authorité corporative vers une économie ordonée', *Chronique sociale de France*, July 1935, pp. 522–4. For the contrary view that 'organisms [...] be mixed' realising 'the participation of workers, not only in the social government of the corporation, but also in its economic government,' see Chanson, *op. cit.*, p. 232.
88 See La Tour, *op. cit.*, p. 145; Azpiazu, *op. cit.*, p. 183; Duthoit, *op. cit.*, pp. 522–3; Pirou, *Le Corporatisme*, pp. 57–9, which also discuss Eugene Mathon; Manoilesco, *op. cit.*, pp. 276–7; De La Rocque, *op. cit.*, pp. 186–7; and W. von Ketteler *Die Katholiken in Deutschem Reiche* (1873), p. 80 quoted in Hogan, *op. cit.*, p. 199–200. The above is merely a selection of references to the regulation of labour conditions.
89 Manoilesco, *op. cit.*, p. 278.
90 Rathenau, 'Die neue Wirtschaft', in *Gesammelte Schriften*, pp. 217–18.
91 De La Rocque, *op. cit.*, p. 184.
92 Bacconnier in *Action Française*, 1 April 1934, quoted also in Elbow, *op. cit.*, p. 147.
93 Bacconnier, *Le Salut par la corporation*, p. 163.
94 *ibid*, pp. 158–66.
95 La Tour, *op. cit.*, p. 29.
96 *ibid*, p. 30.
97 Manoilesco, *op. cit.*, pp. 203–5.
98 For further discussion and examples of professional regulation, see Azpiazu, *op. cit.*, p. 99; Diamant, *op. cit.*, p. 61 (Vogelsang) and p. 239 (Spann); Nitti, *op. cit.*, p. 277 (De Mun); Coutinho, *op. cit.*, p. 421 (Marlo who was one of the few corporatists to advocate requisite qualifications for employers); and Messner, *op. cit.*, p. 442.

 99 De La Rocque, *op. cit.*, p. 189.
100 Azpiazu, *op. cit.*, p. 163.
101 *ibid.*
102 La Tour, *op. cit.*, pp. 27–8. La Tour argued that the fund should not be drawn from the enterprises' profits 'which are the proper realisation of the commercial activity of the enterprise' but from the quantity of production evaluated at cost price.
103 Keller's *L'Encyclique du 8 Décembre 1864 et les principes de 1789, ou l'église, l'état et la liberté* (1865) was one of the major influences on La Tour.
104 Duthoit, *op. cit.*, pp. 522–4.
105 Chanson, *op. cit.*, p. 181. See also Bacconnier *Le Salut par la corporation*.
106 Hogan, *op. cit.*, pp. 106–27 and 133–7.
107 Ketteler *Die Arbeiterfrage und das Christenthum*, pp. 113–14, also quoted in Hogan, *op. cit.*, pp. 123–4. See also M. P. Fogarty *Christian Democracy in Western Europe 1820–1953* (London: Routledge and Kegan Paul, 1957), pp. 164–5.
108 For de Mun's writings on this see his *Discours*, Vol. IV, pp. 21–37.
109 See Pirou *Néo-Liberalisme, Néo-corporatisme, néo-socialisme*, p. 83.
110 Manoilesco, *op. cit.*, pp. 277–8.
111 Bowen, *op. cit.*, pp. 141–2. For other examples of nationalist corporatists see references for De La Rocque and Bacconnier above.
112 Spann, *Der Wahre Staat*, p. 127.
113 La Tour, *Aphorismes de politique social*, p. 10.
114 La Tour, *Vers un Ordre social chrétien*, p. 209.
115 Azpiazu, *op. cit.*, p. 95.
116 De La Rocque, *op. cit.*, p. 104.
117 *ibid*, p. 109.
118 Durkheim, *op. cit.*, p. vi.
119 See E. Durkheim *Suicide* (London: Routledge and Kegan Paul, 1952), pp. 378–84 and 386–91.
120 Durkheim, *De la Division du travail*, p. iii.
121 Diamant, *op. cit.*, pp. 159–63.
122 Ketteler, *op. cit.*, p. 117.
123 For further elaboration of Ketteler's views on this point, see *op. cit.*, pp. 130–6.
124 See Nitti, *op. cit.*, p. 276.
125 Manoilesco, *op. cit.*, p. 279.
126 Spann, *Der wahre Staat*, pp. 269–73.
127 *ibid*, pp. 244–5.
128 Bowen, *op. cit.*, pp. 98–9.
129 Speech of 25 January 1884 in Chamber of Deputies, quoted in Nitti, *op. cit.*, p. 277.
130 Leo XIII, *op. cit.*, pp. 28–9.
131 *ibid*, p. 30.
132 Pirou *Essais sur le corporatisme*, pp. 120–1; see also Elbow, *op. cit.*, p. 148. Brethe de la Gressaye, who was Professor of Law at the University of Aix, was more in sympathy with giving labour a prominent position than his fellow theorists.
133 Perroux, *op. cit.*, pp. 35 and 207–10.
134 Rocco in Lyttleton, *op. cit.*, pp. 281–2.

135 De Michelis, *op. cit.*, pp. 210–11.
136 Manoilesco, *op. cit.*, p. 277.
137 Rathenau *Die neue Wirtschaft*, pp. 58–9.
138 Brethe de la Gressaye, *Syndicalisme* (Paris, 1930), p. 325. Of course Brethe de la Gressaye was against outlawing strikes, and his detailed proposals for arbitration by the state appear to have been designed to reduce substantially the possibility of such action.
139 Messner, *op. cit.*, pp. 439 and 463–6.

Chapter 4

1 Spann, *Der Wahre Staat*, p. 112.
2 *ibid*, pp. 108–9.
3 *ibid*, p. 115.
4 Bowen, *German Theories of the Corporative State* (New York, 1947), pp. 101–2.
5 Quoted in Hogan, *The Development of William Emmanuel von Ketteler's Interpretation of the Social Problem* (Washington, 1946), p. 75.
6 Ketteler, *Die Arbeitefrage und das Christenthum*, p. 72.
7 *ibid*, p. 62.
8 *ibid*, pp. 57 and 77.
9 La Tour, *Vers un ordre social chretien*, p. 253.
10 Rathenau *Der neue Staat*, pp. 28–9.
11 De La Rocque, *The Fiery Cross* (London, 1936), pp. 165–6.
12 Manoilesco, *Le Siècle du Corporatisme* (Paris, 1934), pp. 61–9.
13 W. von Klopp (ed.) *Die socialen Lehren des Freihern. Karl von Vogelsang*, p. 245, quoted Diamant, *Austrian Catholics* (Princeton 1960), p. 45.
14 Manoilesco, *op. cit.*, pp. 330–4 and also 326–30.
15 *ibid*, pp. 334–47, and on selection of 'representatives' see pp. 267–71. To confuse things further, Manoilesco set out proposals for bodies to coordinate the various corporations, the General Confederation of Entrepreneurs in the economic sphere, and the Superior Council of Corporations in the social one (pp. 271–74).
16 Bowen, *op. cit.*, pp. 101–2.
17 La Tour, *op. cit.*, p. 393.
18 For La Tour's changing views see, *ibid*, pp. 260–2, 276–9, 475 and 486.
19 See Rathenau *The New Society*, pp. 12–13 and 28–9 for an outline of these ideal states.
20 See Rathenau *Der neue Staat*, pp. 28–34 for an outline of his scheme, although much is simply rhetoric.
21 See Coutinho, 'The Federalism of Karl Marlo and Konstantin Frantz', *Political Science Quarterly*, Vol. 53 (1938), pp. 414–16.
22 Azpiazu, *The Corporate State* (St Louis, 1951), pp. 245–6.
23 *ibid*, pp. 243–4.
24 Duguit's proposals are set out in several places; see for example, 'L'Election des Senateurs', *Revue politique et parlementaire*, Vol. 3 (1895).
25 Durkheim added that: 'Society instead of remaining what it has become today, an aggregate of distinct juxtaposed electoral districts, would become a vast system of national corporations [...] and it is certain that in this way, political assemblies would express more accurately the diversity of social interests and

their relations; they would be a more faithful résumé of social life in its
ensemble.' See Durkheim, *De la Division du travail*, p. xxxi.

26 For a discussion of such ideas and experiments, both inside and outside
corporatism, in a number of European countries, see K. Lowenstein, 'Occupational Representation and the Idea of an Economic Parliament', *Social Science*,
Vol. 12 (1937).

27 See R. Bonnard, *Syndicalisme, corporatisme et l'état corporatif* (Paris: Librairie Générale de Droit et Jurisprudence, 1937), p. 118.

28 For examples of a national council of corporations, see Brethe de la Gressaye,
Syndicalisme (Paris, 1930), pp. 259, 263 and 344; Chanson, *Les Droits du
travailleur* (Paris, 1935), p. 231; Duthoit, 'Par une authorité' corporative vers
une économie ordonée, *chronique sociale de France*, July 1935, p. 525; De La
Rocque, *op. cit.*, pp. 170–1; and Bonnard, *op. cit.*, p. 120.

29 See G. Viance *Démocratie, dictature, et corporatisme* (Paris: Flammarion,
1938), pp. 189–98.

30 F. Bacconnier *Le Salut par la corporation*, pp. 236–9.

31 See Chroust, 'The Corporate Idea and the Body Politic in the Middle Ages', *The
Review of Politics*, Vol. 9, (1947), for a discussion of the corporate idea.

32 A. Schäffle, *Die Aussichtslosigkeit der Socialdemokratie*, pp. 151–8, quoted in
Bowen, *op. cit.*, pp. 134–6.

33 This was particularly true of French corporatists who sought to return to
France to its pre-1789 glory.

34 From Franz Baader's 'Collected Works', quoted in Moody, *Church and
Society* (New York, 1953), p. 400 (my emphasis).

35 La Tour, *op. cit.*, p. 502.

36 *ibid*, pp. 477–8.

37 *ibid*, p. 257.

38 *ibid*, p. 401.

39 *ibid*, pp. 261 and 473.

40 Muret, *op. cit.*, pp. 200–16.

41 Bacconnier, *op. cit.*, pp. 236–9.

42 See Chanson, *op. cit.*, p. 231; Bonnard *op. cit.*, p. 120; and Brethe de la
Gressaye, *op. cit.*, pp. 259 and 263.

43 De La Rocque, *op. cit.*, pp. 96–7 and 164–5. Women would be allowed to vote
in municipal and Senate elections.

44 *ibid*, pp. 172–3.

45 *ibid*, pp. 164 and 171.

46 Baudin, *op. cit.*, pp. 161–4 and 187.

47 Coutinho, *op. cit.*, pp. 413–16.

48 Manoilesco, *op. cit.*, pp. 349–57.

49 *ibid*, pp. 351–2.

50 Bowen, *op. cit.*, pp. 134–7.

51 Spann, *Der wahre Staat*, pp. 284–5. Spann was against specialisation but
favoured the all-round political leader like the medieval lord (p. 236).

52 See G. L. Mosse, *The Crisis of German Ideology* (London: Weidenfeld and
Nicolson, 1966), pp. 284–5.

53 H. de Man, 'Les Thèses de Pontigny', in P. Dodge (ed.) *A Documentary Study
of Hendrick de Man, Socialist Critic of Marxism* (Princeton, N.J.: Princeton
University Press, 1979), pp. 303–4 (my emphasis).

54 Pirou, *Le Corporatisme*, pp. 62–7. See also Alfred Rolland in G. Boivin and

M. Bouvier-Ajam, *Vers une Economie politique morale*, p. 10 quoted Elbow, French Corporative Theory (New York, 1953), p. 163.

55 See A. H. Birch, *Representation* (London: Macmillan, 1978), pp. 22–4.

56 See H. Noyelle, 'Plans d'une économie Dirigée', in *Revue d'Économie politique*, Vol. 48 (1934), pp. 1663–6. The group, drawn from diverse backgrounds, collaborated under the aegis of Jules Romains to formulate a more effective form of government in the wake of the riots of February 1934. See also *Plan du 9 juillet: Réforme de la France par le groupe du 9 juillet. Avant-propos par Jules Romains* (Paris: Gallimard, 1934).

57 See for example Rathenau, *The New Society*, pp. 137 and 145–6.

58 See Diamant, *op. cit.*, p. 45.

Chapter 5

1 For a discussion of the 'hierarchical' and 'community' conceptions of society see K. Dyson, *The State Tradition in Western Europe* (Oxford: Martin Robertson, 1980), pp. 139–40 and 143–50.

2 G. Pirou *Néo-Liberalisme, néo-corporatisme, néo-socialisme*, pp. 95–110.

3 See Chroust, 'The Corporate Idea and the Body Politic in the Middle Ages', *The Review of Politics*, Vol. 9 (1947), pp. 445–50.

4 M. Weber, *Economy and Society* (New York: Bedminster Press, 1968), Vol. 1, p. 212. Weber defined domination as 'the probability that a command with a given specific content will be obeyed by a given group of persons' (p. 53).

5 Bowen, *German Theories of the Corporate State* (New York, 1947), and Elbow, *French Corporative Theory 1789–1948* (New York, 1953), provide a basis but remain lodged very firmly in the nations which are the subject of their respective studies.

Chapter 6

1 The origins and history of Italian Fascism are subjects of much disagreement and differing interpretation. Many of the references cited in this chapter provide a discussion of these topics. However, a valuable introduction to the origins and early years is provided in A. Lyttleton, *The Seizure of Power* (London: Weidenfeld and Nicolson, 1973).

2 See M. Knox, *Mussolini Unleashed* (Cambridge: Cambridge University Press, 1982), pp. 8–12.

3 A. Aquarone, 'Italy: the Crisis and the Corporate Economy', *Journal of Contemporary History*, Vol. 4 (1969), p. 169.

4 For an outline of the policies pursued under De Stefani see S. La Francesca, *La Politica Economica del Fascismo* (Bari: Laterza, 1972), pp. 6–15.

5 R. De Felice, *Mussolini il Fascista*, 2 (Turin: Einaudi, 1968), pp. 86–9.

6 See A. J. Gregor *Italian Fascism and Developmental Dictatorship* (Guildford: Princeton University Press, 1979), pp. 133–40.

7 A. J. De Grand, *The Italian Nationalist Association and the Rise of Fascism* (London: University of Nebraska Press, 1978), Chs. 9 and 10.

8 C. T. Schmidt, *The Plough and the Sword* (New York: A.M.S. Press, 1966), Ch. 4.

9 Gregor, *op. cit.*, pp. 147–8.

10 See W. Welk, *Fascist Economic Policy* (Cambridge, Mass: Harvard University

Press, 1938), tables 15 and 16, pp. 166–7; and S. B. Clough, *The Economic History of Modern Italy* (London: Columbia University Press, 1964), pp. 229–30.

11 C. T. Schmidt, *The Corporate State in Action* (London: Gollancz, 1939), p. 165; and F. Guarneri *Battaglie Economiche tra le due Grandi Guerre* (Milan: Garzanti, 1953), p. 319.

12 Schmidt, *op. cit.*, pp. 165–166.

13 For details on the Ethiopian war and sanctions, see R. De Felice *Mussolini il Duce*, Vol. 1 (Turin: Einaudi, 1974), pp. 597–757; D. M. Smith *Mussolini's Roman Empire* (London: Longman, 1976), and La Francesca, *op. cit.*, pp. 77–80.

14 Welk, *op. cit.*, pp. 213–18.

15 *ibid*, pp. 177–8.

16 *Survey of Italy's Economy* by UNRRA (Rome: 1947).

17 S. Lombardini, 'Italian Fascism and the Economy', in S. Woolf (ed.) *The Nature of Fascism* (London: Weidenfeld and Nicolson, 1968), pp. 152–3. The small educated elite preferred overwhelmingly careers in law and the state bureaucracy to technology or industry.

18 J. S. Cohen, 'Economic Growth', in E. Tannenbaum and E. Noether (eds) *Modern Italy* (New York: New York University Press, 1974), pp. 177–9.

19 *ibid*, p. 183.

20 See A. Rocco, 'Il problema economico italiano', in *Scritti e discorsi politici*, Vol. 1 (Milan: Giuffre, 1938), pp. 13–19.

21 See again Rocco's 'The Syndicates and the Crisis within the State' in Lyttleton (ed.) *Italian Fascisms*. See also Gregor, *op. cit.*, pp. 103–112.

22 See D. A. Binchy, *Church and State in Fascist Italy* (London: RIIA, 1941); and C. F. Delzell (ed.) *The Papacy and Totalitarianism Between the World Wars* (London: Wiley, 1974).

23 *Law on Syndicates and Collective Relations of Labour* (No. 563, 3 April 1926) arts 3 and 4.

24 *Decree on Functions of Syndicates and Collective Labour Relations* (No. 1130), art 42.

25 *ibid*, art 43.

26 *Law on Reform of National Council of Corporations* (No. 206, 20 March, 1930). See also L. Rosenstock-Franck, *L'Économie corporative fasciste en doctrine et en fait* (Paris: J. Gambier, 1934), pp. 300–3 and 312–30; and G. L. Field, *The Syndical and Corporative Institutions of Italian Fascism* (New York: Columbia University Press, 1938), pp. 144–53.

27 Field, *op. cit.*, pp. 155–86.

28 There were also a number of representatives from the National Fascist Association of Cooperatives, but employer and employee syndicates on average were given jointly over 5/6 of the council places.

29 On the corporations see Field, *op. cit.*, pp. 186–93.

30 G. Salvemini *Under the Axe of Fascism* (London: Gollancz, 1936), Ch. 15.

31 As set out in the *Charter of Labour*, art 6, which was incorporated into law on *Formation and Functions of Corporations*, (No. 163), art 1.

32 Decree No. 563, arts 1–3, and 5–6.

33 From 1926–8 there was a general confederation of labour which did not have an employer counterpart, the trade associations fearing domination by the big industrialists. The division of the general labour confederation in November

1928 marked the virtual end of the remaining power of the Fascist trade unions and their leader Edmondo Rossoni. See Lyttleton, *op. cit.*, p. 248.

34 See D. L. Horowitz, *The Italian Labor Movement* (Cambridge, Mass: Harvard University Press, 1963), pp. 153–80. The trade unions had not been helped by the defeat of the factory occupations in 1920, the political divisions on the left which resulted from this and the arrival by 1921 of a serious post-war depression. These factors, however, only weakened the trade unions – Fascist violence destroyed them. By 1924–5 all effective trade unions had been destroyed. The dominance of the Fascist unions was very largely due to the absence of opposition. See Salvemini, *op. cit.*, Ch. 2.

35 Field, *op. cit.*, p. 70.

36 *ibid*, p. 88(fn).

37 art. 12.

38 Salvemini, *op. cit.*, pp. 41–7.

39 Law No. 563, art 5.

40 *ibid*.

41 *ibid.*, art. 10.

42 A good account of the scheme is available in Field *op. cit.*, pp. 80–1 and 88–95. See also Salvemini, *op. cit.*, Ch. 6.

43 See Lyttleton, *op. cit.*, pp. 223–6, 230–1, 320 and 339–40; and C. Haider, *Capital and Labour under Fascism* (New York: AMS Press, 1968 (repr of 1930 ed)), passim.

44 R. Sarti, *Fascism and the Industrial Leadership in Italy 1919–1940* (London: University of California Press, 1971), pp. 80–8.

45 See Haider, *op. cit.*, pp. 221–5; Field, *op. cit.*, pp. 93–4; and Rosenstock-Franck, *op. cit.*, pp. 90–97.

46 See law on Formation and Functions of Corporations (No. 163), art. 8.

47 See decree No. 206, art. 12.

48 See decree No. 163, arts. 10 and 11.

49 Royal Decree No. 1130, art. 44 (d).

50 Decree No. 163, art. 12.

51 Full details are found in Field, *op. cit.*, pp. 194–203. See also Welk, *op. cit.*, pp. 121–130; Schmidt, *op. cit.*, pp. 173–7; Salvemini, *op. cit.*, pp. 139–45; and Aquarone in *Journal of Contemporary History*, pp. 49–52.

52 Welk, *op. cit.*, p. 147.

53 See Sarti, *op. cit.*, pp. 102–3 and 107–9.

54 See Aquarone in *Journal of Contemporary History*, pp. 50–52; and Sarti, *op. cit.*, pp. 103–4 and 106–7. For Mussolini's personal view see his *Opera Omnia* (Florence: La Fenice, 36 Vols 1951–63), Vol. 27, pp. 241–8.

55 Royal Decree No. 1130, art. 44(a). The corporations also had power to lay down general rules applicable to labour; law No. 563, art. 10.

56 art. 13.

57 Decree No. 563, art. 10 and Royal Decree No. 1130, arts. 47–55 and 58–60.

58 Decree No. 563, arts. 18–23.

59 See *Sindacato e Corporazione* Vol. 62, pp. 277–94 (September 1934).

60 H. Finer, *Mussolini's Italy* (London: Gollancz, 1935), p. 505.

61 See law No. 563, arts. 13–15.

62 Law No. 563, art. 17.

63 Royal Decree (No. 1130), art. 80.

64 *ibid*, art. 80.

65 Sarti, *op. cit.*, pp. 74–5.
66 A. Aquarone, *L'Organizzazione dello Stato Totalitario* (Turin: Einaudi, 1965), pp. 133–6.
67 Rosenstock-Franck, *op. cit.*, p. 122.
68 Salvemini, *op. cit.*, p. 84.
69 Rosenstock-Franck, *op. cit.*, pp. 179–86.
70 *ibid*, pp. 192–203, and Haider, *op. cit.*, pp. 199–205.
71 See Royal Decree on Approval of Electoral Law (No. 1995). The suffrage was also restricted.
72 Lyttleton, *op. cit.*, pp. 125–9.
73 *ibid*, pp. 135–48.
74 *ibid*, Ch. 10.
75 Decree on Powers of Head of the Government (No. 2263), arts. 1–2.
76 *ibid*, arts. 3–4. D. M. Smith, *Mussolini* (London: Weidenfeld and Nicolson, 1981) highlights Mussolini's disposition to take decisions by himself.
77 G. Ciano, *Diario 1937–1943* (Milan: Einaudi, 1980 (ed. De Felice)), 27 March 1939.
78 *ibid*, 3 June 1939.
79 G. Rossoni, 'Fascism Between Legality and Revolution', in R. Sarti (ed.) *The Ax Within* (New York: New Viewpoints, 1974), pp. 15–16. See also Lyttleton, *op. cit.*, Chs. 4–5.
80 R. Sarti, 'Fascist Modernization in Italy: Traditional or Revolutionary?', *American Historical Review*, Vol. 57 (1969–70), p. 1031.
81 The best single work on the behind the scene compromises is Aquarone's *L'Organizzazione dello Stato Totalitario*. The title is, however, misleading as the work indicates that the Fascist state was not totalitarian.
82 A. Lyttleton, 'Italian Fascism', in W. Laquer (ed.) *Fascism, A Reader's Guide* (Harmondsworth: Penguin, 1979), pp. 94–5. See also T. Cole, 'Italy's Fascist Bureaucracy', *American Political Science Review*, Vol. 32 (1938), esp. p. 1157.
83 H. D. Lasswell and R. Serino, 'The Fascists: The Changing Italian Elite', in H. D. Lasswell and D. Lerner (eds) *World Revolutionary Elites* (London: MIT Press, 1966), p. 86.
84 L. Rosenstock-Franck *Les Étapes de l'économie fasciste italienne* (Paris: Librairie Sociale et Économique, 1939), pp. 45–6 and 274–7.
85 D. D. Robertson, *The Syndicalist Tradition and Italian Fascism* (Manchester: Manchester University Press, 1979), pp. 184–5 and 242–75.
86 See R. Sarti, 'Mussolini and the Industrial Leadership in the Battle of the Lira, 1925–1927', *Past and Present* No. 47 (May 1970); and De Felice *Mussolini, il Fascista*, Vol. 2, pp. 246–58.
87 Ciano, *op. cit.*, passim.
88 See Rosenstock-Franck *L'Économie corporative*, pp. 303–330; Aquarone *L'Organizzazione*, pp. 188–94, 215–16 and 271–81; and Field, *op. cit.*, pp. 145–52. See also law on Reform of National Council of Corporations (No. 206) and law erecting the Chamber of Fasces and of Corporations (No. 129). The Chamber did in fact have a role in drafting legislation, but was subordinate to the executive. The Chamber of Fasces and Corporation had 824 members drawn from the National Council of Corporations and the National Council of the PNF. It replaced the Chamber of Deputies.
89 Charter of Labour, art. 12. The same article also stated that 'Wages shall be determined without reference to any general rules' (sic).

90 Rosenstock-Franck, *L'Économie corporative*, pp. 65–77.
91 M. Neufeld, *Italy: School for Awakening Countries* (Ithaca: Cornell University, 1961), pp. 381–4.
92 C. Vannutelli, 'The Living Standards of Italian Workers', in R. Sarti (ed.) *The Ax Within*, pp. 149–50; S. Woolf, 'Did a Fascist Economic System Exist?', in S. Woolf, *op. cit.*, p. 133; and Salvemini, *op. cit.*, pp. 204–20 and 237–55.
93 Vannutelli, *op. cit.*, pp. 150–4. Agricultural workers appeared to have suffered heavier cuts, see Schmidt, *The Corporate State in Action*, p. 107.
94 Clough, *op. cit.*, p. 376.
95 Lombardini, *op. cit.*, p. 161.
96 Woolf, *op. cit.*, p. 134.
97 Gregor, *op. cit.*, pp. 196–206.
98 Clough, *op. cit.*, p. 376.
99 The issue of Fascism as a 'development dictatorship' is discussed in A. Hughes and M. Kolinsky, 'Paradigmatic Fascism and Modernization', *Political Studies*, Vol. 24 (1976), pp. 371–82.
100 P. V. Cannistraro, 'Mussolini's Cultural Revolution: Fascist or Nationalist', *Journal of Contemporary History*, Vol. 7 (1972).
101 M. Neufeld, *Poor Countries and Authoritarian Rule* (New York: Cornell University Press, 1965), p. 151.
102 Cole, *op. cit.*, pp. 1152–5.
103 Cf Charter of Labour.
104 Knox, *op. cit.*, p. 104.
105 E. Tannenbaum *Fascism in Italy* (London: Allen Lane, 1973), p. 117. In 1940 scarcely £20m were being paid out in total.
106 Gregor, *op. cit.*, p. 260.
107 Schmidt, *The Corporate State in Action*, pp. 110–11.
108 On social security in general see Tannenbaum, *op. cit.*, pp. 117–18; and Vannutelli, *op. cit.*, pp. 154–5.
109 Tannenbaum, *op. cit.*, pp. 158–63. For a full discussion see V. De Grazia, *The Culture of Consent* (Cambridge: Cambridge University Press, 1981).
110 *ibid*, Chs. 5 and 6.
111 Schmidt, *The Corporate State in Action*, p. 114.
112 Vannutelli, *op. cit.*, pp. 155–6. See also Salvemini, *op. cit.*, 314–28, 346–53 and 362–70.
113 Clough, *op. cit.*, pp. 240–1.
114 Sarti, *Fascism and the Industrial Leadership in Italy 1919–1940*, pp. 92–93.
115 Salvemini, *op. cit.*, pp. 264–70.
116 Schmidt, *The Corporate State in Action*, p. 111.
117 Tannenbaum, *op. cit.*, pp. 118–19.
118 Aquarone, 'Italy: the Crisis and the Corporative Economy', pp. 40–1.
119 Schmidt, *The Corporate State in Action*, pp. 112–13 and *The Plough and the Sword* (New York: AMS Press, 1966 [originally published in 1938]), Ch. 5; and Salvemini, *op. cit.*, p. 294.
120 Field, *op. cit.*, pp. 107–15, and Schmidt *The Corporate State in Action*, p. 112.
121 Field, *op. cit.*, pp. 116–17.
122 Salvemini, *op. cit.*, pp. 318–19; Welk, *op. cit.*, p. 99; and Tannenbaum, *op. cit.*, p. 118.
123 Gregor, *op. cit.*, pp. 275–6.

124 Cf D. Guerin, *Fascism and Big Business* (New York: Pathfinder, 1973);
     E. Rossi *Padroni del Vapore e Fascismo* (Bari: Laterza, 1966).
125 Aquarone *L'Organizzazione*, pp. 175–88.
126 Knox, *op. cit.*, p. 12.
127 Haider, *op. cit.*, pp. 152–7.
128 Schmidt, *The Corporate State in Action*, p. 109.
129 Sarti, *Fascism and the Industrial Leadership 1919–1940*, p. 94.
130 Salvemini, *op. cit.*, pp. 354–6.
131 Rosenstock-Franck, *L'Économie corporative*, pp. 27–48.
132 Mussolini, *op. cit.*, Vol. 44, p. 410.
133 Knox, *op. cit.*, p. 12.
134 Clough, *op. cit.*, p. 249.
135 K. Allen and A. Stevenson, *An Introduction to the Italian Economy* (London:
     Martin Robertson, 1974), pp. 219–21.
136 *ibid.*
137 R. Romeo, *Breve Storia della Grande Industria in Italia* (Rocco San Cas-
     ciano: Capelli 1967), pp. 168–9.
138 M. Posner and S. Woolf, *Italian Public Enterprise* (London: Duckworth,
     1967), pp. 21–6; and S. Holland, 'The National Context', in S. Holland (ed.),
     The State as Entrepreneur (London: Weidenfeld and Nicolson, 1972),
     pp. 56–62.
139 Sarti, *op. cit.*, pp. 107–9.
140 La Francesca, *op. cit.*, pp. 51–3.
141 Sarti, *op. cit.*, p. 109.
142 Sarti, 'Fascist Modernization in Italy' in *American Historical Review*,
     p. 1043. On price controls see also H. S. Miller, 'Techniques of Price Control
     in Fascist Italy', *Political Science Quarterly*, Vol. 53 (1938), pp. 584–98.
143 Schmidt, *The Corporate State in Action*, pp. 157, 180 and 194–95.
144 Sarti, *Fascism and the Industrial Leadership*, p. 127.
145 Schmidt, *The Plough and the Sword*.

Chapter 7

1 See D. L. Wheeler, *Republican Portugal: A Political History 1910–1926*
   (Madison: University of Wisconsin Press, 1978).
2 D. L. Wheeler, 'The Military and the Portuguese Dictatorship 1926–74: The
   Honor of the Army', in L. S. Graham and H. M. Makler (eds) *Contemporary
   Portugal* (London: University of Texas Press, 1979), p. 199.
3 The rise of Salazar 1928–1933 is described in many sources, several of which
   are cited herein. Basic histories of the period are provided in A. H. de Oliveira
   Marques, *History of Portugal* (New York: Columbia University Press, 1976),
   the seminal liberal history; and S. Payne, *A History of Spain and Portugal*
   (Madison: University of Wisconsin Press, 1973) Vol. 2. See also Oliveira
   Marques, 'The Portuguese 1920s: A General Survey', *Iberian Studies*, Vol. 2
   (1973).
4 H. Kay, *Salazar and Modern Portugal* (London: Eyre and Spottiswoode,
   1970), pp. 48–9; and A. de Figueiredo, *Portugal and its Empire* (London:
   Gollancz, 1961), p. 40.
5 *Political Constitution of the Portuguese Republic*, art. 5.
6 *ibid*, art. 6, (2).

7   *ibid*, art. 6, (3).
8   *ibid*, arts. 31–6.
9   *The Statute of National Labour* (Decree-Law No. 32048), art. 21.
10 *ibid*, arts. 24 and 25.
11 *ibid*, arts. 2 and 3.
12 *ibid*, arts. 4, 6 and 7.
13 Many of the Statute's articles are quoted in F. Cotta, *Economic Planning in Corporative Portugal* (London: King and Son, 1937).
14 H. J. Wiarda *Corporatism and Development* (Amherst: University of Massachusetts Press, 1977), pp. 39–40.
15 *ibid*, pp. 95–8. See also H. Martins, 'Portugal' in S. J. Woolf (ed.) *European Fascism*, p. 314.
16 A single reference that would outline the areas of state regulation over the regime's life is not generally available. Individual references will be given later where appropriate. However, much can be gleaned from F. Pereira da Moura, 'The Development of the Portuguese Economy 1945–73' (Paper presented at Workshop on Modern Portugal, University of New Hampshire, Durham, October 1973).
17 A. de Oliveira Salazar, *Doctrine and Action* (London: Faber and Faber, 1939), pp. 123–4.
18 M. Murteira, 'The Present Economic Situation', in Graham and Makler *op. cit.*, p. 333.
19 See *The Development Plan* (Lisbon: Secretaria de Estado de Informacão e Turismo, 1953), Speech of Salazar, 28 May 1953, pp. 26–7.
20 R. A. Robinson, *Contemporary Portugal* (London: Allen and Unwin, 1979), pp. 140–1; Kay, *op. cit.*, p. 437.
21 Murteira, *op. cit.*, pp. 333–4.
22 V. X. Pintado, *Structure and Growth of the Portuguese Economy* (Geneva: EFTA, 1964), pp. 204–5.
23 Robinson, *op. cit.*, pp. 141–4.
24 A. De Figueiredo, *Portugal: Fifty Years of Dictatorship* (New York: Holmes and Meier, 1976), p. 215.
25 P. T. Pereira, *Memorias* (Lisbon: Verbo, 1972), p. 22.
26 Decree Law, 23,049.
27 Decree Law, 23,050.
28 Decree Law, 23,050.
29 Decree Law, 23,051.
30 Decree Law, 1953.
31 Wiarda, *op. cit.*, pp. 112–13.
32 *ibid*, pp. 113–14.
33 Corporação do Comercio, *As Corporações Na Economia Nacional* (Lisbon: Nacional Ed., 1971), p. 35.
34 A complete list of the corporations and dates of their institution is given in Robinson, *op. cit.*, p. 130.
35 P. C. Schmitter, *Corporatism and Public Policy in Authoritarian Portugal* (London: Sage, 1975), p. 24.
36 M. Lucena, *L'Évolution du système corporatif portugais a travers les lois 1933–71* (Paris: Institut des Sciences du Travail, 1971), Vol. I, pp. 186–92.
37 Cotta, *op. cit.*, pp. 17–18.
38 The early years of the OECs are fully examined in *ibid*, Chs. 4–13.

39 Schmitter, *op. cit.*, p. 29.

40 *ibid*, p. 18.

41 'La CISL internazionale per la libertà sindicale in Portogallo', in *Politica Sindicale*, June 1961, pp. 263–4.

42 Schmitter, *op. cit.*, pp. 17–18.

43 P. Fryer and P. Pinheiro, *Oldest Ally* (London: Dennis Dobson, 1961), p. 124.

44 Schmitter, *op. cit.*, pp. 19–20.

45 J. Riegelhaupt, 'Peasants and Politics in Salazar's Portugal: The Corporate State and Village "Nonpolitics"', in Graham and Makler, *op. cit.*, p. 169.

46 J. Cutileiro, *A Portuguese Rural Society* (Oxford: Clarendon, 1971), pp. 153–4. The *casas dos pescadores* were similarly dominated by a combination of state and employer officials, but were more effective in representing worker-members' interests. Generally they were a more successful and enduring element in the corporatist edifice. (See Wiarda, *op. cit.*, 113–14).

47 Schmitter, *op. cit.*, fn.20.

48 Decree-Law No. 24715.

49 See Cotta, *op. cit.*, Chs. 4–13 passim for shift from *gremios* to OECs.

50 Schmitter, *op. cit.*, p. 29.

51 See M. Pinto and C. Moura, 'Estruturas Sindicais Portuguesas', *Análise Social*, Vol. 9 (1972), No. 33.

52 Martins, *op. cit.*, p. 318.

53 On the *gremio* system and the stratas of business see H. Makler, 'The Portuguese Industrial Elite and its Corporative Relations: A Study of Compartmentalization in an Authoritarian Regime', in Graham and Makler, *op. cit.*

54 Wiarda, *op. cit.*, p. 203.

55 Corporação do Comércio, *op. cit.*, p. 173.

56 See *ibid*; and Wiarda, *op. cit.*, pp. 227–8.

57 H. J. Wiarda, 'The Corporatist Tradition and the Corporative System in Portugal', in Graham and Makler, *op. cit.*, pp. 103–4. Cotta, *op. cit.*, is still valuable.

58 Schmitter, *op. cit.*, p. 29.

59 Wiarda, *Corporatism and Development*, p. 236.

60 L. S. Graham, 'Portugal: The Bureaucracy of Empire' (Paper prepared for the workshop on Modern Portugal, University of New Hampshire, Durham, October 1973), pp. 4–5.

61 H. J. Wiarda, 'The Portuguese Corporative System: Basic Structures and Current Functions', *Iberian Studies*, Vol. 2 (1973), p. 76; and Pinto and Moura, *op. cit.*, pp. 180–2.

62 Cutileiro, *op. cit.*, pp. 154–61.

63 Wiarda, *Corporatism and Development*, p. 272.

64 Wiarda, in *Iberian Studies* Vol. 2, pp. 77–8.

65 Wiarda, *Corporatism and Development*, pp. 243–4; and Makler, in Graham and Makler, *op. cit.*, pp. 141–8.

66 Art. 5.

67 *ibid*, art. 9.

68 *ibid*, art. 23.

69 L. Almeida, 'Labour Organisation Under Salazar's Fascist Regime', *Portuguese and Colonial Bulletin*, June/July 1963, p. 138.

70 The best source on wage determination is Lucena, *op. cit.*

71 See Lucena, *op. cit.*, Vol. 2 passim; and Wiarda, 'Basic Structures and Current Functions', pp. 76–7.

72 For Caetano's ideas of decentralising and reforming the system, see his *Corporative Revolution, Permanent Revolution* (Lisbon: Secretaria de Estado do Informação e Tourismo, 1968).

73 Pinto and Moura, *op. cit.*, pp. 149–53; and Vitoriano, 'Recent Trade Union Developments in Portugal', *Portuguese and Colonial Bulletin*, Vol. 12 (1972), p. 15.

74 *New York Times*, 5 April 1971.

75 A short, but valuable guide to Salazar's background and character is given in P. Sérant, *Salazar et son temps* (Paris: Les Sept Couleurs, 1961).

76 Constitution of 1933, Ch. 2, sections 1–3.

77 Marques, *History of Portugal*, Vol. 2, pp. 192–3; and Figueiredo, *Portugal and its Empire*, pp. 42–3.

78 Robinson, *op. cit.*, pp. 73–5.

79 *ibid*, p. 49.

80 See Constitution, ch. 4.

81 *ibid*, Ch. 3, sect. 3.

82 Martins, *op. cit.*, pp. 319–20; and Marques, *History of Portugal*, Vol. 2, p. 192.

83 Constitution, Ch. 3; quote from art. 102.

84 P. C. Schmitter, 'The Regime d'Exception that Became the Rule', in Graham and Makler, *op. cit.*, p. 8. See also pp. 8–23 for useful background on members of Chamber and National Assembly. For some additional information on the Chamber see Schmitter, *Corporatism and Public Policy*, pp. 30–6.

85 The Assembly however, also coopted certain political groupings Salazar needed to accommodate.

86 For a discussion of Salazar's power in the Council of Ministers see P. H. Lewis, 'Salazar's Ministerial Elite 1932–1968', *The Journal of Politics*, Vol. 40 (1978).

87 On the above see L. Graham, *Portugal: The Decline and Collapse of an Authoritarian Order* (London: Sage, 1975), pp. 5–33.

88 Wiarda, *Corporatism and Development*, p. 56. Kay, *op. cit.*, Ch. 2 gives a brief study of Salazar prior to taking office. See also Salazar's, *Principes d'action* (Paris: Librairie Arthème Fagard, 1956), for a wide selection of writings.

89 Salazar, *Doctrine and Action*, p. 192.

90 See Wheeler in Graham and Makler, *op. cit.*

91 See I. C. Bruneau, 'Church and State in Portugal: crisis of cross and sword', *Journal of Church and State*, Vol. 18 (1976); and also S. Cerqueira, 'L'Église catholique et la dictature corporative portuguaise', *Revue Française de Science Politique*, Vol. 23 (1973); a very critical, but not always accurate, study of the Church is given in P. Blanshard, *Freedom and Catholic Power in Spain and Portugal* (Boston: Beacon Press, 1962), Chs. 11 and 12.

92 Schmitter, in Graham and Makler, *op. cit.*, p. 21.

93 See Graham, *op. cit.*, passim. See also his 'Portugal: The Bureaucracy of Empire' (Paper prepared for the Workshop on Modern Portugal, University of New Hampshire, Durham, October 1973), pp. 34–42.

94 For an accurate description of the final years see D. L. Wheeler, 'Thaw in Portugal', *Foreign Affairs*, Vol. 48 (1969–70). Salazar's own views on the basis of the regime, ignoring the gloss, can be deduced from his 'Realities and

Trends of Portuguese Politics', *Internation·il Affairs*, Vol. 39 (1963), pp. 169–80. The Caetano period is studied in N. Blume, 'Portugal Under Caetano', *Iberian Studies*, Vol. 4 (1975).

95 H. Martins, 'Opposition in Portugal', *Government and Opposition*, Vol. 4 (1969).

96 P. McDonough, 'Structural Factors in the Decline and Fall of Portuguese Corporatism' (Paper presented at Mini-Conference on Contemporary Portugal, Yale University, March, 1975).

97 P. C. Schmitter, 'Liberation by Golpe', *Armed Forces and Society*, Vol. 2 (1975). See also R. M. Fields, *The Portuguese Revolution and the Armed Forces Movement* (London: Praeger, 1976), Chs. 1–3.

98 Constitution of 1933, art.3.

99 See Statute, arts. 21 and 24. It was even suggested that firms unable to pay fair wages should go out of existence; see Cotta, *op. cit.*, pp. 14–16.

100 Wiarda, *Corporatism and Development*, pp. 130 and 134–5.

101 Robinson, *op. cit.*, p. 135.

102 Wage legislation of the period can be found in *Boletim do INTP*, Vols. 2–4.

103 Decree-Law 32749. Of course, article I of the Decree continued to pay lip service to social justice.

104 *The Times*, 23 and 25 July 1942.

105 *The Times*, 18 February and 30 July 1943.

106 J. R. Migueis, 'Salazar of Portugal: Forgotten Fascist', *The Nation*, No. 159 (9 December 1944), pp. 715–16.

107 See E. Morris, 'Portugal's Politics Remain Unaltered', *World Today*, Vol. 20 (1964), p. 21; and Fryer and Pinheiro, *op. cit.*, pp. 140–1.

108 Robinson, *op. cit.*, p. 158; and Schmitter, *Corporatism and Public Policy*, p. 5 for figures.

109 Martins in Woolf (ed), p. 331.

110 'R.C.', 'Portugal: A Political and Economic Survey', *Balsa Review*, Vol. 5 (1971), p. 465.

111 Robinson, *op. cit.*, p. 174.

112 See V. M. Godinho, *O Socialismo e o Futoro da Peninsula* (Lisbon: 1969).

113 Salazar, *Doctrine and Action*, pp. 67–85 for a statement of the faith.

114 Figueiredo, *Portugal: Fifty Years of Dictatorship*, pp. 160–1.

115 See H. Martins, 'Portugal', in M. Archer and S. Giner (eds) *Contemporary Europe* (London: Weidenfeld and Nicolson, 1971).

116 McDonough, *op. cit.*

117 J. B. Pereira Neto, 'Social Evolution in Portugal Since 1945', in R. S. Sayers (ed) *Portugal and Brazil in Transition* (Minneapolis: University of Minnesota Press, 1968).

118 Morris, *op. cit.*, p. 21.

119 McDonough, *op. cit.*, Table 12.

120 Wiarda *Corporatism and Development*, pp. 210–18.

121 Wiarda, 'Basic Structures and Current Functions', p. 78.

122 Wiarda in Graham and Makler, *op. cit.*, pp. 108 and 110.

123 McDonough, *op. cit.*, pp. 16 and 26.

124 Pintado, *op. cit.*, p. 41.

125 Morris, *op. cit.*, p. 23; and Figueiredo, *Portugal and Its Empire* p. 51.

126 Pintado, *op. cit.*, p. 176 and ff. See also Moura, *op. cit.*; and Robinson, *op. cit.*, pp. 135–40.

127 E. N. Baklanoff, *The Economic Transformation of Spain and Portugal* (London: Praeger, 1978), pp. 119–27.
128 J. R. Logan, 'Worker Mobilization and Party Politics: Revolutionary Portugal in Perspective', in L. S. Graham and D. L. Wheeler (eds) *In Search of Modern Portugal* (London: University of Wisconsin Press, 1983), p. 138.
129 Baklanoff, *op. cit.*, pp. 127–30.
130 The Constitution of 1933, art. 35.
131 *Statute of National Labour*, art. 12.
132 *ibid*, arts. 13–15.
133 Pintado, *op. cit.*, pp. 200–1.
134 M. Derrick, *The Portugal of Salazar* (London: Paladin, 1938), p. 67. This work is an out and out apologia for Salazar.
135 L. Simas, 'Salazar: A Political Inquest', *Portuguese and Colonial Bulletin*, Vol. 11 (1971), pp. 29–30.
136 Pintado, *op. cit.*, pp. 201–2.
137 Baklanoff, *op. cit.*, p. 108.
138 See Makler, in Graham and Makler (eds) *op. cit.*; and 'A Case Study of the Portuguese Business Elite, 1964–1966', in Sayers (ed).
139 See H. Makler, 'Educational Levels of the Portuguese Industrial Elite', *International Studies of Management and Organisation*, Vol. 4 (1974), Part 1 and 2.
140 B. Lomax, 'Ideology and Illusion in the Portuguese Revolution', in Graham and Wheeler (eds), pp. 110–12.
141 Makler, in Graham and Makler (eds), pp. 148–9.
142 M. Murteira, 'The Present Economic Situation', in Graham and Makler (eds), pp. 333–4.
143 Baklanoff, *op. cit.*, p. 110. To place CUF into a wider context it was only 173rd in *Fortune*'s listing of non-US companies.
144 Robinson, *op. cit.*, pp. 145–6.
145 Wiarda, *Corporatism and Development*, pp. 303–4. See also M. B. Martins, *Sociedades e Grupos em Portugal* (Lisbon: Estampa, 1973).
146 Baklanoff, *op. cit.*, p. 111. In 1972 of 43 000 enterprises, 30 470 had 4 or less employees.
147 *ibid*, p. 112.
148 A. Ramos, 'Portuguese Industry', in *Portuguese and Colonial Bulletin*, Vol. 3 (1963–4), parts 3 and 4.
149 Pintado, *op. cit.*, pp. 28–32.
150 *IBRD World Tables*, January 1971.
151 OECD, *The Industrial Policies of 14 Member Countries* (Paris: 1971), pp. 276–8.
152 Simas, *op. cit.*, p. 30.

Chapter 8

1 For a distinction drawn between Fascism and other authoritarian regimes see H. R. Trevor-Roper, 'The Phenomenon of Fascism', in S. Woolf (ed.), *The Nature of Fascism* (London: Weidenfeld and Nicolson, 1969).
2 On the economic background see A. De Grand, *Italian Fascism* (London: University of Nebraska Press, 1982), Part 1; and Schmitter in Graham and Makler (eds) *Contemporary Portugal* (London, 1979), pp. 23–28.

3 On this point in relation to Portugal see Wiarda in Graham and Makler (eds), pp. 117–18.
4 See C. W. Anderson, *The Political Economy of Modern Spain* (London: The University of Wisconsin Press, 1970); F. B. Pike, 'The New Corporatism in Franco's Spain and some Latin American Perspectives', in F. B. Pike and T. Stritch (eds.) *The New Corporatism* (London: University of Notre Dame Press, 1974); S. G. Payne *Franco's Spain* (London: Routledge and Kegan Paul, 1968); K. N. Medhurst, *Government in Spain: The Executive at Work* (New York: Pergamon, 1973), and J. Linz, 'A century of politics and interests in Spain', in Berger (ed), *Organizing Interests in Western Europe* (Cambridge: Cambridge University Press, 1981).
5 See K. P. Erikson, *The Brazilian Corporative State and Working Class Politics* (London: University of California Press, 1977); A. Stephen (ed.), *Authoritarian Brazil* (London: Yale University Press, 1973); P. C. Schmitter, *Interest Conflict and Political Change in Brazil* (Stanford, Calif.: Stanford University Press, 1971).
6 See A. Stefan, *The State and Society: Peru in Comparative Perspective* (Princeton, N.J.: Princeton University Press, 1978); D. S. Palmer, *Peru: the Authoritarian Tradition* (New York: Praeger, 1980); A. F. Lowenthal (ed.), *The Peruvian Experiment: Continuity and Change under a Military Regime* (Princeton, N.J.: Princeton University Press, 1975); and J. M. Malloy, 'Authoritarian Corporatism and Mobilisation in Peru', in Pike and Stritch (eds), *op. cit.*
7 See W. J. Cornelius, 'Nation Building, Participation and Distribution: The Politics of Social Reform Under Cárdenas', in G. A. Almond, S. C. Tharagan and R. J. Mundt, *Crisis, Choice and Change* (Boston: Little Brown, 1973); B. Anderson and J. D. Cockeraft, 'Control and Cooption in Mexican Politics' *International Journal of Comparative Sociology*, Vol. 7 (1976); and M. Clark, *Organized Labour in Mexico* (Chapel Hill: University of North Carolina Press, 1934).
8 See J. Malloy (ed.) *Authoritarianism and Corporatism in Latin America* (Pittsburg, Pen.: University of Pittsburg Press, 1977); V. Alba, *Politics and the Labor Movement in Latin America* (Stanford, Calif.: Stanford University Press, 1968); C. W. Anderson, *Politics and Economic Change in Latin America: The Governing of Restless Nations* (Princeton, N.J.: Van Nostrand, 1967) and M. Davis and L. W. Goodman (eds.), *Workers and Managers in Latin America* (Lexington, Ma.: D. C. Heath, 1972).
9 H. J. Wiarda, *The Corporative Origins of the Iberian and Latin American Labor Relations System* (Amherst: University of Massachusetts, 1975).
10 Erikson, *op. cit.*
11 Wiarda, *op. cit.*, p. 36.
12 *ibid*, p. 35.
13 See Stefan, *op. cit.*; and Malloy in Pike and Stritch (ed.).
14 But see Stefan, *op. cit.*

Chapter 9

1 See A. G. Jordan, *Corporatism: The Unity and Utility of the Concept* (Glasgow: Strathclyde Papers on Government and Politics, 1983) pp. 2–3.
2 For example S. H. Beer, *Britain Against Itself* (London: Faber, 1982),

pp. 64–6; J. Hayward, 'National Aptitudes for Planning in Britain, France and Italy', *Government and Opposition*, Vol. 9 (1974), p. 401; H. M. Drucker, 'Devolution and Corporatism', *Government and Opposition*, Vol. 12 (1977), and S. A. Walkland, 'Whither the Commons?', in S. Walkland and M. Ryle (eds). *The Commons Today* (Glasgow: Collins, 1981), p. 283.

3 See J. T. Winkler, 'Corporatism', *Archives Européennes de Sociologie*, Vol. 17 (1976); A. Fox, 'Corporatism and Industrial Democracy', in Social Science Research Council, *Industrial Democracy: International Views* (Coventry: SSRC, 1978); D. Coombes, 'Parliamentary Politics in Britain and the Representation of Industrial Interest' (Paper for PSI Seminar, 2 April 1980), p. 14.

4 See most obviously P. C. Schmitter, 'Still the Century of Corporatism?', in Schmitter and Lehmbruch (eds), *Trends Towards Corporatist Intermediation* (London, 1979), pp. 14–15.

5 T. Lowi, 'American Business, Public Policy, Case-Studies, and Political Theory', *World Politics*, Vol. 16 (1964), p. 681.

6 See C. E. Lindblom, 'Another State of Mind', *American Political Science Review* Vol. 76 (1982), pp. 9–21.

7 J. Playford, 'The Myth of Pluralism', in F. G. Castles, D. J. Murray, D. C. Potter and C. J. Pollitt (eds.), *Decisions, Organisations and Society* (Harmondsworth: Penguin, 1976), pp. 381–5.

8 N. Polsby, *Community Power and Political Theory* (New Haven, Conn.: Yale University Press, 1963) and R. Prethus, 'Pluralism and Elitism', in F. G. Castles, D. J. Murray and D. C. Potter (eds.), *Decisions, Organisation and Society* (Harmondsworth: Penguin, 1971) p. 336.

9 R. A. Dahl, *Who Governs?* (New Haven, Conn.: Yale University Press, 1961), Books 4 and 5.

10 D. B. Truman, *The Governmental Process* (New York: Knopf, 1971), Ch. 16.

11 P. Bachrach and M. Baratz, 'Two Faces of Power', *American Political Science Review*, Vol. 46 (1962) and, 'Decisions and Non-Decisions: An Analytical Framework', *American Political Science Review*, Vol. 47 (1963).

12 See *Pluralist Democracy in the United States* (Chicago: Rand McNally, 1967); *Polyarchy* (London: Yale University Press, 1971); and with Charles Lindblom the new edition of *Politics, Economics and Welfare* (Chicago: University of Chicago Press, 1976). See also S. Ehrlich *Pluralism on and off course* (Oxford: Pergamon, 1982), pp. 118–29 for a wider discussion of changes in pluralism.

13 *Dilemmas of Pluralist Democracy* (New Haven: Yale University Press, 1982), pp. 40–1 and Appendix A.

14 R. Dahl, 'Pluralism Revisited' in S. Ehrlich and G. Wooten (eds) *Three Faces of Pluralism* (Farnborough: Gower, 1980), p. 28.

15 (New York: Basic Books, 1977), Part 4.

16 C. Lindblom, 'Comment on Manley', *American Political Science Review*, Vol. 77 (1983), p. 384.

17 See again Ehrlich, *op. cit.*

18 Lindblom is possibly exempt now, but then he is hardly a committed advocate of pluralist theory.

19 Dahl and Lindblom, *op. cit.*, p. xxxvi.

20 J. Manley, 'Neopluralism: A Class Analysis of Pluralism I and II', *American Political Science Review*, Vol. 77 (1983), pp. 379–80.

21 *ibid.*, p. 379. It is interesting that Dahl does not pick up this point in his reply (pp. 386–9).

22 See S. Lukes, *Power: A Radical View* (London: Macmillan, 1978); and
   P. Morriss, 'Power in New Haven: A Reassessment of "Who Governs"',
   British Journal of Political Science, Vol. 2 (1972).
23 A. Wolfe, *The Limits of Legitimacy* (London: Free Press, 1977), pp. xi–xii.
24 R. Alford, 'Paradigms of Relations Between State and Society', in L. Lindberg,
   R. Alford, C. Crouch and C. Offe (eds), *Stress and Contradiction in Modern
   Capitalism* (London: Lexington, 1975), p. 147.
25 See C. Lindblom, 'Another State of Mind', *American Political Science Review*,
   Vol. 76 (1982), pp. 9–21 on the marked impact of the challenge.
26 W. E. Connolly, 'The Challenge to Pluralist Theory', in W. E. Connolly (ed),
   The Bias of Pluralism (New York: Atherton Press, 1969).
27 See J. K. Galbraith, *The New Industrial Estate* (Harmondsworth: Penguin,
   1969); and D. Bell, *The Coming of Post-Industrial Society* (New York: Basic
   Books, 1973).
28 J. Lively, 'Pluralism and Consensus', in P. Birnbaum, J. Lively and G. Parry
   (eds), *Democracy, Consensus and Social Contract* (London: Sage, 1978).
29 M. Heisler, 'Corporate Pluralism Revisited: Where is the Theory', *Scandinavian Political Studies*, Vol. 2 (1979), p. 284.
30 *ibid*, p. 284–5.
31 A. G. Jordan, 'Iron triangles, woolly corporatism and elastic nets; Images of
   the policy process', *Journal of Public Policy*, Vol. 1 (1981), pp. 109–13.
32 *ibid*, p. 109.
33 *ibid*, p. 110.
34 Schmitter, in Schmitter and Lehmbruch (eds), *op. cit.*, p. 23.
35 Jordan, 'Iron Triangles', p. 110.
36 *ibid*, pp. 98 and 112–13.
37 *Corporatism: The Unity and Utility of the Concept?*, passim.
38 R. Martin, 'Pluralism and the New Corporatism', *Political Studies*, Vol. 31
   (1983), p. 99.
39 *ibid*, pp. 91–5.
40 *ibid*, p. 99.
41 See A. Cawson, *Corporatism and Welfare* (London: Heinemann, 1982), p. 39.
42 Martin, *op. cit.*, pp. 99–102.
43 S. H. Beer, 'Pressure Groups and Parties in Britain', *American Political Science
   Review*, Vol. 50 (1956), pp. 6–11.
44 P. C. Schmitter, 'Interest intermediation and regime governability in contemporary Western Europe and North America', in S. Berger (ed.), *Organizing
   interests in Western Europe* (Cambridge: Cambridge University Press, 1981),
   p. 327 (n. 28).
45 C. F. Sable, 'The internal politics of trade unions', in Berger (ed), *op. cit.*,
   p. 212.
46 *ibid*, p. 214.
47 *ibid*, p. 212.
48 A. Cox, 'Corporatism as Reductionism: the Analytic Limits of the Corporatist
   Thesis', *Government and Opposition*, Vol. 16 (1981), p. 90.
49 *ibid*, p. 92.
50 W. Grant, 'Studying Business Interest Associations: Does Neo-Corporatism
   Tell us Anything We didn't Know Already' (Paper presented to Political
   Studies Association Annual Conference, University of Newcastle, April 1983),
   p. 13.

51 P. Birnbaum, 'The State versus Corporatism', *Politics and Society*, Vol. 11 (1982).
52 Schmitter and Lehmbruch (eds.), *op. cit.*, p. 3.
53 Heisler, *op. cit.*, pp. 285–6. See also A. Diamant, 'Bureaucracy and Public Policy in Neo-corporatist Settings', *Comparative Politics*, Vol. 14 (1981).
54 L. Panitch, 'Recent Theorisations of Corporatism: reflections on a growth industry', *The British Journal of Sociology*, Vol. 31 (1980), p. 184.
55 *ibid*, pp. 183–4.
56 B. Nedelman and K. Meier, 'Theories of Contemporary Corporatism: Static or Dynamic?', *Comparative Political Studies*, Vol. 10 (1977), p. 40.
57 *ibid*, pp. 40–9.
58 Schmitter, 'Still the Century of Corporatism?' in Schmitter and Lehmbruch (eds), *op. cit.*, p. 13.
59 *ibid*, p. 21.
60 *ibid*, p. 15.
61 Schmitter in Berger (ed), *op. cit.*, p. 291.
62 P. Schmitter, 'Reflections on Where the Theory of Neo-Corporatism has Gone and Where the Praxis of Neo-Corporatism May be Going', in G. Lehmbruch and P. Schmitter (eds) *Patterns of Corporatist Policy Making* (London: Sage, 1982), p. 260. One of Schmitter's latest tracts is *Democratic Theory and Neo-Corporatist Practice* (Florence: EUI, 1983). This work does a 'Jordan' and claims negotiation exclusively for corporatism (p. 22).
63 Schmitter, 'Still the Century of Corporatism?', p. 21.
64 Prethus, *op. cit.*, pp. 336–7; and Connolly, *op. cit.*, p. 13.
65 Dahl, *Who Governs?* and *Dilemmas of Pluralist Democracies*; Polsby, *op. cit.*; Truman, *op. cit.*; J. La Polambara *Interest Groups in Italian Politics* (Princeton, N.J.: Princeton University Press, 1964); and Dahl and Lindblom, *op. cit.*
66 W. McConnel *Private Power and American Democracy* (New York: Knopf, 1966); H. Kariel, *The Decline of American Pluralism* (Stanford, Calif.: Stanford University Press, 1961); W. Connolly (ed.), *The Bias of Pluralism*; R. Miliband *The State in Capitalist Society* (London: Quartet, 1973).
67 C. W. Mills, *The Power Elite* (London: OUP, 1956).
68 Schmitter, 'Still the Century of Corporatism?', p. 10.
69 *ibid*, p. 24.
70 Schmitter, 'Modes of Interest Intermediation and Models of Societal Change in Western Europe', in Schmitter and Lehmbruch (eds.), *op. cit.*
71 Panitch, *op. cit.*, pp. 166–73.
72 Schmitter, in Lehmbruch and Schmitter (eds.), *op. cit.*
73 Heisler, *op. cit.*, p. 278.
74 See A. Cox, 'Introduction' in A. Cox (ed.), *Politics, Policy and the European Recession* (London: Macmillan, 1982), p. 29.
75 See J. J. Richardson and A. G. Jordan, *Governing Under Pressure* (Oxford: Martin Robertson, 1979).
76 See for early recognition of this aspect in Britain S. H. Beer, 'The British Legislature and the Problem of Mobilising Consent', in B. Crick (ed.) *Essays in Reform* (London: OUP, 1967).
77 G. Ionescu, *Centripetal Politics* (London: Hart-Davis, 1975), p. 1.
78 *ibid*, pp. 1–2.
79 *ibid*, p. 2.
80 Schmitter, in Berger (ed.), *op. cit.*, p. 295.

81 For example, Schmitter, 'Still the Century of Corporatism?', p. 13; A. G. Jordan and J. J. Richardson, 'The British Policy Style: or the logic of negotiation?', in J. Richardson (ed.), *Policy Styles in Western Europe* (London: Allen and Unwin, 1982), pp. 93–6; Cawson, *Corporatism and Welfare*, p. 39; J. P. Olsen 'Integrated organizational participation in government', in P. Nystrom and W. Starbuck (eds.), *Handbook of Organizational Design*, Vol. 2 (London: OUP, 1981), p. 493; M. Heisler (with R. Kvavik), 'Patterns of European Politics', in M. Heisler (ed.), *Politics in Europe* (New York: McKay, 1974), pp. 52–3; and L. Panitch, 'The Development of Corporatism in Liberal Democracies', in Schmitter and Lehmbruch (eds), *op. cit.*, p. 123.

82 H. Eckstein, *Pressure Group Politics* (London: Allen and Unwin, 1960) pp. 22–5.

83 L. Dion, 'The Politics of Consultation', *Government and Opposition*, Vol. 8 (1973).

84 S. Levine and P. E. White, 'Exchange as a conceptual Framework for the Study of Interorganizational Relationships', *Administrative Science Quarterly*, Vol. 5 (1961).

85 Support for this line comes from Olsen, *op. cit.*

86 For a discussion of bargaining see Dahl and Lindblom, *op. cit.*, Chs. 12 and 17.

87 See L. Panitch, 'The Development of Corporatism in Liberal Democracies', in Schmitter and Lehmbruch (eds.), *op. cit.*, for similar arguments.

88 L. Panitch, 'Trade Unions and the State', *New Left Review*, No. 125, Jan.–Feb. 1981, p. 24.

89 A. Cawson, 'Pluralism, Corporatism and the Role of the State', *Government and Opposition*, Vol. 13 (1978), p. 187.

90 B. Jessop, 'Corporatism, Parliamentarism and Social Democracy', in Schmitter and Lehmbruch (eds.), *op. cit.*, p. 204.

91 G. Lehmbruch, 'Liberal Corporatism and Party Government', in Schmitter and Lehmbruch (eds.), *op. cit.*, p. 151.

92 *ibid*, p. 153.

93 D. H. Wrong, *Power* (Oxford: Blackwell, 1979), p. 73.

94 A. Dunsire, *Control in a Bureaucracy* (Oxford: Martin Robertson, 1978) p. 106.

95 Lukes, *op. cit.*, p. 23.

96 *ibid*, p. 43.

97 B. Jessop, 'The Capitalist State and the Rule of Capital: Problems in the Analysis of Business Associations', in D. Marsh (ed.), *Capital and Politics in Western Europe* (London: Cass, 1983), p. 155.

Chapter 10

1 Lehmbruch in Schmitter and Lehmbruch (eds.) *Trends Towards Corporatist Mediation* (London, 1979), p. 150.

2 *ibid*, pp. 150–1.

3 *ibid*, pp. 152–7.

4 *ibid*, p. 150.

5 Though this itself enjoys a highly ambiguous treatment by Lehmbruch, see his 'Concluding Remarks' in Schmitter and Lehmbruch (eds.), pp. 304–5.

6 Panitch, in Schmitter and Lehmbruch (eds.), pp. 138–9.

7   L. Panitch, 'Trade Unions and the State', *New Left Review*, No. 125, Jan.–Feb. 1981, pp. 33–4.
8   *ibid*, pp. 32 and 34–7.
9   C. Offe and H. Wiesenthal, 'Two Logics of Collective Action', *Political Power and Social Theory*, Vol. 1 (1980), pp. 67–115.
10 W. E. Connolly, *The Terms of Political Discourse* (Oxford: Martin Robertson, 1983), pp. 88–93.
11 C. Crouch, *Class Conflict and the Industrial Relation Crisis* (London: Heinemann, 1977) pp. 34–5.
12 *ibid*, pp. 39–40.
13 C. Crouch, *The Politics of Industrial Relations* (Glasgow: Fontana, 1979), p. 189.
14 C. Crouch, 'Pluralism and the New Corporatism: A Rejoinder', *Political Studies* Vol. 31 (1983), p. 457.
15 *ibid*, pp. 457–8.
16 *ibid*, p. 458.
17 This is not the case, however, with Crouch's authoritarian corporatism where government imposes its regulations and the interest organisations' role therein (p. 458). Here a power relation would be regarded as more significant politically than simply self-administration.
18 C. Crouch, 'Corporatism in Industrial Relations: A Formal Model', Draft chapter for W. Grant (ed.) *The Political Economy of Corporatism* (Forthcoming). The author is indebted to Colin Crouch for permission to refer to this draft.
19 A. Cawson, 'Representational Crises and Corporatism in Capitalist societies' (Paper prepared for Joint PSA/ECPR Conference on Authority in Industrial Societies, Brussels, April 1979), p. 14.
20 A. Cawson, 'Pluralism, Corporatism and the role of the state', *Government and Opposition*, Vol. 13 (1978), p. 184.
21 A. Cawson, *Corporatism and Welfare* (London: Heinemann, 1982), p. 39.
22 *ibid*, p. 43.
23 *ibid*, pp. 43–4.
24 *ibid*, pp. 108–12.
25 *ibid*, p. 40.
26 *ibid*, p. 72.
27 A. Cawson and P. Saunders, 'Corporatism, Collective Politics and Class Struggle', in R. King (ed.), *Capital and Politics* (London: Routledge and Kegan Paul, 1983).
28 Offe and Wiesenthal, *op. cit.*, pp. 94–5.
29 G. R. Epsing-Anderson, G. R. Friedland and E. C. Wright, 'Modes of Class Struggle and the Capitalist state', in *Kapitalstate* No. 4/5 (1976), p. 191.
30 M. Crozier, 'The Problem of Power', *Social Research*, vol. 40 (1973), p. 219.
31 *ibid*, pp. 220–1.
32 *ibid*, p. 221.
33 S. Clegg, 'Power, Organization Theory, Marx and Critique', in S. Clegg and D. Dunkerley (eds.), *Critical Issues in Organizations* (London: Routledge and Kegan Paul, 1977) p. 32. Clegg's *The Theory of Power and Organization* (London: Routledge and Kegan Paul, 1979), provides many insights which can be drawn upon here.
34 Some might argue for the abandonment of 'power' for 'control' or 'domi-

nation', particularly Clegg in *The Theory of Power and Organization*. We, however, will stick with power along lines similar to Lukes, *Power: A Radical View* (London, 1978).

35 An interesting account of power, interests and values within organisations is provided by K. Walsh, B. Hinings, R. Greenwood and S. Ranson, 'Power and Advantage in Organizations', *Organization Studies*, Vol. 2 (1981), pp. 131–52.

36 K. Benson, 'A Framework for Policy Analysis', in D. Rogers and D. Whetton (eds.), *Interorganisational Co-ordination* (Ames: Iowa State Univesity Press, 1981), p. 164.

37 Jessop, 'The Capitalist State and the Rule of Capital', in D. Marsh (ed.), *Capital and Politics in Western Europe* (London, 1983), pp. 149–50.

38 Walsh, et al., pp. 136–7.

39 See J. P. Olsen, 'Integrated organisational participation in government', in P. C. Nystrom and W. G. Starbuck (eds.), *Handbook of Organizational Design* (London: OUP, 1981).

40 See Schmitter, in Lehmbruch and Schmitter (eds.), p. 260.

41 Olsen, *op. cit.*, pp. 499–500.

42 Panitch in Schmitter and Lehmbruch (eds.), pp. 144–5.

43 W. Streeck, 'Between Pluralism and Corporatism: German Business Associations and the State', *Journal of Public Policy*, Vol. 3 (1983), p. 272 supplies some supporting empirical evidence.

44 C. Offe, 'The Attribution of Public Status to Interest Groups: observations on the West German Case', in Berger (ed.); *Organizing Interests in Western Europe* (Cambridge, 1981), and Schmitter *ibid*, p. 291.

45 Streeck, *op. cit.*, p. 270.

46 C. Hood, *The Limits of Administration* (London: Wiley, 1976), pp. 9–11.

47 C. Offe, 'The Theory of the Capitalist State and the Problem of Policy Formation', in Lindberg et al., *Stress and Contradiction in Modern Capitalism* (London, 1975).

48 A. Cawson, 'Functional Representation and Democratic Politics: towards a Corporatist Democracy?', in G. Duncan (ed.), *Democratic Theory and Practice* (Cambridge: CUP, 1983), p. 179.

49 *ibid*, p. 181.

50 *ibid*, p. 182.

51 N. Poulantzas, *Classes in Contemporary Capitalism* (London: New Left Books, 1975); J. Holloway and S. Picciotto, 'Towards a Materialist Theory of the State', in J. Holloway and S. Picciotto (eds.) *State and Capital* (London: Edward Arnold 1978).

52 Holloway and Picciotto, *op. cit.*, p. 24.

53 J. O'Connor, *The Fiscal Crisis of the State* (New York: St Martin's Press, 1973); I. Gough, *The Political Economy of the Welfare State* (London: Macmillan, 1979); and J. Habermas, *Legitimation Crisis* (London: Heinemann, 1976) are among the most notable examples.

54 A short but succinct case for the need for making 'theory' testable by the use of counterfactuals is given in Cawson and Saunders, *op. cit.*, pp. 12–13.

55 C. J. Gray, J. K. Stringer and P. J. Williamson, 'Policy Analysis and Policy Change: An Analytic Framework' (Paper presented to Annual Conference of Political Studies Association, University of Newcastle, April 1983) pp. 42–4.

56 T. Forester, 'Neutralising the Industrial Strategy', in K. Coates (ed.) *What Went Wrong?* (Nottingham: Spokesman, 1979).

57 Gray et al., *op. cit.*, pp. 36–48.
58 P. Dunleavy, 'Professions and Policy Change: Notes Towards a Model of Ideological Corporatism', *Public Administration Bulletin* No. 36, August 1981. But see also P. J. Williamson and J. K. Stringer, 'Professions and Policy change: A Comment', *Public Administration Bulletin* No. 39, August 1982.
59 Benson, *op. cit.*
60 See for example B. Jessop, 'The Transformation of the State in Britain', in R. Scase (ed.), *The State in Western Europe* (London: Croom Helm, 1980).
61 See again Jessop in Marsh (ed.), pp. 149–50.
62 C. Offe and V. Ronge, 'Thesis on the Theory of the State', in C. Offe *Contradiction of the Welfare State* (London: Hutchinson, 1984) (ed. by J. Keans), p. 120.
63 *ibid*, p. 123.
64 See B. Jessop, *The Capitalist State* (Oxford: Martin Robertson, 1982).
65 Lehmbruch in Schmitter and Lehmbruch (eds.), p. 150; Panitch, *ibid*, p. 123; Jessop *ibid*, p. 195; Streeck, *op. cit.*; and Schmitter in Lehmbruch and Schmitter (eds.) pp. 260–1.
66 Cawson and Saunders, *op. cit.*, p. 17.
67 Panitch in Schmitter and Lehmbruch (eds.), p. 142.
68 *ibid*, pp. 140–5.
69 *Pace* O. A. Hirschman, *Exit, Voice and Loyalty* (Cambridge, Mass.: Harvard University Press, 1970).
70 See Walsh et al., pp. 131–3 for a shift away from bureaucratic authority perspectives.
71 For discussion of this point see A. F. Wasserspring, 'Neo-Corporatism and the Quest for Control: The Cuckoo Game', in Lehmbruch and Schmitter (eds.).
72 Offe in Berger (ed.), p. 137.
73 *ibid*, pp. 136–7.
74 *ibid*, pp. 137–8.
75 For such an example see R. King, 'Corporatism, Capital and Local Politics' (Paper presented to Annual Conference of Political Studies Association, University of Newcastle, April, 1983).
76 See P. C. Schmitter, *Democratic Theory and Neo-Corporatist Practice*, pp. 24–5.
77 Grant, 'Studying Business Interest Associations: Does Neo-Corporatism Tell us anything We Don't Already Know?' (Paper presented to the Annual Conference of the Political Studies Assoication, University of Newcastle, April 1983), p. 9.

Chapter 11

1 P. C. Schmitter, *Neo-Corporatism and the State* (Florence: EUI, 1984), pp. 2–9.
2 *ibid*, p. 11.
3 *ibid*, pp. 11–12 and 20.
4 *ibid*, p. 23. See also pp. 21–6.
5 For a full discussion of the associative-corporatist order see W. Streeck and P. C. Schmitter, *Community, Market, State – and Associations?* (Florence: EUI, 1984).

6 See Richardson (ed.), *Policy Styles in Western Europe* (London: Allen & Unwin, 1982).
7 Streeck and Schmitter, *op. cit.*, p. 25.
8 *ibid*, pp. 22–8.
9 Schmitter, *Neo-Corporatism and the State*, pp. 7 and 14–18.
10 See again C. Crouch, 'Pluralism and the New Corporatism: A Rejoinder', *Political Studies*, Vol. 31 (1983), pp. 457–8.
11 Schmitter, *op. cit.*, p. 30.
12 ESRC, *Programme of the Corporatism and Accountability Sub-Committee*, para 3.3.
13 Hegel, *The Philosophy of Right* (Oxford, 1942), p. 154.
14 *ibid*, pp. 152–4.
15 C. A. Gulick, *Austria: From Hapsburg to Hitler*, Vol. 2 (London: University of California Press, 1948); J. Dobrestberger, *Katholische Sozialpolitik am Scheideweg* (Graz: Ulrich Moser, 1947).
16 Fondation Nationale des Sciences Politiques, *Le Gouvernement de Vichy, 1940–1942* (Paris: Armand Colin, 1972); and Elbow, *French Corporative Theory* (New York, 1953), ch. 6.
17 The most quoted example of missing out on the corporatist resurgence is the United States. See R. H. Salisbury, 'Why No Corporatism in America?' in Schmitter and Lehmbruch (eds.); and G. K. Wilson, 'Why is there No Corporatism in the United States?' in Lehmbruch and Schmitter (eds.). The United States has not been exempt, however; see D. R. Fusfeld, 'The Rise of the Corporate State in America', *Journal of Economic Issues*, Vol. 6 (1972); N. H. Keehn, 'A World Becoming: From Pluralism to Corporatism', *Polity*, Vol. 9 (1976); and Milward and Francisco, 'Subsystem Politics and Corporatism in the United States', *Policy and Politics*, Vol. 11 (1983).
18 Schmitter, *Democratic Theory and Neo-Corporatist Practice*.
19 See Schmitter in Berger (ed.), *Organising Interests in Western Europe* (Cambridge, 1981), pp. 292–5, and Lehmbruch in Lehmbruch and Schmitter (eds.), *Patterns of Corporatist Policy making* (London, 1982), pp. 6–23.
20 Schmitter in Berger (ed.), *op. cit.*, p. 294, and Lehmbruch in Lehmbruch and Schmitter (eds.), *op. cit.*, pp. 16–34. Lehmbruch is less explicit in outlining exactly what he is seeking to address, it is only clear once he has actually addressed it.
21 A good example is H. L. Wilensky, *The New Corporatism: Centralization and the Welfare state* (London: Sage, 1976). See also H. Paloheimo, 'Pluralism, Corporatism and the Distributive Conflict in Developed Capitalist Countries', *Scandinavian Political Studies*, Vol. 7 (1984), No. 1 for a broader approach.
22 See A. Bentley, *The Process of Government* (Cambridge, Mass.: Harvard University Press, 1967).
23 J. P. Olsen, *Organised Democracy: Political Institutions in a Welfare State – The Case of Norway* (Bergen: Universitetsforlaget, 1983), pp. 166–76.
24 *ibid*, pp. 178–9.
25 *ibid*, pp. 179–83.
26 In addition to Olsen's book, which contrasts Norway with other Scandinavian countries, and Britain and the U.S.A., see R. B. Kvavik, *Interest Groups in Norwegian Politics* (Oslo: Universitetsforlaget, 1976) and D. S. Schiverin, *Corporatism and Protest: Organizational Politics in the Norwegian Trade*

Unions (Kent, Oh.: Kent Popular Press, 1981). See also I. Christensen and
M. Eyeberg, 'Organised Group – Government Relations in Norway', *Scandinavian Political Studies*, Vol. 2 (1979), No. 3.

27 Kvavik, *op. cit.*, p. 156.

28 R. Huntford, *The New Totalitarians* (London: Allen Lane, 1971) provides a
description, but with a rather silly commentary. See also O. Ruin, 'Participatory Democracy and Corporativism: The Case of Sweden', *Scandinavian
Political Studies*, Vol. 9 [Old Series] (1974), pp. 171–84; and M. D. Hancock,
Sweden: The Politics of Postindustrial Change (Hinsdale: Dryden Press,
1972). Several issues of *Scandinavian Political Studies* have essays on specific
areas of policy in Sweden. F. G. Castles, 'Policy Innovation and Institutional
Stability in Sweden', *British Journal of Political Science*, Vol. 6 (1976),
pp. 203–16, also highlights certain important aspects; as does C. von Otter,
'Swedish Welfare Capitalism: The Role of the State', in R. Scase (ed.) *The
State in Western Europe* (London: Croom Helm, 1980).

29 O. Ruin, 'Sweden in the 1970s: Policy Making Becomes More Difficult' in
Richardson (ed.) pp. 155–6.

30 L. N. Johansen and O. P. Kristensen, 'Corporatist Traits in Denmark,
1946–1976', in Lehmbruch and Schmitter (eds.). See also L. N. Johansen,
'The Corporatist Elite in Denmark 1946–1975' (Paper prepared by ECPR
Joint Sessions of Workshops, Florence, March 1980, 'Interests Groups and
Government').

31 J. G. Buksti and L. N. Johansen, 'Variations in Organizational Participation in
Government: The Case of Denmark', *Scandinavian Political Studies*, Vol. 2
(1979), p. 218. There is much valuable empirical information in this article.

32 V. Helander, 'Interest Representation in the Finnish Committee system in the
post-War era', *Scandinavian Political Studies* Vol. 2 (1979), pp. 221–37. See
also his 'A Liberal-Corporatist Sub-system in Action: The Incomes Policy
System in Finland', in Lehmbruch and Schmitter (eds.).

33 For a general summary of Scandinavian politics, see N. Elder, A. H. Thomas
and D. Arter, *The Consensual Democracies?* (Oxford: Martin Robertson,
1982).

34 See J. van Putten, 'Policy Styles in the Netherlands: Negotiation and Conflict',
in Richardson (ed.). See also J. Kooiman, 'Departments under Pressure:
Governing Problems of Ministries in the Netherlands', *European Journal of
Political Research*, Vol. 11 (1983), No. 4.

35 A. L. MacMullen, 'Netherlands', in F. F. Ridley (ed.) *Government and
Administration in Western Europe* (Oxford: Martin Robertson, 1979),
pp. 230–1.

36 Materials on Austria are rather sparse. But see Lehmbruch in Schmitter and
Lehmbruch (eds.); K. McRae (ed.) *Consociational Democracy* (Toronto:
McClelland and Stewart, 1976); and K. Waldheim, *The Austrian Example*
(New York: Macmillan, 1973).

37 J. Hayward, 'Interest Groups and the Demand for state action', in J. E.
Hayward and R. N. Berki, *State and Society in Contemporary Europe*
(Oxford: Martin Robertson, 1978), p. 38.

38 G. Jordan, 'Pluralistic Corporatisms and Corporate Pluralism', *Scandinavian
Political Studies*, Vol. 7 (1984), No. 3, p. 152.

39 This point is made by Alan Cawson in 'Varieties of Corporatism: The
Importance of the Mid-Level of Interest Intermediation', draft chapter of a

book edited by Alan Cawson on corporatism and industrial policy to be published by Sage.

40 Schmitter in Berger (ed.), p. 313.
41 Mannoilesco, *Le Siècle du Corporatisme*, p. 25.

Index

DATE DUE